T0336183

A Second Course in Formal Languages and Automata Theory

Intended for graduate students and advanced undergraduates in computer science, *A Second Course in Formal Languages and Automata Theory* treats topics in the theory of computation not usually covered in a first course.

After a review of basic concepts, the book covers combinatorics on words, regular languages, context-free languages, parsing and recognition, Turing machines, and other language classes. Many topics often absent from other textbooks, such as repetitions in words, state complexity, the interchange lemma, 2DPDAs, and the incompressibility method, are covered here. The author places particular emphasis on the resources needed to represent certain languages. The book also includes a diverse collection of more than 200 exercises, suggestions for term projects, and research problems that remain open.

JEFFREY SHALLIT is professor in the David R. Cheriton School of Computer Science at the University of Waterloo. He is the author of *Algorithmic Number Theory* (co-authored with Eric Bach) and *Automatic Sequences: Theory, Applications, Generalizations* (coauthored with Jean-Paul Allouche). He has published approximately 90 articles on number theory, algebra, automata theory, complexity theory, and the history of mathematics and computing.

A Second Course in Formal Languages and Automata Theory

JEFFREY SHALLIT
University of Waterloo

CAMBRIDGE
UNIVERSITY PRESS

CAMBRIDGE
UNIVERSITY PRESS

32 Avenue of the Americas, New York NY 10013-2473, USA

Cambridge University Press is part of the University of Cambridge.

It furthers the University's mission by disseminating knowledge in the pursuit of
education, learning and research at the highest international levels of excellence.

www.cambridge.org
Information on this title: www.cambridge.org/9780521865722

© Jeffrey Shallit 2009

First published 2009

A catalogue record for this publication is available from the British Library

Library of Congress Cataloguing in Publication data
Shallit, Jeffrey Outlaw.
A second course in formal languages and automata theory / Jeffrey Shallit.
p. cm.
Includes bibliographical references and index.
ISBN 978-0-521-86572-2 (hardback)
1. Formal languages. 2. Machine theory. I. Title.
QA267.3.S53 2009
005.13'1–dc22 2008030065

ISBN 978-0-521-86572-2 Hardback

Contents

Preface

Goals of this book

This is a textbook for a second course on formal languages and automata theory.

Many undergraduates in computer science take a course entitled "Introduction to Theory of Computing," in which they learn the basics of finite automata, pushdown automata, context-free grammars, and Turing machines. However, few students pursue advanced topics in these areas, in part because there is no really satisfactory textbook.

For almost 20 years I have been teaching such a second course for fourth-year undergraduate majors and graduate students in computer science at the University of Waterloo: CS 462/662, entitled "Formal Languages and Parsing." For many years we used Hopcroft and Ullman's *Introduction to Automata Theory, Languages, and Computation* as the course text, a book that has proved very influential. (The reader will not have to look far to see its influence on the present book.)

In 2001, however, Hopcroft and Ullman released a second edition of their text that, in the words of one professor, "removed all the good parts." In other words, their second edition is geared toward second- and third-year students, and omits nearly all the advanced topics suitable for fourth-year students and beginning graduate students.

Because the first edition of Hopcroft and Ullman's book is no longer easily available, and because I have been regularly supplementing their book with my own handwritten course notes, it occurred to me that it was a good time to write a textbook on advanced topics in formal languages. The result is this book.

The book contains many topics that are not available in other textbooks. To name just a few, it addresses the Lyndon–Schützenberger theorem, Thue's results on avoiding squares, state complexity of finite automata, Parikh's theorem, the interchange lemma, Earley's parsing method, Kolmogorov complexity, and Cook's theorem on the simulation of 2DPDAs. Furthermore, some well-known theorems have new (and hopefully simpler) proofs. Finally, there are almost 200 exercises to test students' knowledge. I hope this book will prove useful to advanced undergraduates and beginning graduate students who want to dig a little deeper in the theory of formal languages.

Prerequisites

I assume the reader is familiar with the material contained in a typical first course in the theory of computing and algorithm design. Because not all textbooks use the same terminology and notation, some basic concepts are reviewed in Chapter 1.

Algorithm descriptions

Algorithms in this book are described in a "pseudocode" notation similar to Pascal or C, which should be familiar to most readers. I do not provide a formal definition of this notation. The readers should note that the scope of loops is denoted by indentation.

Proof ideas

Although much of this book follows the traditional theorem/proof style, it does have one nonstandard feature. Many proofs are accompanied by "proof ideas," which attempt to capture the intuition behind the proofs. In some cases, proof ideas are all that is provided.

Common errors

I have tried to point out some common errors that students typically make when encountering this material for the first time.

Exercises

There are a wide variety of exercises, from easy to hard, in no particular order. Most readers will find the exercises with one star challenging and exercises with two stars *very* challenging.

Projects

Each chapter has a small number of suggested projects that are suitable for term papers. Students should regard the provided citations to the literature only as starting points; by tracing forward and backward in the citation history, many more papers can usually be found.

Research problems

Each chapter has a small number of research problems. Currently, no one knows how to solve these problems, so if you make any progress, please contact me.

Acknowledgments

Over the last 18 years, many students in CS 462/662 at the University of Waterloo have contributed to this book by finding errors and suggesting better arguments. I am particularly grateful to the following students (in alphabetical order): Margareta Ackerman, Craig Barkhouse, Matthew Borges, Tracy Damon, Michael DiRamio, Keith Ellul, Sarah Fernandes, Johannes Franz, Cristian Gaspar, Ryan Golbeck, Mike Glover, Daniil Golod, Ryan Hadley, Joe Istead, Richard Kalbfleisch, Jui-Yi Kao, Adam Keanie, Anita Koo, Dalia Krieger, David Landry, Jonathan Lee, Abninder Litt, Brendan Lucier, Bob Lutz, Ian MacDonald, Angela Martin, Glen Martin, Andrew Martinez, Gyanendra Mehta, Olga Miltchman, Siamak Nazari, Sam Ng, Lam Nguyen, Matthew Nichols, Alex Palacios, Joel Reardon, Joe Rideout, Kenneth Rose, Jessica Socha, Douglas Stebila, Wenquan Sun, Aaron Tikuisis, Jim Wallace, Xiang Wang, Zhi Xu, Colin Young, Ning Zhang, and Bryce Zimny.

Four people have been particularly influential in the development of this book, and I single them out for particular thanks: Jonathan Buss, who taught from this book while I was on sabbatical in 2001 and allowed me to use his notes on the closure of CSLs under complement; Narad Rampersad, who taught from this book in 2005, suggested many exercises, and proofread the final draft; Robert Robinson, who taught from a manuscript version of this book at the University of Georgia and identified dozens of errors; and Nic Santean, who carefully read the draft manuscript and made dozens of useful suggestions. All errors that remain, of course, are my responsibility. If you find an error, please send it to me. The current errata list can be found on my homepage; http://www.cs.uwaterloo.ca/~shallit/ is the URL.

This book was written at the University of Waterloo, Ontario, and the University of Arizona. This work was supported in part by grants from the Natural Sciences and Engineering Research Council (Canada).

Waterloo, Ontario; January 2008 Jeffrey Shallit

1

Review of formal languages
and automata theory

In this chapter we review material from a first course in the theory of computing. Much of this material should be familiar to you, but if not, you may want to read a more leisurely treatment contained in one of the texts suggested in the notes (Section 1.12).

1.1 Sets

A set is a collection of elements chosen from some domain. If S is a finite set, we use the notation $|S|$ to denote the number of elements or *cardinality* of the set. The empty set is denoted by $\emptyset$. By $A \cup B$ (respectively $A \cap B$, $A - B$) we mean the union of the two sets A and B (respectively intersection and set difference). The notation $\overline{A}$ means the complement of the set A with respect to some assumed universal set U; that is, $\overline{A} = \{x \in U \ : \ x \notin A\}$. Finally, 2^A denotes the *power set*, or set of all subsets, of A.

Some special sets that we talk about include $\mathbb{N} = \{0, 1, 2, 3, \ldots\}$, the natural numbers, and $\mathbb{Z} = \{\ldots, -3, -2, -1, 0, 1, 2, 3, \ldots\}$, the integers.

1.2 Symbols, strings, and languages

One of the fundamental mathematical objects we study in this book is the *string*. In the literature, a string is sometimes called a *word* or *sentence*. A string is made up of *symbols* (or *letters*). (We treat the notion of symbol as primitive and do not define it further.) A nonempty set of symbols is called an *alphabet* and is often denoted by Σ; in this book, Σ will almost always be finite. An alphabet is called *unary* if it consists of a single symbol. We typically denote elements of Σ by using the lowercase italic letters a, b, c, d.

A *string* is a finite or infinite list of symbols chosen from Σ. The symbols themselves are usually written using the typewriter font. If unspecified, a string is assumed to be finite. We typically use the lowercase italic letters s, t, u, v, w, x, y, z to represent finite strings. We denote the *empty string* by ϵ. The set of all finite strings made up of letters chosen from Σ is denoted by Σ^*. For example, if $\Sigma = \{a, b\}$, then $\Sigma^* = \{\epsilon, a, b, aa, ab, ba, bb, aaa, \ldots\}$. Note that Σ^* does not contain infinite strings. By Σ^+ for an alphabet Σ, we understand $\Sigma^* - \{\epsilon\}$, the set of all nonempty strings over Σ.

If w is a finite string, then its *length* (the number of symbols it contains) is denoted by $|w|$. (There should be no confusion with the same notation used for set cardinality.) For example, if $w = \texttt{five}$, then $|w| = 4$. Note that $|\epsilon| = 0$. We can also count the number of occurrences of a particular letter in a string. If $a \in \Sigma$ and $w \in \Sigma^*$, then $|w|_a$ denotes the number of occurrences of a in w. Thus, for example, if $w = abbab$, then $|w|_a = 2$ and $|w|_b = 3$.

We say a string y is a *subword* of a string w if there exist strings x, z such that $w = xyz$. We say x is a *prefix* of w if there exists y such that $w = xy$. The prefix is *proper* if $y \neq \epsilon$ and *nontrivial* if $x \neq \epsilon$. For example, if $w = \texttt{antsy}$, then the set of prefixes of w is $\{\epsilon, \texttt{a}, \texttt{an}, \texttt{ant}, \texttt{ants}, \texttt{antsy}\}$ (see Exercise 4). The set of proper prefixes of w is $\{\epsilon, \texttt{a}, \texttt{an}, \texttt{ant}, \texttt{ants}\}$, and the set of nontrivial prefixes of w is $\{\texttt{a}, \texttt{an}, \texttt{ant}, \texttt{ants}, \texttt{antsy}\}$.

Similarly, we say that z is a *suffix* of w if there exists y such that $w = yz$. The suffix is *proper* if $y \neq \epsilon$ and *nontrivial* if $z \neq \epsilon$.

We say that x is a *subsequence* of y if we can obtain x by striking out 0 or more letters from y. For example, gem is a subsequence of enlightenment.

If $w = a_1 a_2 \cdots a_n$, then for $1 \leq i \leq n$, we define $w[i] = a_i$. If $1 \leq i \leq n$ and $i - 1 \leq j \leq n$, we define $w[i..j] = a_i a_{i+1} \cdots a_j$. Note that $w[i..i] = a_i$ and $w[i..i-1] = \epsilon$.

If $w = ux$, we sometimes write $x = u^{-1}w$ and $u = wx^{-1}$.

Now we turn to sets of strings. A *language* over Σ is a (finite or infinite) set of strings—in other words, a subset of Σ^*.

Example 1.2.1. The following are examples of languages:

PRIMES2 $= \{10, 11, 101, 111, 1011, 1101, 10001, \ldots\}$ (the primes represented in base 2)

EQ $= \{x \in \{0, 1\}^* : |x|_0 = |x|_1\}$ (strings containing an equal number of each symbol)

$= \{\epsilon, 01, 10, 0011, 0101, 0110, 1001, 1010, 1100, \ldots\}$

EVEN $= \{x \in \{0, 1\}^* : |x|_0 \equiv 0 \pmod{2}\}$ (strings with an even number of 0s)

SQ $= \{xx : x \in \{0, 1\}^*\}$ (the language of squares)

Given a language $L \subseteq \Sigma^*$, we may consider its prefix and suffix languages. We define

$\mathrm{Pref}(L) = \{x \in \Sigma^* :$ there exists $y \in L$ such that x is a prefix of $y\}$;

$\mathrm{Suff}(L) = \{x \in \Sigma^* :$ there exists $y \in L$ such that x is a suffix of $y\}$.

One of the fundamental operations on strings is *concatenation*. We concatenate two finite strings w and x by juxtaposing their symbols, and we denote this by wx. For example, if $w = $ book and $x = $ case, then $wx = $ bookcase. Concatenation of strings is, in general, not commutative; for example, we have $xw = $ casebook. However, concatenation is associative: we have $w(xy) = (wx)y$ for all strings w, x, y.

In general, concatenation is treated notationally like multiplication, so that, for example, w^n denotes the string $www \cdots w$ (n times).

If $w = a_1 a_2 \cdots a_n$ and $x = b_1 b_2 \cdots b_n$ are finite words of the same length, then by $w \amalg x$ we mean the word $a_1 b_1 a_2 b_2 \cdots a_n b_n$, the *perfect shuffle* of w and x. For example, shoe $\amalg$ cold $= $ schooled, and clip $\amalg$ aloe $= $ calliope, and (appropriately for this book) term $\amalg$ hoes $= $ theorems.

If $w = a_1 a_2 \cdots a_n$ is a finite word, then by w^R we mean the *reversal* of the word w; that is, $w^R = a_n a_{n-1} \cdots a_2 a_1$. For example, $(\text{drawer})^R = $ reward. Note that $(wx)^R = x^R w^R$. A word w is a *palindrome* if $w = w^R$. Examples of palindromes in English include radar, deified, rotator, repaper, and redivider.

We now turn to orders on strings. Given a finite alphabet Σ, we can impose an order on the elements. For example, if $\Sigma = \Sigma_k = \{0, 1, 2, \ldots, k - 1\}$, for some integer $k \geq 2$, then $0 < 1 < 2 < \cdots < k - 1$. Suppose w, x are equal-length strings over Σ. We say that w is *lexicographically smaller* than x, and write $w < x$, if there exist strings z, w', x' and letters a, b such that $w = zaw', x = zbx'$, and $a < b$. Thus, for example, trust $<$ truth. We can extend this order to the *radix order* defined as follows: $w < x$ if $|w| < |x|$, or $|w| = |x|$ and w precedes x in lexicographic order. Thus, for example, rat $<$ moose in radix order.

1.3 Regular expressions and regular languages

As we have seen earlier, a language over Σ is a subset of Σ^*. Languages may be of finite or infinite cardinality. We start by defining some common operations on languages.

Let $L, L_1, L_2 \subseteq \Sigma^*$ be languages. We define the *product* or *concatenation* of languages by

$$L_1 L_2 = \{wx : w \in L_1, x \in L_2\}.$$

Common Error 1.3.1. Note that the definition of language concatenation implies that $L\emptyset = \emptyset L = \emptyset$. Many students mistakenly believe that $L\emptyset = L$.

We define $L^0 = \{\epsilon\}$ and define L^i as LL^{i-1} for $i \geq 1$. We define

$$L^{\leq i} = L^0 \cup L^1 \cup \cdots \cup L^i.$$

We define L^* as $\bigcup_{i \geq 0} L^i$; the operation L^* is sometimes called *Kleene closure*. We define $L^+ = L\,L^*$; the operation $+$ in the superscript is sometimes called *positive closure*. If L is a language, then the reversed language is defined as follows: $L^R = \{x^R : x \in L\}$.

We now turn to a common notation for representing some kinds of languages. A *regular expression* over the base alphabet Σ is a well-formed string over the larger alphabet $\Sigma \cup A$, where $A = \{\epsilon, \emptyset, (,), +, *\}$; we assume $\Sigma \cap A = \emptyset$. In evaluating such an expression, $*$ represents Kleene closure and has highest precedence. Concatenation is represented by juxtaposition, and has next highest precedence. Finally, $+$ represents union and has lowest precedence. Parentheses are used for grouping. A formal definition of regular expressions is given in Exercise 33.

If the word u is a regular expression, then $L(u)$ represents the language that u is shorthand for. For example, consider the regular expression $u = (0 + 10)^*(1 + \epsilon)$. Then $L(u)$ represents all finite words of 0s and 1s that do not contain two consecutive 1s. Frequently we will abuse the notation by referring to the language as the naked regular expression without the surrounding $L(\ )$. A language L is said to be *regular* if $L = L(u)$ for some regular expression u.

1.4 Finite automata

A *deterministic finite automaton*, or DFA for short, is the simplest model of a computer. We imagine a finite control equipped with a read head and a tape, divided into cells, which holds a finite input. At each step, depending on the machine's internal state and the current symbol being scanned, the machine can change its internal state and move right to the next square on the tape. If, after scanning all the cells of the input the machine is in any one of a number of *final states*, we say the input is *accepted*; otherwise it is *rejected* (see Figure 1.1).

Formally, a DFA is a 5-tuple $(Q, \Sigma, \delta, q_0, F)$, where

- Q is a finite nonempty set of states;
- Σ is a finite nonempty input alphabet;
- $\delta : Q \times \Sigma \to Q$ is a transition function;

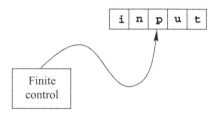

Figure 1.1: A deterministic finite automaton

- $q_0 \in Q$ is the start or initial state;
- $F \subseteq Q$ is the set of final states.

The transition function δ can be extended to a transition function $\delta^* : Q \times \Sigma^* \to Q$ as follows:

- $\delta^*(q, \epsilon) = q$ for all $q \in Q$;
- $\delta^*(q, xa) = \delta(\delta^*(q, x), a)$ for all $q \in Q, x \in \Sigma^*$, and $a \in \Sigma$.

Since δ^* agrees with δ on the domain of δ, we often just write δ for δ^*.

Now we give the formal definition of $L(M)$, the language accepted by a DFA M. We have

$$L(M) = \{x \in \Sigma^* \ : \ \delta(q_0, x) \in F\}.$$

We often describe deterministic finite automata by providing a *transition diagram*. This is a directed graph where states are represented by circles, final states represented by double circles, the initial state is labeled by a headless arrow entering a state, and transitions represented by directed arrows, labeled with a letter. For example, the transition diagram in Figure 1.2 represents the DFA that accepts the language EVEN $= \{x \in \{0, 1\}^* \ : \ |x|_0 \equiv 0 \ (\mathrm{mod} \ 2)\}$.

Representation as a transition diagram suggests the following natural generalization of a DFA: we allow the automaton to have multiple choices (or none at all) on what state to enter on reading a given symbol. We accept an input if and only if *some* sequence of choices leads to a final state. For example, the

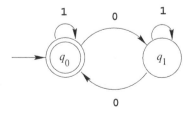

Figure 1.2: Transition diagram for a DFA

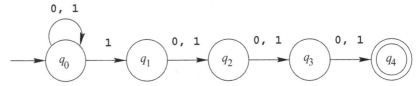

Figure 1.3: Transition diagram for an NFA

transition diagram in Figure 1.3 represents a *nondeterministic* finite automaton (NFA) that accepts the language L_4, where

$$L_n := \{x \in \{0, 1\}^* \ : \ \text{the } n\text{th symbol from the right is } 1\}.$$

It is possible to show that the smallest DFA accepting L_n has at least 2^n states (see Exercise 3.14), so NFAs, while accepting the same class of languages as DFAs, can be exponentially more concise.

Formally, an NFA is a 5-tuple $M = (Q, \Sigma, \delta, q_0, F)$, where $\delta : Q \times \Sigma \to 2^Q$. We define the extended transition function δ^* by

- $\delta^*(q, \epsilon) = \{q\}$;
- $\delta^*(q, xa) = \bigcup_{r \in \delta^*(q,x)} \delta(r, a)$.

The language accepted by an NFA, $L(M)$, is then given by

$$L(M) = \{x \in \Sigma^* \ : \ \delta^*(q_0, x) \cap F \neq \emptyset\}.$$

The following theorem shows that NFAs accept exactly the regular languages.

Theorem 1.4.1. *If M is an NFA, then there exists a DFA M' such that $L(M) = L(M')$.*

Proof Idea. We let the states of M' be all subsets of the state set of M. The final states of M' are those subsets containing at least one final state of M. ∎

Exercise 31 asks you to show that the subset construction for NFA-to-DFA conversion can be carried out in $O(kn2^n)$ time, where $k = |\Sigma|$ and $n = |Q|$.

Yet another generalization of DFA is to allow the DFA to change state spontaneously without consuming a symbol of the input. This can be represented in a transition diagram by allowing arrows labeled ϵ, which are called ϵ-transitions. An NFA-ϵ is a 5-tuple $M = (Q, \Sigma, \delta, q_0, F)$, where $\delta : Q \times (\Sigma \cup \{\epsilon\}) \to 2^Q$.

The most important theorem on regular languages is Kleene's theorem:

Theorem 1.4.2. *The following language classes are identical:*

(a) the class of languages specified by regular expressions;
(b) the class of languages accepted by DFAs;

(c) the class of languages accepted by NFAs;
(d) the class of languages accepted by NFA-ϵ's.

As a corollary, we can deduce some important *closure properties* of regular languages. We say a class of languages is *closed* under an operation if whenever the arguments to the operation are in the class, the result is also. If there are any counterexamples at all, we say the class is *not closed*.

Corollary 1.4.3. *The class of regular languages is closed under the operations of union, concatenation, Kleene $*$, and complement.*

The pumping lemma is an important tool for proving that certain languages are not regular.

Lemma 1.4.4. *Suppose L is a regular language. Then there exists a constant $n \geq 1$, depending on L, such that for all $z \in L$ with $|z| \geq n$, there exists a decomposition $z = uvw$ with $|uv| \leq n$ and $|v| \geq 1$ such that $uv^i w \in L$ for all $i \geq 0$. In fact, we may take n to be the number of states in any DFA accepting L.*

Proof Idea. The basic idea of the proof is that the path through the transition diagram for any sufficiently long accepted word must contain a loop. We may then go around this loop any number of times to obtain an infinite number of accepted words of the form $uv^i w$.   ∎

Example 1.4.5. Let us show that the language

$$\text{PRIMES1} = \{a^2, a^3, a^5, \ldots\},$$

the prime numbers represented in unary, is not regular. Let n be the pumping lemma constant, and choose a prime $p > n$; we know such a prime exists by Euclid's theorem that there are infinitely many primes. Let $z = a^p$. Then there exists a decomposition $z = uvw$ with $|uv| \leq n$ and $|v| \geq 1$ such that $uv^i w \in \text{PRIMES1}$ for all $i \geq 0$. Suppose $|v| = r$. Then choose $i = p + 1$. We have $|uv^i w| = p + (i - 1)r = p(r + 1)$. Since $r \geq 1$, this number is not a prime, a contradiction.

Example 1.4.6. Here is a deeper application of the pumping lemma. Let us show that the language

$$\text{PRIMES2} = \{10, 11, 101, 111, 1011, 1101, 10001, \ldots\},$$

the prime numbers represented in binary, is not regular. Let n be the pumping lemma constant and p be a prime $p > 2^n$. Let z be the base-2 representation of p. If t is a string of 0s and 1s, let $[t]_2$ denote the integer whose base-2 representation is given by t. Write $z = uvw$. Now

$$[z]_2 = [u]_2 2^{|vw|} + [v]_2 2^{|w|} + [w]_2,$$

while

$$[uv^i w]_2 = [u]_2 2^{i|v|+|w|} + [v]_2 (2^{|w|} + 2^{|vw|} + \cdots + 2^{|v^{i-1}w|}) + [w]_2.$$

Now $2^{|w|} + 2^{|vw|} + \cdots + 2^{|v^{i-1}w|}$ is, by the sum of a geometric series, equal to $2^{|w|} \frac{2^{i|v|}-1}{2^{|v|}-1}$. Now by Fermat's theorem, $2^p \equiv 2 \pmod{p}$ if p is a prime. Hence, setting $i = p$, we get $[uv^p w]_2 - [uvw]_2 \equiv 0 \pmod{p}$. But since z has no leading zeroes, $[uv^p w]_2 > [uvw]_2 = p$. (Note that $2^{|v|} - 1 \not\equiv 0 \pmod{p}$ since $|v| \geq 1$ and $|uv| \leq n \Rightarrow 2^{|v|} \leq 2^n < p$.) It follows that $[uv^p w]_2$ is an integer larger than p that is divisible by p, and so cannot represent a prime number. Hence, $uv^p w \notin \texttt{PRIMES2}$. This contradiction proves that $\texttt{PRIMES2}$ is not regular.

1.5 Context-free grammars and languages

In the previous section, we saw two of the three important ways to specify languages: namely, as the language accepted by a machine or the language specified by a regular expression. In this section, we explore a third important way, the *grammar*. A machine receives a string as input and processes it, but a grammar actually constructs a string iteratively through a number of rewriting rules. We focus here on a particular kind of grammar, the *context-free grammar* (CFG).

Example 1.5.1. Consider the CFG given by the following production rules:

$$S \to \text{a}$$
$$S \to \text{b}$$
$$S \to \text{a}S\text{a}$$
$$S \to \text{b}S\text{b}.$$

The intention is to interpret each of these four rules as rewriting rules. We start with the symbol S and can choose to replace it by any of a, b, aSa, bSb. Suppose we replace S by aSa. Now the resulting string still has an S in it, and so we can choose any one of four strings to replace it. If we choose the rule $S \to \text{b}S\text{b}$, we get ab$S$ba. Now if we choose the rule $S \to \text{b}$, we get the string abbba, and no more rules can be performed.

It is not hard to see that the language generated by this process is the set of palindromes over {a, b} of odd length, which we call ODDPAL.

Example 1.5.2. Here is a somewhat harder example. Let us create a CFG to generate the *nonpalindromes* over {a, b}.

$$S \rightarrow aSa \mid bSb \mid aTb \mid bTa$$

$$T \rightarrow aTa \mid aTb \mid bTa \mid bTb \mid \epsilon \mid a \mid b.$$

The basic idea is that if a string is a nonpalindrome, then there must be at least one position such that the character in that position does not match the character in the corresponding position from the end. The productions $S \rightarrow aSa$ and $S \rightarrow bSb$ are used to generate a prefix and suffix that match properly, but eventually one of the two productions involving T on the right-hand side must be used, at which point a mismatch is introduced. Now the remaining symbols can either match or not match, which accounts for the remaining productions involving T.

Example 1.5.3. Finally, we conclude with a genuinely challenging example. Consider the language

$$L = \{x \in \{0, 1\}^* : x \text{ is not of the form } ww\} = \overline{SQ}$$

$$= \{0, 1, 01, 10, 000, 001, 010, 011, 100, 101, 110, 111, 0001, 0010,$$

$$0011, 1000, \dots\}.$$

Exercise 25 asks you to prove that this language can be generated by the following grammar:

$$S \rightarrow AB \mid BA \mid A \mid B$$

$$A \rightarrow 0A0 \mid 0A1 \mid 1A0 \mid 1A1 \mid 0$$

$$B \rightarrow 0B0 \mid 0B1 \mid 1B0 \mid 1B1 \mid 1.$$

Formally, we define a CFG G to be a 4-tuple $G = (V, \Sigma, P, S)$, where V is a nonempty finite set of variables, Σ is a nonempty finite set of terminal symbols, P is a finite set of productions of the form $A \rightarrow \alpha$, where $A \in V$ and $\alpha \in (V \cup \Sigma)^*$ (i.e., a finite subset of $V \times (V \cup \Sigma)^*$), and S is a distinguished element of V called the *start symbol*. We require that $V \cap \Sigma = \emptyset$. The term *context-free* comes from the fact that A may be replaced by α, independent of the context in which A appears.

A *sentential form* is any string of variables and terminals. We can go from one sentential form to another by applying a rule of the grammar. Formally, we write $\alpha B \gamma \Longrightarrow \alpha \beta \gamma$ if $B \rightarrow \beta$ is a production of P. We write $\overset{*}{\Longrightarrow}$ for the reflexive, transitive closure of $\Longrightarrow$. In other words, we write $\alpha \stackrel{*}{\Longrightarrow} \beta$ if there exist sentential forms $\alpha = \alpha_0, \alpha_1, \ldots, \alpha_n = \beta$ such that

$$\alpha_0 \Longrightarrow \alpha_1 \Longrightarrow \alpha_2 \Longrightarrow \cdots \Longrightarrow \alpha_n.$$

A *derivation* consists of 0 or more applications of $\Longrightarrow$ to some sentential form. If G is a CFG, then we define

$$L(G) = \{x \in \Sigma^* : S \stackrel{*}{\Longrightarrow} x\}.$$

A *leftmost derivation* is a derivation in which the variable replaced at each step is the leftmost one. A *rightmost derivation* is defined analogously. A grammar G is said to be *unambiguous* if every word $w \in L(G)$ has exactly one leftmost derivation and *ambiguous* otherwise.

A *parse tree* or *derivation tree* for $w \in L(G)$ is an ordered tree T where each vertex is labeled with an element of $V \cup \Sigma \cup \{\epsilon\}$. The root is labeled with a variable A and the leaves are labeled with elements of Σ or ϵ. If a node is labeled with $A \in V$ and its children are (from left to right) $X_1, X_2, \ldots, X_r$, then $A \to X_1 X_2 \cdots X_r$ is a production of G. The *yield* of the tree is w and consists of the concatenation of the leaf labels from left to right.

Theorem 1.5.4. *A grammar is unambiguous if and only if every word generated has exactly one parse tree.*

The class of languages generated by CFGs is called the *context-free languages* (CFLs).

We now recall some basic facts about CFGs. First, productions of the form $A \to \epsilon$ are called ϵ-*productions* and productions of the form $A \to B$ *unit productions*. There is an algorithm to transform a CFG G into a new grammar G' without ϵ-productions or unit productions, such that $L(G') = L(G) - \{\epsilon\}$ (see Exercise 27). Furthermore, it is possible to carry out this transformation in such a way that if G is unambiguous, G' is also.

We say a grammar is in *Chomsky normal form* if every production is of the form $A \to BC$ or $A \to a$, where A, B, C are variables and a is a single terminal. There is an algorithm to transform a grammar G into a new grammar G' in Chomsky normal form, such that $L(G') = L(G) - \{\epsilon\}$; (see Exercise 28).

We now recall a basic result about CFLs, known as the pumping lemma.

Theorem 1.5.5. *If L is context-free, then there exists a constant n such that for all $z \in L$ with $|z| \geq n$, there exists a decomposition $z = uvwxy$ with $|vwx| \leq n$ and $|vx| \geq 1$ such that for all $i \geq 0$, we have $uv^i wx^i y \in L$.*

Proof Idea. If L is context-free, then we can find a Chomsky normal form grammar G generating $L - \{\epsilon\}$. Let $n = 2^k$, where k is the number of variables

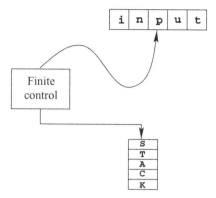

Figure 1.4: A pushdown automaton

in G. If $z \in L$ and $|z| \geq n$, then the parse tree for z must contain a relatively long path—long enough, in fact, that some variable A gets repeated. We then have derivations of the form

$$S \overset{*}{\Longrightarrow} uAy$$
$$A \overset{*}{\Longrightarrow} vAx$$
$$A \overset{*}{\Longrightarrow} w$$

for some strings u, v, w, x, y. Thus, $uv^i wx^i y \in L$ for all $i \geq 0$. (The length conditions on $|vwx|$ and $|vx|$ come from a more precise analysis of the path.) ∎

We now turn to a machine model for the CFLs. Consider augmenting an NFA-ϵ with the ability to store symbols on a *stack* or *pushdown store* (see Figure 1.4). (Recall that in a stack we are only able to push elements on top of the stack and pop an element from the top of the stack.)

Formally, a pushdown automaton (or PDA) is a 7-tuple $M = (Q, \Sigma, \Gamma, \delta, q_0, Z_0, F)$. Here $Q, \Sigma, q_0,$ and F are defined as earlier, and Γ is a finite alphabet of symbols that may appear in the stack, Z_0 is the symbol representing the initial stack contents, and δ is the transition function. The function δ maps $Q \times (\Sigma \cup \{\epsilon\}) \times \Gamma$ to finite subsets of $Q \times \Gamma^*$. The meaning of

$$\delta(q, a, X) = \{(p_1, \gamma_1), \ldots, (p_r, \gamma_r)\}$$

is that the machine M in state q with X on top of the stack may on input a consume that symbol from the input and nondeterministically choose an i such that it changes state to p_i, pops X from the stack, and pushes the symbols of γ_i on top of the stack in its place.

We now define the notion of *configuration*, which is intended to be a complete description of the current state of the machine. A configuration is an element of $Q \times \Sigma^* \times \Gamma^*$. A triple of the form (q, w, α) means that the machine is currently in state q, with w the input not yet read (and the tape head currently scanning the first symbol of w) and α the stack contents. We write the contents of the stack with the top at the left.

Moves of the machine take us from one configuration to the next. We write

$$(q, aw, X\alpha) \vdash (p, w, \beta\alpha)$$

for $q \in Q, a \in \Sigma \cup \{\epsilon\}, w \in \Sigma^*, X \in \Gamma, \alpha, \beta \in \Gamma^*$ if there exists a transition of the form $(p, \beta) \in \delta(q, a, X)$. We write $\overset{*}{\vdash}$ for the reflexive, transitive closure of $\vdash$.

We are now ready to define acceptance by final state in a PDA. We have

$$L(M) = \{x \in \Sigma^* : (q_0, x, Z_0) \overset{*}{\vdash} (q, \epsilon, \alpha) \text{ for some } q \in F \text{ and } \alpha \in \Gamma^*\}.$$

Note that this definition requires that in order for a string to be accepted, all of its symbols must actually be processed by the PDA.

There is another possible definition of acceptance in a PDA, namely, acceptance by empty stack. We have $L_e(M) = \{x \in \Sigma^* : (q_0, x, Z_0) \overset{*}{\vdash} (q, \epsilon, \epsilon)$ for some $q \in Q\}$.

Theorem 1.5.6. *The two conventions of acceptance (final-state, empty stack) are equivalent in the sense that for all PDAs M, there exists a PDA M' such that $L(M) = L_e(M')$ and vice versa.*

We now come to the most important theorem of this section.

Theorem 1.5.7. *For all CFGs G, there exists a PDA M such that $L(G) = L_e(M)$. For all PDAs M, there exists a CFG G such that $L_e(M) = L(G)$.*

Proof Idea.   Let $G = (V, \Sigma, P, S)$ be a CFG. We create a one-state PDA $M = (\{q\}, \Sigma, V \cup \Sigma, \delta, q, S, \emptyset)$, which accepts $L(G)$ by empty stack, as follows: for each $A \in V$, we define

$$\delta(q, \epsilon, A) = \{(q, \alpha) : A \rightarrow \alpha \text{ is a production}\}.,$$

and for each $a \in \Sigma$, we define

$$\delta(q, a, a) = \{(q, \epsilon)\}.$$

An easy induction now proves that M accepts exactly $L(G)$.

For the other direction, assume $M = (Q, \Sigma, \Gamma, \delta, q_0, Z_0, \emptyset)$. Create a grammar $G = (V, \Sigma, P, S)$, where

$$V = \{S\} \cup \{[q, A, p] : p, q \in Q, A \in \Gamma\},$$

and the productions P are given by

$$S \to [q_0, Z_0, q] \quad \text{for each } q \in Q$$
$$[q, A, q_{m+1}] \to a[q_1, B_1, q_2][q_2, B_2, q_3] \cdots [q_m, B_m, q_{m+1}] \text{ for each } q,$$
$$q_1, \ldots, q_m, q_{m+1} \in Q, \text{ each } a \in \Sigma \cup \{\epsilon\}, \text{ each } A, B_1, \ldots,$$
$$B_m \in \Gamma \text{ such that } (q_1, B_1 B_2 \cdots B_m) \in \delta(q, a, A).$$

A nontrivial argument now proves that $L_e(M) = L(G)$. ∎

Theorem 1.5.7 is useful for proving some theorems where CFGs are not a useful characterization of the CFLs. For example:

Theorem 1.5.8. *If L is a CFL and R is regular, then $L \cap R$ is a CFL.*

Proof Idea. If L is a CFL, then $L = L(M_1)$ for some PDA $M_1 = (Q_1, \Sigma, \Gamma, \delta_1, q_1, Z_1, F_1)$. If R is regular then $R = L(M_2)$ for some DFA $M_2 = (Q_2, \Sigma, \delta_2, q_2, F_2)$. We create a PDA $M = (Q_1 \times Q_2, \Sigma, \Gamma, \delta, q_0, Z_1, F_1 \times F_2)$ accepting $L \cap R$. The idea is that M simulates M_1 in the first component of its state and M_2 in the second component. We define $q_0 = [q_1, q_2]$ and

$$\delta([p, q], a, A) = \{([p', q'], \gamma) : (p', \gamma) \in \delta_1(p, a, A) \text{ and } \delta_2(q, a) = q'\}.$$

To complete the proof, prove by induction on $|x|$ that $([q_1, q_2], x, Z_1) \overset{*}{\vdash} ([p, q], \epsilon, \alpha)$ in M if and only if $(q_1, x, Z_1) \overset{*}{\vdash} (p, \epsilon, \alpha)$ in M_1 and $\delta(q_2, x) = q$ in M_2. ∎

Corollary 1.5.9. *If $R \subseteq \Sigma^*$ is a regular language, then R is a CFL.*

Proof. In Theorem 1.5.8 take $L = \Sigma^*$. Then $R = L \cap R$ is a CFL. ∎

1.6 Turing machines

In previous sections we have reviewed machine models such as the finite automaton and pushdown automaton. We now turn to a more powerful model of computation, the Turing machine.

A Turing machine (or TM for short) is a computing device equipped with an unbounded tape divided into individual cells. For purposes of reference,

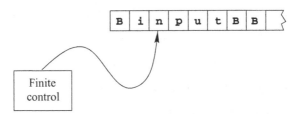

Figure 1.5: A Turing machine

we number the cells $0, 1, 2, \ldots$, but the TM itself has no access to the cell numbers. The TM has a finite control, and based on its current state and the current symbol being scanned, the TM can change state, rewrite the symbol, and move either left or right. The input initially appears in cells $1, 2, \ldots, n$. Cell 0 and cells $n + 1, n + 2, \ldots$ initially hold a distinguished character called the blank symbol, which we will write as B. This character, as well as all others, can be rewritten during the course of the computation (see Figure 1.5).

Formally, a TM is a 6-tuple $(Q, \Sigma, \Gamma, \delta, q_0, h)$, where Q is a finite set of states, $\Sigma \subseteq \Gamma$ is the input alphabet, Γ is the tape alphabet, q_0 is the initial state, and $h \in Q$ is a special distinguished state called the *halting state*. By convention we have B $\notin \Sigma$, but B $\in \Gamma$. The transition function δ is a partial function from $Q \times \Gamma$ to $Q \times \Gamma \times \{L, R, S\}$. By partial function, we mean that it may not be defined for some pairs (q, α) in its domain. By convention, a TM has no transitions leaving its halting state.

In a single move, the TM examines the current cell, and based on the contents and its current state, it rewrites the current cell, changes state, and moves either left (L), right (R), or stays stationary (S).

Informally, a TM M accepts its input if, when M starts with x as its input, scanning cell 0, it eventually enters the halting state h. Note we do not require that M actually read all its input.

In order to define acceptance formally, we need to define the notion of configuration. A *configuration* of a TM is a string of the form wqx, where $w, x \in \Gamma^*$ and $q \in Q$. The meaning of wqx is that the M is in state q, the current contents of the tape is wx, and q is scanning the first symbol of x. Since the tape is unbounded, some clarification is needed about the string wx representing the tape contents. Our convention is that all characters to the right of the rightmost character of x must be B. This means that our definition of configuration is not unique, but is unique up to trailing blank symbols.

Transitions of the TM correspond to moving from one configuration to another:

(a) If $\delta(p, X) = (q, Y, L)$, then $\alpha Z p X \beta \vdash \alpha q Z Y \beta$.
(b) If $\delta(p, X) = (q, Y, R)$, then $\alpha p X \beta \vdash \alpha Y q \beta$.
(c) If $\delta(p, X) = (q, Y, S)$, then $\alpha p X \beta \vdash \alpha q Y \beta$.

We use $\overset{*}{\vdash}$ for the reflexive, transitive closure of $\vdash$, and we define $L(M) = \{x \in \Sigma^* : q_0 B x \overset{*}{\vdash} \alpha h \beta \text{ for some } \alpha, \beta \in \Gamma^*\}$.

Starting with a given input, a TM may eventually either

(a) enter a configuration that has no further move (i.e., for which δ is undefined);
(b) attempt to move left off the edge of its tape;
(c) enter an infinite loop; or
(d) enter the halting state h.

In cases (a)–(c) we say that M does not accept its input. In the last case we say that M accepts its input. In cases (a)–(b) we say that M crashes.

If $L = L(M)$ for some TM M, then we say L is *recursively enumerable* (often abbreviated r.e.). (The origin of this somewhat obscure term appears in Exercise 32.) If $L = L(M)$ for some TM M that has the property that M never enters an infinite loop on any input, then we say L is *recursive*.

There are many variations on TMs, such as allowing extra tracks on a single tape, or allowing multiple tapes, or allowing tapes to be unbounded to both the right and the left, or allowing two-dimensional tapes, or allowing nondeterminism. All of these variations can be shown to be equivalent in computing power to the vanilla TM model (see Exercise 29).

There is a special TM, M_U, called the universal TM. This TM has the property that it takes an input consisting of an encoded version of some TM T and an encoded version of an input x and simulates T on x, accepting if and only if T accepts x.

Which encoding should be used? To some extent it is not important, as long as all machines use the same convention. One possible encoding is as follows: we fix an infinite universal alphabet $\Sigma_U = \{a_1, a_2, \ldots\}$ and assume that all inputs and tape symbols are drawn from Σ_U. Similarly, we fix an infinite universal set of states $Q_U = \{q_0, q_1, \ldots\}$ and assume that all TMs use state names chosen from Q_U. We then encode an element $a_i \in \Sigma_U$ by the string $e(a_i) = 0^{i+1}$ and encode the blank symbol B by the string 0. We encode an alphabet $\Sigma = \{b_1, b_2, \ldots, b_r\}$ by the string

$$e(\Sigma) = 111 e(b_1) 1 e(b_2) 1 \cdots 1 e(b_r) 111.$$

We encode an element $q_i \in Q_U$ by the string $e(q_i) = 0^{i+1}$. We encode the directions of moves of a TM by $e(L) = 0$, $e(R) = 00$, and $e(S) = 000$. To encode a move m of a TM, say $\delta(q, a) = (p, b, D)$, we write

$$e(m) = 11e(q)1e(a)1e(p)1e(b)1e(D)11.$$

Finally, to encode an entire TM M with moves $m_1, m_2, \ldots, m_t$, we define

$$e(M) = 11111e(q_0)1e(h)1e(\Sigma)1e(\Gamma)1e(m_1)1 \cdots 1e(m_t)11111.$$

Theorem 1.6.1. *There exists a universal TM M_U that has the following behavior: on input $e(T)e(x)$, M_U simulates T on input x and halts if and only if T halts on x.*

Proof Idea. The TM M_U uses three tapes. The first tape is used to hold the input $e(T)e(x)$. The second tape holds an encoded version of T's tape and the third tape holds the encoded state that T is in. A step of M_U consists of determining if any moves on tape 1 match the current configuration and then performing the move on tape 2. If the simulated machine enters the halt state, so does M_U. A move may require replacing an encoded version of one symbol with another. Since these encodings could be of different lengths, some shifting of tape 2 may be required. Finally, the new state is written on tape 3. ∎

We now turn to two classes of languages that are based on TMs. The following theorem gives an alternative characterization of the class of recursive languages.

Theorem 1.6.2. *A language L is recursive if and only if there exists a TM M that on input x halts with either 1 or 0 written in cell 1 on its tape (and blank symbols on the rest of the tape) such that 1 is written if $x \in L$ and 0 is written if $x \notin L$.*

Such a TM is sometimes said to *decide L*.
The following theorems are easy exercises.

Theorem 1.6.3. *The class of recursive languages is closed under the operations of union, intersection, complement, Kleene *, and concatenation.*

Theorem 1.6.4. *The class of r.e. languages is closed under the operations of union, intersection, Kleene *, and concatenation.*

We can view the TM in Theorem 1.6.2 as computing a function—in that case, a function from Σ^* to $\{0, 1\}$. We can generalize this to allow TMs to compute a function from Σ^* to Δ^*.

1.7 Unsolvability

A decision problem is a problem with at least one parameter that takes infinitely many values, and for which the answer is always "yes" or "no."

We can associate a language with a decision problem as follows: we take the set of all encodings of instances of the decision problem for which the answer is "yes." Of course, this raises the question of what encoding to use, but often there is a "natural" encoding that suggests itself.

Example 1.7.1. Consider the following decision problem: given an integer n, decide whether or not n is a prime number. The input n can take infinitely many values (all $n \geq 2$, for example), and the answer is "yes" (the number is prime) or "no" (the number is not).

A natural encoding of an integer n is representation in base 2. The language associated with the previous decision problem is therefore

$$\text{PRIMES2} = \{10, 11, 101, 111, 1011, 1101, 10001, \ldots\}.$$

We say a decision problem is *solvable* if its associated language L is recursive—in other words, if there is a TM M that decides L. Note that a solvable decision problem corresponds to what we ordinarily think of as solvable by mechanical means: there exists a finite deterministic procedure that, given an instance of the problem, will halt in a finite amount of time and answer either "yes" or "no."

Turing's fundamental paper of 1936 proved that there exist unsolvable (or "uncomputable") decision problems. The next theorem concerns what is probably the most famous one.

Theorem 1.7.2. *The decision problem "Given a Turing machine T and an input w, does T halt on w?" is unsolvable.*

Proof. Let us assume that this problem, called the halting problem, is solvable. This means that there exists a TM, call it M_H, that takes an input of the form $e(T)e(w)$ and eventually halts, writing 1 on its output tape if T halts on w and 0 otherwise. This is illustrated by Figure 1.6.

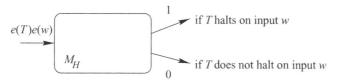

Figure 1.6: Hypothetical TM M_H

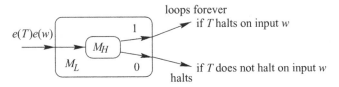

Figure 1.7: Constructing TM M_L from M_H

Now let us create a new TM M_L as follows: it simulates M_H and then examines the tape after M_H halts. If the tape contains a 1, then M_L enters an infinite loop (e.g., by moving right on every tape symbol). If the tape contains a 0, then M_L halts. This is illustrated by Figure 1.7.

Finally, we make a new TM M_D as follows: on input $e(T)$, M_D computes the encoding of $e(T)$, that is, $e(e(T))$, and writes it on the tape after $e(T)$. Then it calls M_L. This is illustrated in Figure 1.8.

We are now ready to obtain a contradiction. Feed M_D with $e(M_D)$ as input. The result is that M_D halts on input $e(M_D)$ if and only if it does not halt. This contradiction proves that our original assumption, the existence of M_H, must not hold.   ■

Another way to state Turing's theorem is the following.

Corollary 1.7.3. *The halting language $L_H = \{e(T)e(w) : T \text{ halts on } w\}$ is recursively enumerable but not recursive.*

We can obtain additional unsolvable problems by using reductions. We say a problem P_1 *Turing-reduces* to a problem P_2, and we write $P_1 \leq P_2$, if, given a TM T_2 that solves P_2, we could use T_2 as a subroutine in a TM T_1 that solves P_1. Similarly, we say a language L_1 *Turing-reduces* to a language L_2, and we write $L_1 \leq_T L_2$, if, given a TM T_2 deciding L_2, we could use T_2 as a subroutine in another TM deciding L_1.

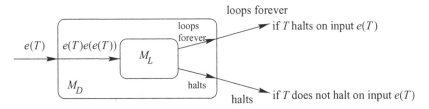

Figure 1.8: Constructing TM M_D from M_L

Theorem 1.7.4

(a) If P_1 is unsolvable, and $P_1 \leq P_2$, then P_2 is unsolvable.
(b) If L_1 is not recursive, and $L_1 \leq_T L_2$, then L_2 is not recursive.

Proof. We prove only (a), leaving (b) to the reader.
Suppose P_2 were solvable, say by a TM T_2. Since $P_1 \leq_T P_2$, we could use T_2 as a subroutine in a TM T_1 to solve P_1, a contradiction. ∎

Example 1.7.5. Let us use reductions to show that the decision problem

$$P_{\text{nonempty}} : \text{Given a TM } T, \text{ is } L(T) \neq \emptyset?$$

is unsolvable. It suffices to show that the halting problem reduces to P_{nonempty}. Suppose there were a TM M solving P_{nonempty}; M takes an encoding of a TM $e(T)$ as input and eventually writes 1 on its output tape if T accepts some string, and writes 0 if T accepts no string. Then we could use M to solve the halting problem as follows: on input $e(T)$ and w, create the encoding $e(T')$ of a TM T' that ignores its input, writes w out on its tape, and then simulates T on w. If T accepts w, then T' halts; otherwise it crashes. Thus, $L(T') = \Sigma^*$ if T accepts w and $L(T') = \emptyset$ otherwise.

To solve the halting problem, we now run M on $e(T')$ and answer whatever M answers.

1.8 Complexity theory

In the previous section, we exhibited some problems (such as the halting problem) that are, in general, unsolvable by a TM no matter how much time and space are allocated to the solution. We might instead consider what problems are solvable using only a *reasonable* amount of time and space. By putting restrictions on the amount of time and space used by a TM, we obtain various *complexity classes* of languages.

Many of the most important complexity classes deal with time. We say that a TM M is of *time complexity* $T(n)$ if, whenever M is started with an input w of length n on its tape, it eventually halts after making at most $T(n)$ moves.

The complexity class P is defined to be the set of all languages that are accepted by a deterministic TM of time complexity $T(n)$, where T is a polynomial. This complexity class includes many of the languages discussed in this book, such as PRIMES1, EQ, EVEN, SQ, and ODDPAL. Roughly speaking, the class P represents those languages in which membership is feasibly solvable, that is, solvable in a reasonable length of time, in terms of the size of the input.

Similarly, the complexity class NP is defined to be the set of all languages that are accepted by a nondeterministic TM of time complexity $T(n)$, where T is a polynomial. Of course, a nondeterministic TM may have many computational paths, and these paths could be of different lengths. Here, then, the time complexity of a nondeterministic TM on a given input is taken to be the length of the longest computational path over all nondeterministic choices.

A classical example of a language in NP is SAT, the language of encodings of Boolean formulas in conjunctive normal form that have a satisfying assignment, that is, an assignment to the variables that makes the formula evaluate to "true" (or 1). Here a Boolean formula is an expression consisting of variables connected with the operations "and" ($\land$), "or" ($\lor$), and "not" (typically represented by an overline). A formula is said to be in conjunctive normal form if it consists of clauses joined by $\land$, where each clause is an $\lor$ of variables or their negations. For example, a typical formula in conjunctive normal form is

$$f = (x_1 \lor \overline{x_2} \lor x_4) \land (x_2 \lor x_3 \lor \overline{x_5}) \land (\overline{x_1} \lor x_3 \lor x_4),$$

and $(x_1, x_2, x_3, x_4, x_5) = (1, 1, 0, 1, 0)$ is a satisfying assignment for f.

In order to define the class NPC, the NP-complete languages, we need the notion of Karp reduction. We say L_1 *Karp-reduces* to L_2, and we write $L_1 \leq L_2$, if there is a polynomial-time computable function f such that $x \in L_1$ if and only if $f(x) \in L_2$.

Theorem 1.8.1. *If $L_1 \in P$ and $L_1 \leq L_2$, then $L_2 \in P$.*

Proof. On input x, run a TM for f, obtaining $f(x)$. Since f is polynomial-time computable, we have $|f(x)| \leq T(|x|)$ for some polynomial T. Now run a polynomial-time algorithm M_2 to decide L_2 on $f(x)$. Return whatever M_2 says. The total time is bounded by a polynomial. ∎

We say a language L is NP-*complete* if

(a) $L \in$ NP;
(b) for all $L' \in$ NP, we have $L' \leq L$.

Thus, in some sense, the NP-complete problems are the "hardest" problems in NP.

Theorem 1.8.2. SAT *is* NP-*complete.*

Proof Idea.   It is easy to see that SAT is in NP, for all we need do is guess a satisfying assignment and then verify it. To show that every problem in NP reduces to SAT, take a polynomial-time-bounded TM M. We need to transform an input x to a Boolean formula φ_x, such that φ_x is satisfiable if and only if M accepts x. We encode the computation of M on x as a string s of configurations separated by delimiters and then create Boolean variables $c_{i,a}$ that are true if and only if the ith symbol of s equals a. Using these variables, we can construct φ_x to enforce the conditions that the configurations are legal, that the first configuration represents the initial state, that a final state is eventually reached, and that each configuration follows from the previous one by a legitimate move of the machine. ∎

A useful variation on SAT is 3-SAT; in this variant we force every clause to have exactly three literals.

Theorem 1.8.3. 3-SAT *is* NP-*complete.*

Proof Idea. The basic idea is to introduce new variables to create a formula where every clause has exactly three literals in such a way that the new formula is satisfiable if and only if the old formula is satisfiable. A clause such as $(x_1 \vee x_2)$ can be replaced by $(x_1 \vee x_2 \vee y_1) \wedge (x_1 \vee x_2 \vee \overline{y_1})$. Similarly, a clause such as $(x_1 \vee x_2 \vee x_3 \vee x_4 \vee x_5)$ can be replaced by $(x_1 \vee x_2 \vee y_1) \wedge (\overline{y_1} \vee x_3 \vee y_2) \wedge (\overline{y_2} \vee x_4 \vee x_5)$. ∎

We now turn to space complexity. If a TM uses at most $f(n)$ cells on any input of length n, we say it is of space complexity $f(n)$. One of the most important theorems about space complexity is *Savitch's theorem.*

Theorem 1.8.4 (Savitch). *If L is decidable in $f(n)$ nondeterministic space, and $f(n) \geq n$, then it is decidable in $O(f(n)^2)$ deterministic space.*

Proof Idea. Use the divide-and-conquer strategy coupled with recursion to decide if a nondeterministic TM M accepts x. ∎

We define PSPACE to be the class of languages decidable in space bounded by a polynomial on a deterministic TM and NPSPACE to be the class of languages decidable in space bounded by a polynomial on a nondeterministic TM.

Corollary 1.8.5. PSPACE = NPSPACE.

1.9 Exercises

1. Prove that for all words $u, v \in \Sigma^*$ and integers $e \geq 0$ we have $(uv)^e u = u(vu)^e$.

2. Let A, B, and C be languages. For each of the following identities, prove it or give a counterexample:
   (a) $(A \cup B)C = AC \cup BC$.
   (b) $(A \cap B)C = AC \cap BC$.
3. Find palindromes in languages other than English.
4. The English word antsy has the property that every nontrivial prefix is a valid English word. Can you find a longer English word with this property?
5. What is the smallest class of languages over Σ containing each singleton $\{a\}$ for $a \in \Sigma$ and closed under the operations of union, intersection, and complement?
6. Give regular expressions for each of the following languages:
   (a) The set of strings over $\{a, b, c\}$ in which all the a's precede all the b's, which in turn precede all the c's.
   (b) The complement of the language in (a).
   (c) The same as in (a), but only the *nonempty* strings satisfying the conditions.
   (d) The set of strings over $\{a, b\}$ that do not contain the substring aa.
   (e) The set of strings over $\{a, b\}$ that do not contain the substring aab.
   (f) The set of strings over $\{a, b\}$ containing both an even number of a's and an even number of b's.
   (g) The set of strings over $\{a, b\}$ that do not contain two or more consecutive occurrences of the same letter.
   (h) The set of strings that contain at least one occurrence of ab and at least one occurrence of ba. (These occurrences may overlap.)
   (i) The set of strings over $\{a, b\}$ that contain exactly one occurrence of the string bbb. *Note:* Overlapping occurrences should be counted more than once, so that the string abbbbba contains three occurrences of bbb.
   (j) The set of strings over $\{a, b\}$ having an equal number of occurrences of ab and ba.
   (k) The set of strings over $\{a, b\}$ containing at least one a and at least one b.
7. Let $L = \{x \in (a + b)^* : |x|_a \neq |x|_b\}$. Give a regular expression for L^2.
8. Suppose $M = (Q, \Sigma, \delta, q_0, F)$ is a DFA, and suppose there exists a state $q \in Q$, a string $z \in \Sigma^*$, and integers $i, j > 0$ such that $\delta(q, z^i) = q = \delta(q, z^j)$. Prove that $\delta(q, z^{\gcd(i,j)}) = q$.
9. Let x, y be words. Prove that $xy = yx$ if and only if there exists a word z such that $x^2 y^2 = z^2$.

10. A regular expression r is said to be in *disjunctive normal form* if it can be written in the form $r = r_1 + r_2 + \cdots + r_n$ for some $n \geq 1$, where none of the regular expressions $r_1, r_2, \ldots, r_n$ contains the symbol $+$ (union). For example, the regular expression $\text{a*b*} + (\text{ab})^* + (\text{c}(\text{acb})^*)^*$ is in disjunctive normal form, but $(\text{a} + \text{b})^*$ is not. Prove that every regular language can be specified by a regular expression in disjunctive normal form.

11. In an *extended regular expression*, intersection and complementation may be used. Show how to write $(\text{aba})^*$ as a *star-free* extended regular expression. (That is, your expression can use intersection, union, concatenation, and complementation, but may not use the Kleene closure or positive closure operators.)

*12. Show that allowing intersection in a regular expression can permit dramatically more concise regular expressions. More precisely, show that the shortest regular expression for $(\cdots(((a_0^2 a_1)^2 a_2)^2 a_3)^2 \cdots a_n)^2$ is of length $\Omega(2^n)$, while there exists a regular expression involving intersection of length $O(n^2)$.

13. Prove that each of the following languages is not regular:
    (a) $\{\text{a}^i\,\text{b}^j\ :\ \gcd(i, j) = 1\}$;
    (b) $\{\text{a}^i\text{b}^j\text{c}^k\ :\ i^2 + j^2 = k^2\}$.

14. Consider the language

$$L = \{xcy\ :\ x, y \in \{a, b\}^*\text{ and }y\text{ is a subsequence of }x\}.$$

    Show that L is not context-free.

15. Consider the language

$$L = \{x^R cy\ :\ x, y \in \{a, b\}^*\text{ and }y\text{ is a subsequence of }x\}.$$

    Show that L is context-free but not regular.

16. Prove that each of the following languages is not context-free:
    (a) $\{xx\ :\ x \in \{\text{a}, \text{b}\}^*\}$;
    (b) $\{x \in \{\text{a}, \text{b}, \text{c}\}^*\ :\ |x|_a = |x|_b = |x|_c\}$;
    (c) $\{wxw\ :\ w, x \in \{\text{a}, \text{b}\}^+\}$;
    (d) $\{x \in \{\text{a}, \text{b}, \text{c}\}^*\ :\ |x|_a = \max(|x|_b, |x|_c)\}$;
    (e) $\{x \in \{\text{a}, \text{b}, \text{c}\}^*\ :\ |x|_a = \min(|x|_b, |x|_c)\}$.

17. Let L_1 and L_2 be languages, and define

$$\text{join}(L_1, L_2) = \{z\ :\ \text{there exist }x_1 \in L_1,\ x_2 \in L_2,\text{ with }|x_1| = |x_2|,$$
$$\text{such that }z = x_1 x_2\}.$$

    Prove that if L_1 and L_2 are regular, then $\text{join}(L_1, L_2)$ is context-free.

18. The *order* of a language L is the smallest integer k such that $L^k = L^{k+1}$. (Note that the order may be infinite.) Show that for each $k \geq 0$, there exists a regular language of order k.

19. Prove that the converse of the pumping lemma holds if L is a unary language. Prove that it does not hold, in general, for larger alphabets.

20. Consider the following CFG: $G = (\{S\}, \{a, b\}, P, S)$, where the set of productions P is given by $S \rightarrow SSa \mid b$.

    Give an interpretation for $L(G)$ based on the evaluation of an algebraic expression.

    Give another characterization for $L(G)$ in terms of the number of a's and b's in any word $w \in L(G)$. Prove that your characterization is correct.

21. In our definition of CFG we demanded that $V \cap \Sigma = \emptyset$. What happens if we do not make this restriction?

22. Give CFGs for the following languages:
    (a) the set of strings over $\{a, b\}$ containing twice as many a's as b's;
    (b) the complement of $\{(a^n b)^n : n \geq 1\}$;
    (c) $\{a^i b^j : i, j \geq 0$ and $i \neq j$ and $i \neq 2j\}$;
    (d) $\{a^i b^j : j \leq i \leq 2j\}$.

23. Show that the following decision problems are unsolvable:
    (a) Given a TM T, does T enter an infinite loop on input ϵ?
    (b) Given a TM T, does T accept ϵ in an even number of moves?
    (c) Given a TM T and an input w, does T accept both w and w^R?

24. Show that the following decision problems are solvable:
    (a) Given a TM T, does T ever enter a state other than the initial state q_0?
    (b) Given a TM T, does T ever make a right move on input ϵ?
    (c) Given a TM T, does T ever make a left move on input ϵ?

25. Give a formal proof that the grammar in Example 1.5.3 is correct.

26. A symbol of a CFG is called *useless* if it never participates in the derivation of any terminal string. Give an algorithm that, on input a CFG G, outputs a CFG G' such that $L(G') = L(G)$ and G' contains no useless symbols. Your algorithm should not introduce any new ambiguities.

27. Give an algorithm that, on input a CFG G, outputs a CFG G' such that $L(G') = L(G) - \{\epsilon\}$ and G' has no ϵ-productions or unit productions. Your algorithm should not introduce any new ambiguities.

28. Give an algorithm that, on input a CFG G, outputs a CFG G' such that $L(G') = L(G) - \{\epsilon\}$ and G' is in Chomsky normal form. Your algorithm should not introduce any new ambiguities. Suppose G has m productions and the length of the longest production is k. Show that G' can be constructed in time polynomial in m and k.

29. In this exercise we explore some variations on the TM model and show that they are all equivalent in computing power to the vanilla TM model. For each suggested model, give a formal definition and proof that the model accepts the same class of languages as an ordinary TM.

    (a) *A multitrack TM.* Here the TM has a single tape that is divided into parallel tracks. In a single move, the TM can read all the tracks at once and, based on the contents, move and change the contents of the tracks.

    (b) *A multitape TM.* Here the TM has an arbitrary, but fixed, number of tapes with independent heads. At any step the TM can read the contents of the symbols under all the tape heads and move the heads independently in any direction (or stay stationary).

    (c) *A TM with doubly infinite tape.* Here the tape has no "left edge" and the head can move arbitrarily far in either direction.

    (d) *A TM with two-dimensional tape.* Here the head is assumed to be scanning a cell in an infinite array of cells and, at any point, can move up, down, right, or left one cell, or remain stationary.

    (e) *A nondeterministic TM.* Here the machine accepts if some series of choices leads to the halting state.

30. Show that every TM can be simulated by a TM that never writes the blank symbol B on the tape. *Hint:* Instead of writing a blank symbol, write an alternate symbol $\bar{B}$.

31. Show that the subset construction for NFA-to-DFA conversion can be performed in $O(kn2^n)$ time, where k is the alphabet size and n is the number of states. *Hint:* Precompute all the possible unions.

32. Show that a language L is recursively enumerable if and only if there exists a TM M with a special output tape, such that M never moves left on its output tape, writes out a string of the form $\#x_1\#x_2\#x_3\#x_4\cdots$ on its output tape, where each $x_i \in L$, and every element of L eventually appears on the output tape and exactly once.

33. Consider the following CFG for regular expressions:

$$S \rightarrow E_+ \mid E_{\bullet} \mid G$$
$$E_+ \rightarrow E_+ + F \mid F + F$$
$$F \rightarrow E_{\bullet} \mid G$$
$$E_{\bullet} \rightarrow E_{\bullet} G \mid GG$$
$$G \rightarrow E_* \mid C \mid P$$
$$C \rightarrow \emptyset \mid \epsilon \mid a \quad (a \in \Sigma)$$
$$E_* \rightarrow G *$$
$$P \rightarrow (S)$$

The meaning of the variables is as follows:

- S generates all regular expressions.
- E_+ generates all unparenthesized expressions where the last operator was $+$.
- $E_\bullet$ generates all unparenthesized expressions where the last operator was $\cdot$ (implicit concatenation).
- E_* generates all unparenthesized expressions where the last operator was $*$ (Kleene closure).
- C generates all unparenthesized expressions where there was no last operator (i.e., the constants).
- P generates all parenthesized expressions.

Here, by *parenthesized* we mean there is at least one pair of enclosing parentheses. Note this grammar allows $a * *$ but disallows (   ). Prove that this grammar is correct and unambiguous.

34. Let L be a language. Show that the following are equivalent:
   (a) $\epsilon \in L$ and if $x, y \in L$, then $xy \in L$;
   (b) $L = L^*$;
   (c) there exists a language T such that $L = T^*$.

1.10 Projects

1. Read some of the foundational papers in the theory of computing, such as Turing [1936], Rabin and Scott [1959], and Cook [1971], and contrast the presentation you find there with the presentation found in more recent books. Did Turing actually state the halting problem in his 1936 paper?

1.11 Research problems

1. Is there an infinite family of distinct unary languages $(L_n)_{n \geq 1}$ and constants c, d such that L_n is accepted by an NFA with $\leq cn$ states, but every regular expression for L_n has $\geq dn^2$ symbols?

1.12 Notes on Chapter 1

There are many excellent textbooks that introduce the reader to the theory of computation, for example, Martin [1997], Hopcroft, Motwani, and Ullman [2001], and Lewis and Papadimitriou [1998].

1.2 Some textbooks use the symbols λ or Λ to denote the empty string. We use ϵ in this book.

Some writers, particularly Europeans, use the term "factor" for what we have called "subword" and the term "subword" for what we have called "subsequence."

1.3 Brzozowski [1962b] is a good introduction to the properties of regular expressions.

1.4 The origins of finite automata include the neural net model of McCulloch and Pitts [1943]. Rabin and Scott [1959] is the fundamental paper in this area.

Although most writers agree on the conventions for finite automata as specified here, there are some minor differences. For example, some writers do not enforce the condition that the transition function of a DFA be a complete function (defined on all elements of its domain $Q \times \Sigma$). Some writers allow an NFA to have an initial "state" that is actually a set of states.

1.5 The Indian philologist Panini (ca. 400 B.C.E.) used grammars to describe the structure of Sanskrit. The modern mathematical treatment is due to Chomsky [1956].

For a delightful collection of examples of ambiguous English sentences, see Thornton [2003].

1.6 TMs were introduced by Turing [1936].

1.7 Oddly enough, Turing's original paper [1936] did not state exactly what we call the halting problem today. The first use of the term seems to be in Davis [1958, p. 70]. Also see Strachey [1965].

What we have called "unsolvable" is, in the literature, also called "undecidable" or "uncomputable."

1.8 The classic reference for NP-completeness and related topics is Garey and Johnson [1979]. The book of Papadimitriou [1994] is a good general reference on computational complexity. In this text, we have used polynomial-time reductions, although it is more fashionable these days to use logspace reductions.

2

Combinatorics on words

In 1906, the Norwegian mathematician Axel Thue initiated the study of what is now called *combinatorics on words*—the properties of finite and infinite strings of symbols over a finite alphabet. Although combinatorics on words does not directly involve machine models, its results have implications for many areas of computer science and mathematics.

2.1 Basics

We start by defining infinite strings (or infinite words or infinite sequences—we use the terms interchangeably). We let $\mathbb{Z}$ denote the integers, $\mathbb{Z}^+$ denote the positive integers $\{1, 2, 3, \ldots\}$, and $\mathbb{N}$ denote the nonnegative integers $\{0, 1, 2, \ldots\}$. Then we usually take an infinite string $a_0a_1a_2\cdots$ to be a map from $\mathbb{N}$ to Σ (a finite alphabet), although occasionally we instead use a map from $\mathbb{Z}^+$ to Σ.

Example 2.1.1. The following is an example of a right-infinite string:

$$\mathbf{p} = (p_n)_{n \geq 1} = 0110101000101 \cdots,$$

where $p_n = 1$ if n is a prime number and 0 otherwise. The sequence $\mathbf{p}$ is called the *characteristic sequence* of the primes.

The set of all infinite strings over Σ is denoted by Σ^ω. We define $\Sigma^\infty = \Sigma^* \cup \Sigma^\omega$. In this book, infinite strings are typically given in boldface.

The notions of subword, prefix, and suffix for finite strings have evident analogues for infinite strings. Let $\mathbf{w} = a_0a_1a_2\cdots$ be an infinite string. For $i \geq 0$, we define $\mathbf{w}[i] = a_i$. Also, for $i \geq 0$ and $j \geq i - 1$, we define $\mathbf{w}[i..j] = a_ia_{i+1}\cdots a_j$.

For a sequence of words (w_i), we let

$$\prod_{i \geq 1} w_i$$

denote a string $w_1 w_2 w_3 \cdots$, which is infinite if and only if $w_i \neq \epsilon$ infinitely often. We can also concatenate a finite string on the left with an infinite string on the right, but not vice versa. If x is a nonempty finite string, then x^ω is the infinite string $xxx \cdots$. Such a string is called *purely periodic*. An infinite string **w** of the form $x y^\omega$ for $y \neq \epsilon$ is called *ultimately periodic*. If **w** is ultimately periodic, then we can write it uniquely as $x y^\omega$ where $|x|, |y|$ are as small as possible. In this case y is referred to as the *period* of **w**, and x is called the *preperiod* of **w**. In some cases, the word *period* refers to the length $|y|$, and similarly for "preperiod."

If L is a language, we define

$$L^\omega = \{w_1 w_2 w_3 \cdots \ : \ w_i \in L - \{\epsilon\} \text{ for all } i \geq 1\}.$$

2.2 Morphisms

In this section we introduce a fundamental tool of formal languages, the *homomorphism*, or just *morphism* for short. Let Σ and Δ be alphabets. A morphism is a map h from Σ^* to Δ^* that obeys the identity $h(xy) = h(x)h(y)$ for all strings $x, y \in \Sigma^*$. Typically, we use the roman letters f, g, h and the Greek letters μ, τ to denote morphisms.

Clearly if h is a morphism, then we must have $h(\epsilon) = \epsilon$. Furthermore, once h is defined for all elements of Σ, it can be uniquely extended to a map from Σ^* to Δ^*. Henceforth, when we define a morphism, we usually give it by specifying its action only on Σ.

Example 2.2.1. Let $\Sigma = \{\text{e}, \text{m}, \text{o}, \text{s}\}$ and $\Delta = \{\text{a}, \text{e}, \text{l}, \text{n}, \text{r}, \text{s}, \text{t}\}$, and define

$$h(\text{m}) = \text{ant};$$
$$h(\text{o}) = \epsilon;$$
$$h(\text{s}) = \text{ler};$$
$$h(\text{e}) = \text{s}.$$

Then $h(\text{moose}) = \text{antlers}$.

If $\Sigma = \Delta$, then we can iterate the application of h. We define $h^0(a) = a$ and $h^i(a) = h(h^{i-1}(a))$ for all $a \in \Sigma$.

Example 2.2.2. Let $\Sigma = \Delta = \{0, 1\}$. Define the *Thue–Morse morphism* $\mu(0) = 01$ and $\mu(1) = 10$. Then $\mu^2(0) = 0110$ and $\mu^3(0) = 01101001$.

We can also apply morphisms to infinite strings. If $\mathbf{w} = c_0 c_1 c_2 \cdots$ is an infinite string, then we define

$$h(\mathbf{w}) = h(c_0)h(c_1)h(c_2)\cdots.$$

2.3 The theorems of Lyndon–Schützenberger

In this section, we prove two beautiful and fundamental theorems due to Lyndon and Schützenberger.

We start with one of the simplest and most basic results on strings, sometimes known as Levi's lemma:

Lemma 2.3.1. *Let $u, v, x, y \in \Sigma^*$, and suppose that $uv = xy$. If $|u| \geq |x|$, there exists $t \in \Sigma^*$ such that $u = xt$ and $y = tv$. If $|u| < |x|$, there exists $t \in \Sigma^+$ such that $x = ut$ and $v = ty$.*

Proof. Left to the reader. ∎

To motivate the first theorem of Lyndon–Schützenberger, consider the following problem: under what conditions can a string have a nontrivial proper prefix and suffix that are identical? Examples in English include `reader`, which begins and ends with `r`, and `alfalfa`, which begins and ends with `alfa`. The answer is given by the following theorem.

Theorem 2.3.2. *Let $x, y, z \in \Sigma^+$. Then $xy = yz$ if and only if there exist $u \in \Sigma^+$, $v \in \Sigma^*$, and an integer $e \geq 0$ such that $x = uv$, $z = vu$, and $y = (uv)^e u = u(vu)^e$.*

Proof. ($\Leftarrow$): This direction is easy. We have

$$xy = uv(uv)^e u = (uv)^{e+1} u;$$
$$yz = u(vu)^e vu = u(vu)^{e+1};$$

and these strings are equal by Exercise 1.1.

($\Rightarrow$): The proof is by induction on $|y|$. If $|y| = 1$, then $y = a$ for $a \in \Sigma$. Then $xa = az$. Thus, x begins with a and z ends with a, so we can write $x = ax'$ and $z = z'a$. Thus, $ax'a = xa = az = az'a$, and so $x' = z'$. Thus we can take $u = a$, $v = x'$, and $e = 0$.

Now suppose that $|y| > 1$. There are two cases:

Case I: If $|x| \geq |y|$, then we have a situation like the following:

By Levi's lemma there exists $w \in \Sigma^*$ such that $x = yw$ and $z = wy$. Now take $u = y$, $v = w$, $e = 0$, and we are done.

Case II: Now suppose that $|x| < |y|$. Then we have a situation like the following:

By Levi's lemma there exists $w \in \Sigma^+$ such that $y = xw = wz$. By induction (since $0 < |w| = |y| - |x| < |y|$), we know there exist $u \in \Sigma^+$, $v \in \Sigma^*$, $e \geq 0$ such that

$$x = uv;$$
$$z = vu;$$
$$w = (uv)^e u = u(vu)^e.$$

so it follows that $y = xw = uv(uv)^e u = (uv)^{e+1} u$. ■

To motivate the second theorem of Lyndon and Schützenberger, consider the following problem: what are the solutions in strings to the equation $x^2 = y^3$? If we take the positive integers as an analogy, then unique factorization into primes suggests that the only possible solutions are when x is a cube of some string z and y is the square of z.

Another motivation comes from the problem of determining when words can commute: when can $xy = yx$? There are not too many nontrivial examples in English; some examples are $x = \mathtt{do}$, $y = \mathtt{dodo}$ and $x = \mathtt{tar}$, $y = \mathtt{tartar}$.

The general case is given by the following result.

Theorem 2.3.3. *Let* $x, y \in \Sigma^+$. *Then the following three conditions are equivalent:*

1. $xy = yx$.
2. *There exist* $z \in \Sigma^+$ *and integers* $k, l > 0$ *such that* $x = z^k$ *and* $y = z^l$.
3. *There exist integers* $i, j > 0$ *such that* $x^i = y^j$.

Proof. We show that $(1) \Rightarrow (2)$, $(2) \Rightarrow (3)$, and $(3) \Rightarrow (1)$.

$(1) \Rightarrow (2)$: By induction on $|xy|$. If $|xy| = 2$, then $|x| = |y| = 1$, so $x = y$ and we may take $z = x = y$, $k = l = 1$.

Now assume that the implication is true for all x, y with $|xy| < n$. We prove it for $|xy| = n$. Without loss of generality, assume $|x| \geq |y|$. Then we have a situation like the following:

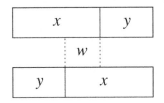

Hence there exists $w \in \Sigma^*$ such that $x = wy = yw$. If $|w| = 0$, then $x = y$, so we may take $z = x = y$ and $k = l = 1$. Otherwise $w \in \Sigma^+$. Now $|wy| = |x| < |xy| = n$, so the induction hypothesis applies, and there exist $z \in \Sigma^+$ and integers $k, l > 0$ such that $w = z^k$, $y = z^l$. It follows that $x = wy = z^{k+l}$.

$(2) \Rightarrow (3)$: By (2) there exist $z \in \Sigma^+$ and integers $k, l > 0$ such that $x = z^k$ and $y = z^l$. Hence, taking $i = l$, $j = k$, we get

$$x^i = (z^k)^i = z^{kl} = (z^l)^k = (z^l)^j = y^j,$$

as desired.

$(3) \Rightarrow (1)$: We have $x^i = y^j$. Without loss of generality, assume $|x| \geq |y|$. Then we have a situation like the following:

Hence there exists $w \in \Sigma^*$ such that $x = yw$. Hence, $x^i = (yw)^i = y^j$, and so $y(wy)^{i-1}w = y^j$. Therefore, $(wy)^{i-1}w = y^{j-1}$ and so, by multiplying by y

on the right, we get $(wy)^i = y^j$. Hence, $(yw)^i = (wy)^i$, and hence $yw = wy$. It follows that $x = yw = wy$ and $xy = (yw)y = y(wy) = yx$. ∎

We now make the following definition: a string $w \in \Sigma^+$ is a *power* if there exists a string z and an integer $k \geq 2$ such that $w = z^k$. A string $w \in \Sigma^+$ that is not a power is called *primitive*. For example, door is primitive, but dodo $= (\text{do})^2$ is not.

Theorem 2.3.4. *Every nonempty string w can be expressed uniquely in the form $w = x^n$, where $n \geq 1$ and x is primitive.*

Proof. Choose n as large as possible so that $w = x^n$ has a solution; clearly, $1 \leq n \leq |w|$. We claim that the resulting x is primitive. For if not, we could write $x = y^k$ for some $k \geq 2$ and then $w = y^{kn}$, where $kn > n$.

To prove uniqueness, suppose that w has two representations $w = x^n = y^m$, where both x, y are primitive and $n, m \geq 1$. Then by Theorem 2.3.3, there exists z with $|z| \geq 1$ such that $x = z^k$ and $y = z^\ell$. Since x, y are primitive, however, we must have $k = \ell = 1$. But then $x = y = z$, and hence $n = m$, and the two representations are actually the same. ∎

If $w = x^n$, where x is primitive, then x is sometimes called the *primitive root* of w.

The following theorem can be thought of as a generalization of Theorem 2.3.3.

Theorem 2.3.5. *Let w and x be nonempty words. Let $\mathbf{y} \in w\{w, x\}^\omega$ and $\mathbf{z} \in x\{w, x\}^\omega$. Then the following conditions are equivalent:*

(a) $\mathbf{y}$ and $\mathbf{z}$ agree on a prefix of length at least $|w| + |x| - \gcd(|w|, |x|)$.
(b) $wx = xw$.
(c) $\mathbf{y} = \mathbf{z}$.

Proof.

(a) $\Rightarrow$ (b): We prove the contrapositive. Suppose $wx \neq xw$.

Then we prove that $\mathbf{y}$ and $\mathbf{z}$ differ at a position $\leq |w| + |x| - \gcd(|w|, |x|)$. The proof is by induction on $|w| + |x|$.

The base case is $|w| + |x| = 2$. Then $|w| = |x| = 1$ and $|w| + |x| - \gcd(|w|, |x|) = 1$. Since $wx \neq xw$, we must have $w = a$, $x = b$ with $a \neq b$. Then $\mathbf{y}$ and $\mathbf{z}$ differ at the first position.

Now assume the result is true for $|w| + |x| < k$. We prove it for $|w| + |x| = k$. If $|w| = |x|$, then $\mathbf{y}$ and $\mathbf{z}$ must disagree at the $|w|$th position or earlier, for otherwise $w = x$ and $wx = xw$; since $|w| \leq |w| + |x| - \gcd(|w|, |x|) = |w|$, the result follows. So, without loss of generality, assume $|w| < |x|$. If w is not a prefix of x, then $\mathbf{y}$ and $\mathbf{z}$ disagree on the $|w|$th position or earlier, and again $|w| \leq |w| + |x| - \gcd(|w|, |x|)$.

So w is a proper prefix of x. Write $x = wt$ for some nonempty word t. Now any common divisor of $|w|$ and $|x|$ must also divide $|x| - |w| = |t|$, and similarly any common divisor of both $|w|$ and $|t|$ must also divide $|w| + |t| = |x|$. So $\gcd(|w|, |x|) = \gcd(|w|, |t|)$.

Now $wt \neq tw$, for otherwise we have $wx = wwt = wtw = xw$, a contradiction. Then $\mathbf{y} = ww \cdots$ and $\mathbf{z} = wt \cdots$. By induction (since $|w| + |t| < k$), $w^{-1}\mathbf{y}$ and $w^{-1}\mathbf{z}$ disagree at position $|w| + |t| - \gcd(|w|, |t|)$ or earlier. Hence, $\mathbf{y}$ and $\mathbf{z}$ disagree at position $2|w| + |t| - \gcd(|w|, |t|) = |w| + |x| - \gcd(|w|, |x|)$ or earlier.

(b) $\Rightarrow$ (c): If $wx = xw$, then by the second theorem of Lyndon–Schützenberger, both w and x are in u^+ for some word u. Hence, $\mathbf{y} = u^\omega = \mathbf{z}$.

(c) $\Rightarrow$ (a): Trivial. ∎

There is another possible generalization of Theorem 2.3.3. To state it, we need the notion of fractional power. If $z = x^n x'$, where $n \geq 1$, $1 \leq |x'| \leq |x|$, and x' is a prefix of x, then we say z is a $|z|/|x|$ power. For example, `alfalfa` is a 7/3 power, as it equals $(\texttt{alf})^2\texttt{a}$. Similarly, if p/q is a rational number > 1, and $|x|$ is divisible by q, then by $x^{p/q}$ we mean $z = x^a x'$, where $a = \lfloor p/q \rfloor$, x' is a prefix of x, and $|z|/|x| = p/q$. For example, $(\texttt{entanglem})^{4/3} = $ `entanglement`.

Theorem 2.3.6. *Let x and y be nonempty words. Then $xy = yx$ if and only if there are rational numbers $\alpha, \beta \geq 2$ such that $x^\alpha = y^\beta$.*

Proof. Suppose $xy = yx$. Then by Theorem 2.3.3, there must be integers $i, j \geq 1$ such that $x^i = y^j$. Hence we can take $\alpha = 2i$, $\beta = 2j$.

Now suppose $x^\alpha = y^\beta$. Without loss of generality, we can assume $|x| \geq |y|$. Then x^ω and y^ω agree on a prefix of length $\geq \alpha|x| \geq 2x \geq |x| + |y| > |x| + |y| - \gcd(|x|, |y|)$. Hence by Theorem 2.3.5, $xy = yx$. ∎

2.4 Conjugates and borders

We say a word w is a *conjugate* of a word x if w is a cyclic shift of x, that is, if there exist words u, v such that $w = uv$ and $x = vu$, and we write $w \sim x$. For example, `enlist` and `listen` are conjugates (take $u = $ en, and $v = $ list).

Theorem 2.4.1. *The conjugacy relation $\sim$ is an equivalence relation.*

Proof. Left to the reader as Exercise 10. ∎

Theorem 2.4.2. *Let w and x be conjugates. Then w is a power if and only if x is a power. Furthermore, if $w = y^k$, $k \geq 2$, then $x = z^k$, where z is a conjugate of y.*

Proof. Since w and x are conjugates, there exist u, v such that $w = uv$, $x = vu$. Furthermore, since w is a power, there exists a word y and an integer $k \geq 2$ such that $w = y^k$. Hence, $y^k = uv$.

If $|u|$ is a multiple of $|y|$, then $u = y^i$ for some i, and so $v = y^{k-i}$. Thus, $x = vu = y^k$.

Otherwise, assume $|u|$ is not a multiple of $|y|$. Then we can write $u = y^i r$, $v = s y^{k-i-1}$, where $r, s \neq \epsilon$ and $rs = y$. Then $x = vu = s y^{k-i-1} y^i r = s(rs)^{k-1} r = (sr)^k$. Thus, x is a power. Letting $z = sr$, we also see that $x = z^k$, and z is a conjugate of y. ∎

Now we turn to borders. A word $w \in \Sigma^+$ is said to be *bordered* if it can be written as $w = xyx$, where $x \in \Sigma^+$, $y \in \Sigma^*$. Alternatively, a word w is bordered if and only if it is an α-power, for α a rational number > 1. Examples of bordered words in English include outshout and photograph. If a word is not bordered, it is *unbordered*.

Theorem 2.4.3. *Let w be a nonempty word. Then w is primitive if and only if w has an unbordered conjugate.*

Proof. Suppose w is primitive. Let x be the lexicographically least conjugate of w. I claim x is unbordered. For if x were bordered, we could write $x = uvu$, where $u \in \Sigma^+$ and $v \in \Sigma^*$. Now $z = uuv$ is a conjugate of x and so is a conjugate of w. If $x = z$, then $uv = vu$. If $v = \epsilon$, then $x = u^2$. Otherwise, by Theorem 2.3.3, there exist a string t and integers $i, j \geq 1$ such that $u = t^i$, $v = t^j$. Then $x = uvu = t^{2i+j}$. By Theorem 2.4.2, w is also a power, a contradiction.

Now $x < z$, since x was lexicographically least among all conjugates of w. Then $uvu < uuv$, so $vu < uv$. Then $vuu < uvu = x$, so we have found a conjugate of w that is lexicographically smaller than x, a contradiction.

For the other direction, suppose w is not primitive, and let x be any conjugate of w. By Theorem 2.4.2, x is also a power; that is, $x = t^k$ for some nonempty t and integer $k \geq 2$. Then $x = tt^{k-2}t$, so x is bordered. ∎

We now apply our results about conjugates and borders to determine the solutions to the equation in words $x^i y^j = z^k$. But first, we need a technical lemma.

Lemma 2.4.4. *Let x be a power, $x = z^k$, $k \geq 2$, and let w be a subword of x with $|w| > |z|$. Then w is bordered.*

Proof. Since w is a subword of x, we have $x = ywz$ for some words y, z. Now consider wzy, a conjugate of x. By Theorem 2.4.2, since x is a kth power of z, we know that wzy is a kth power of some conjugate t of z. Write $w = t^j t'$, where $j \geq 1$ and t' is a nonempty prefix of t (possibly equal to t). Then w begins and ends with t'. ∎

Now we turn to a famous equation in words, which might be considered as the noncommutative version of Fermat's last theorem.

Theorem 2.4.5. *The equation*

$$x^i = y^j z^k \tag{2.1}$$

holds for strings $x, y, z \in \Sigma^+$ and $i, j, k \geq 2$ if and only if there exist a word $w \in \Sigma^+$ and integers $l, m, n \geq 1$ such that $x = w^l$, $y = w^m$, $z = w^n$, with $li = mj + nk$.

Proof. Suppose $x = w^l$, $y = w^m$, and $z = w^n$ and $li = mj + nk$. Then $x^i = w^{li} = w^{mj+nk} = w^{mj} w^{nk} = y^j z^k$.

For the other direction, without loss of generality, assume x, y, and z are primitive; otherwise, replace a nonprimitive string with its primitive root and adjust the exponent. Assume x is of minimal length, satisfying an equation of the form (2.1), and also assume, contrary to what we want to prove, that there is no $w \in \Sigma^+$ with $x, y, z \in w^+$.

If $y^p \in x^+$ for some p, $1 \leq p \leq j$, then by Theorem 2.3.3, y and x are both powers of a word w, which can be assumed to be primitive. Now we can cancel powers of w on both sides of Eq. (2.1) to get an equation of the form $w^s = z^k$. It follows that z is also a power of w, a contradiction. By symmetry, the same conclusion follows if $z^q \in x^+$ for some q, $1 \leq q \leq k$. Thus we can assume $y^p, z^q \notin x^+$ for $1 \leq p \leq j$, $1 \leq q \leq k$. In particular, $|x| \neq |y|$ and $|x| \neq |z|$.

If $|y| > |x|$, then we have, by looking at a prefix of Eq. (2.1), that $x^\alpha = y^2$ for some rational $\alpha > 2$. Then by combining Theorems 2.3.6 and 2.3.3, we see that there exists a string w and integers $r, s \geq 1$ such that $y = w^r$, $x = w^s$. Since $|y| > |x|$, we must have $r \geq 2$. So y is not primitive, a contradiction. A similar conclusion follows if $|z| > |x|$, by considering the reversal of Eq. (2.1). So we can assume that $|y|, |z| < |x|$.

Suppose $i > 2$. By Theorem 2.4.3, x has an unbordered conjugate f. Write $x = uv$ and $f = vu$. Then $x^i = (uv)^i = u(vu)^{i-1}v$. Thus at least two copies of f lie within $x^i = y^j z^k$, so at least one copy is either entirely within y^j or entirely within z^k. By Lemma 2.4.4, f is bordered. This is a contradiction.

It remains to consider the case $i = 2$. If $|y^j| = |z^k|$, then $x = y^j = z^k$, a contradiction. Without loss of generality, we can assume $|y^j| > |z^k|$. Hence, $y^j = xu^r$ for some primitive word u and integer $r \geq 1$. Similarly, $u^r z^k = x$. Thus, multiplying both sides by u^r, we get $u^{2r} z^k = u^r x$. Thus, $u^{2r} z^k$ is a conjugate of y^j. Hence, by Theorem 2.4.2, $u^{2r} z^k = v^j$ for some v a conjugate of y. Now we have an equation of the form (2.1) with $|v| = |y| < |x|$, contradicting the minimality of x.

Thus our original assumption that there is no $w \in \Sigma^+$ with $x, y, z \in w^+$ is false, and such a w must exist. ∎

2.5 Repetitions in strings

A *square* is a string of the form xx, such as the English word hotshots. If w is a (finite or infinite) string containing no nonempty subword of this form, then it is said to be *squarefree*. Note that the string square is squarefree, while the string squarefree is not.

It is easy to verify (see Exercise 3) that there are no squarefree strings of length >3 over a two-letter alphabet. However, there are infinite squarefree strings over a three-letter alphabet. We construct one later in Theorem 2.5.2.

Similarly, a *cube* is a string of the form xxx, such as the English sort-of-word shshsh. If w contains no nonempty cube, it is said to be *cubefree*. The string cubefree is not squarefree, since it contains two consecutive occurrences of the string e, but it is cubefree.

An *overlap* is a string of the form $cxcxc$, where x is a string and c is a single letter. (The term *overlap* refers to the fact that such a string can be viewed as two overlapping occurrences of the string cxc.) The English string alfalfa, for example, is an overlap with $c = $ a and $x = $ lf. If w contains no overlap, it is said to be *overlap-free*.

In this section, we prove some simple results in the theory of repetitions in strings. We start by constructing an infinite overlap-free string over an alphabet of size 2.

Define

$$t_n = \begin{cases} 0, & \text{if the number of 1s in the base-2 expansion of } n \text{ is even;} \\ 1, & \text{if the number of 1s in the base-2 expansion of } n \text{ is odd.} \end{cases}$$

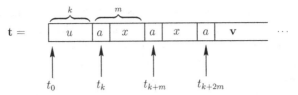

Figure 2.1: Hypothesized overlap in **t**

Note that $t_{2n} = t_n$, because the base-2 expansions of n and $2n$ have the same number of 1s. Similarly, $t_{2n+1} = 1 - t_n$, since we get the base-2 expansion of $2n + 1$ by concatenating the base-2 expansion of n with a 1.

We define $\mathbf{t} = t_0 t_1 t_2 \cdots = 01101001 \cdots$. The infinite string **t** is usually called the *Thue–Morse* sequence, named after Axel Thue and Marston Morse, two of the first mathematicians to study its properties. This infinite sequence occurs in many different areas of mathematics, physics, and computer science (for a brief tour, see Section 2.6). In a moment we will prove Thue's theorem that **t** is overlap-free. It is interesting to note that Thue published his result in an obscure Norwegian journal and it was overlooked for many years. In the meantime, many people rediscovered the sequence and its properties.

Theorem 2.5.1. *The Thue–Morse sequence* **t** *is overlap-free.*

Proof Idea.   Assume that **t** has an overlap; this implies that a certain set of equations holds on the symbols of **t**. Use the identities $t_{2n} = t_n$ and $t_{2n+1} = 1 - t_n$ for $n \geq 0$ to derive a contradiction.

Proof.   Assume, contrary to what we want to prove, that **t** contains an overlap. Then we would be able to write $\mathbf{t} = uaxaxav$ for some finite strings u, x, an infinite string **v**, and a letter a (see Figure 2.1).

In other words, we would have $t_{k+j} = t_{k+m+j}$ for $0 \leq j \leq m$, where $m = |ax|$ and $k = |u|$. Assume $m \geq 1$ is as small as possible. Then there are two cases: (i) m is even and (ii) m is odd.

(i) If m is even, then let $m = 2m'$. Again there are two cases: (a) k is even and (b) k is odd.

    (a) If k is even, then let $k = 2k'$. Then we know $t_{k+j} = t_{k+m+j}$ for $0 \leq j \leq m$, so it is certainly true that $t_{k+2j'} = t_{k+m+2j'}$ for $0 \leq j' \leq m/2$. Hence, $t_{2k'+2j'} = t_{2k'+2j'+2m'}$ for $0 \leq j' \leq m'$, and so $t_{k'+j'} = t_{k'+j'+m'}$ for $0 \leq j' \leq m'$. But this contradicts the minimality of m.

    (b) If k is odd, then let $k = 2k' + 1$. Then as before we have $t_{k+2j'} = t_{k+m+2j'}$ for $0 \leq j' \leq m/2$. Hence, $t_{2k'+2j'+1} = t_{2k'+2j'+2m'+1}$ for $0 \leq$

$j' \le m'$, and so $t_{k'+j'} = t_{k'+j'+m'}$ for $0 \le j' \le m'$, again contradicting the minimality of m.

(ii) If m is odd, then there are three cases: (a) $m \ge 5$, (b) $m = 3$, and (c) $m = 1$. For $n \ge 1$, we define $b_n = (t_n + t_{n-1}) \bmod 2$. Note that $b_{4n+2} = (t_{4n+2} + t_{4n+1}) \bmod 2$. Since the base-2 representations of $4n + 2$ and $4n + 1$ are identical, except that the last two bits are switched, we have $t_{4n+2} = t_{4n+1}$, and so $b_{4n+2} = 0$. On the other hand, $b_{2n+1} = (t_{2n+1} + t_{2n}) \bmod 2$, and the base-2 representations of $2n + 1$ and $2n$ are identical except for the last bit; hence, $b_{2n+1} = 1$.

(a) m odd, ≥ 5. We have $b_{k+j} = b_{k+m+j}$ for $1 \le j \le m$. Since $m \ge 5$, we can choose j such that $k + j \equiv 2 \pmod 4$. Then for this value of $k + j$, we have from earlier that $b_{k+j} = 0$, but $k + j + m$ is odd, so $b_{k+m+j} = 1$, a contradiction.

(b) $m = 3$. Again, $b_{k+j} = b_{k+j+3}$ for $1 \le j \le 3$. Choose j such that $k + j \equiv 2$ or $3 \pmod 4$. If $k + j \equiv 2 \pmod 4$, then the reasoning of the previous case applies. Otherwise $k + j \equiv 3 \pmod 4$ and then $b_{k+j} = 1$, while $b_{k+j+3} = 0$.

(c) $m = 1$. Then $t_k = t_{k+1} = t_{k+2}$. Hence, $t_{2n} = t_{2n+1}$ for $n = \lceil k/2 \rceil$, a contradiction.

This completes the proof. ■

Using the fact that $\mathbf{t}$ is overlap-free, we may now construct a squarefree infinite string over the alphabet $\Sigma_3 = \{0, 1, 2\}$.

Theorem 2.5.2. *For $n \ge 1$, define c_n to be the number of 1s between the nth and $(n + 1)$th occurrence of 0 in the string $\mathbf{t}$. Set $\mathbf{c} = c_1 c_2 c_3 \cdots$. Then $\mathbf{c} = 210201 \cdots$ is an infinite squarefree string over the alphabet Σ_3.*

Proof. First, observe that $\mathbf{c}$ is over the alphabet $\{0, 1, 2\}$. For if there were three or more 1s between two consecutive occurrences of 0 in $\mathbf{t}$, then $\mathbf{t}$ would not be overlap-free, a contradiction.

Next, assume that $\mathbf{c}$ is not squarefree. Then it contains a square of the form xx, with $x = x_1 x_2 \cdots x_n$ and $n \ge 1$. Then, from the definition of $\mathbf{c}$, the string $\mathbf{t}$ would contain a subword of the form

$$01^{x_1} 01^{x_2} 0 \cdots 01^{x_n} 01^{x_1} 01^{x_2} 0 \cdots 01^{x_n} 0,$$

which constitutes an overlap, a contradiction. ■

For alternate definitions of $\mathbf{c}$, see Exercise 25.

2.6 Applications of the Thue–Morse sequence and squarefree strings

Both the Thue–Morse sequence and squarefree strings turn out to have many applications in many different fields of mathematics and computer science. In this section we briefly survey some of these applications.

2.6.1 The Tarry–Escott problem

Let us begin with the Tarry–Escott problem (also known as the problem of multigrades). This old problem, still not completely solved, asks for solutions to the equation

$$\sum_{i \in I} i^k = \sum_{j \in J} j^k$$

for $k = 0, 1, 2, \ldots, n$, where I and J are disjoint sets of integers.

Example 2.6.1. The equation

$$0^k + 3^k + 5^k + 6^k = 1^k + 2^k + 4^k + 7^k$$

holds for $k = 0, 1, 2$ (but not for $k = 3$). Of course, we define $0^0 = 1$.

Although Escott and Tarry discussed the problem in 1910 and 1912, respectively, Étienne Prouhet found an interesting connection between the Thue–Morse sequence and the Tarry–Escott problem in 1851. Here is (a weak version of) what Prouhet discovered.

Theorem 2.6.2. *Let* $\mathbf{t} = t_0 t_1 t_2 \cdots$ *be the Thue–Morse sequence and* N *be a positive integer. Define*

$$I = \{i \in \{0, 1, \ldots, 2^N - 1\} : t_i = 0\};$$
$$J = \{j \in \{0, 1, \ldots, 2^N - 1\} : t_j = 1\}.$$

Then for $0 \le k < N$, *we have*

$$\sum_{i \in I} i^k = \sum_{j \in J} j^k.$$

Example 2.6.1 is the case $N = 3$ of this theorem. The proof is not terribly difficult, but is left to the reader as Exercise 21.

2.6.2 Certain infinite products

Next we turn to some interesting infinite products. Consider the following infinite sequence:

$$1/2, \quad \frac{1}{2}/\frac{3}{4}, \quad \frac{\frac{1}{2}}{\frac{3}{4}}/\frac{\frac{5}{6}}{\frac{7}{8}}, \quad \cdots$$

What is the limit of this sequence? Computing the first few terms suggests that the limit is about 0.7071, which you may recognize as $\sqrt{2}/2$. But how can we prove this?

The first step is to recognize the hidden occurrence of the Thue–Morse sequence. In fact, it is not hard to see that we can write the limit as

$$\prod_{n=0}^{\infty} \left(\frac{2n+1}{2n+2} \right)^{\varepsilon_n}, \tag{2.2}$$

where $\varepsilon_n = (-1)^{t_n}$ and t_n is the nth symbol of the Thue–Morse sequence. We now prove that this infinite product equals $\sqrt{2}/2$.

Let P and Q be the infinite products defined by

$$P = \prod_{n=0}^{\infty} \left(\frac{2n+1}{2n+2} \right)^{\varepsilon_n}, \quad Q = \prod_{n=1}^{\infty} \left(\frac{2n}{2n+1} \right)^{\varepsilon_n}.$$

Then

$$PQ = \frac{1}{2} \prod_{n=1}^{\infty} \left(\frac{n}{n+1} \right)^{\varepsilon_n} = \frac{1}{2} \prod_{n=1}^{\infty} \left(\frac{2n}{2n+1} \right)^{\varepsilon_{2n}} \prod_{n=0}^{\infty} \left(\frac{2n+1}{2n+2} \right)^{\varepsilon_{2n+1}}.$$

(We have to check convergence, but this is left to the reader.) Now, since $\varepsilon_{2n} = \varepsilon_n$ and $\varepsilon_{2n+1} = -\varepsilon_n$, we get

$$PQ = \frac{1}{2} \prod_{n=1}^{\infty} \left(\frac{2n}{2n+1} \right)^{\varepsilon_n} \left(\prod_{n=0}^{\infty} \left(\frac{2n+1}{2n+2} \right)^{\varepsilon_n} \right)^{-1} = \frac{1}{2} \frac{Q}{P}.$$

Since $Q \neq 0$, this gives $P^2 = 1/2$, and the result follows since P is positive.

2.6.3 Chess and music

Now let us turn to applications of squarefree words. One of the first applications was to the game of chess.

Modern-day chess has several rules to avoid the possibility of infinite games. Rule 9.3 of the *FIDE Laws of Chess* states that if 50 consecutive moves are made by each player without a pawn being moved or a piece being captured, then a draw can be claimed. Rule 9.2 states that if the same position occurs three times, then a draw can be claimed.

Max Euwe (1901–1981), the Dutch chess grandmaster and world chess champion from 1935 to 1937, discussed what would happen if Rule 9.3 were discarded and Rule 9.2 were weakened to the following "German rule": if the same *sequence* of moves occurs twice in succession and is immediately followed by the first move of a third repetition, then a draw occurs. Could an infinite game of chess then be played?

Euwe showed the answer is yes, and his technique was based on what we now call the Thue–Morse sequence. If we take the Thue-Morse sequence, and replace each 0 by the following sequence of four moves

$$\text{Ng1–f3} \quad \text{Ng8–f6}$$
$$\text{Nf3–g1} \quad \text{Nf6–g8}$$

and each 1 by the following sequence of four moves

$$\text{Nb1–c3} \quad \text{Nb8–c6}$$
$$\text{Nc3–b1} \quad \text{Nc6–b8}$$

then the fact that **t** is overlap-free means that the German rule can never apply. This may not be the world's most interesting chess game, but it *is* infinite.

The Thue–Morse sequence even appears in music. The Danish composer Per Nørgård (1932–) independently rediscovered the Thue–Morse sequence and used it in some of his compositions, such as the first movement of his *Symphony No. 3*.

2.6.4 The Burnside problem

Finally, we mention the occurrence of repetition-free sequences in the solution of the Burnside problem for groups.

Recall that a group G is a nonempty set together with a binary operation $\cdot$ that satisfies the following properties:

(a) $a \cdot b \in G$ for all $a, b \in G$.
(b) $a \cdot (b \cdot c) = (a \cdot b) \cdot c$.
(c) There exists a distinguished element $e \in G$ such that $e \cdot g = g \cdot e = g$ for all $g \in G$.
(d) For all $g \in G$ there exists an element $g' \in G$ such that $g \cdot g' = g' \cdot g = e$. We usually write $g' = g^{-1}$.

For group multiplication we often write gg' for $g \cdot g'$.

If G is a group and X a nonempty subset of G, then $\langle X \rangle$, the *subgroup generated* by X, is the set

$$\{a_1^{e_1} a_2^{e_2} \cdots a_t^{e_t} \ : \ a_i \in X, t \geq 0, \text{ and } e_i \in \{1, -1\}\}.$$

If there exist finitely many elements $b_1, b_2, \ldots, b_n$ such that $G = \langle b_1, b_2, \ldots, b_n \rangle$ then G is said to be *finitely generated*.

The *exponent* of a group G is the least integer $n > 0$ such that $x^n = e$ for all $x \in G$. If no such n exists then G has exponent ∞. Note that it is possible for each element to have finite order (i.e., for there to exist an r, depending on x, such that $x^r = e$) and yet the group's exponent is infinite (see Exercise 31). If every element has finite order, the group is called "periodic" or "torsion."

Burnside asked in 1902 if every group of finite exponent n with a finite number of generators m is necessarily finite.

For $m = 1$ the answer is trivially yes, and for $m > 1$ and $n = 2, 3$, the answer is also yes, although more work is needed. Sanov proved in 1940 that the answer is yes for $m > 1$ and $n = 4$, and Hall proved in 1957 that the answer is yes for $m > 1$ and $n = 6$. However, in 1968 Novikov and Adian proved that the answer is no for $m > 1$ and $n \geq 4381$ and odd. Later, Adian improved the bound from 4381 to 665. The proof is based in part on the existence of cubefree sequences.

2.7 Exercises

1. Define the strings F_n $(n \geq 1)$ as follows:

$$F_1 = 0;$$
$$F_2 = 1;$$
$$F_n = F_{n-1}F_{n-2} \quad \text{for } n \geq 3.$$

   Thus, for example, we find $F_3 = 10$, $F_4 = 101$, and so on.
   (a) Prove that no F_i contains either 00 or 111 as a substring.
   (b) Guess the relationship between $F_i F_{i+1}$ and $F_{i+1} F_i$, and prove your guess by induction.
2. Is the decimal expansion of π a squarefree string? Is it cubefree? Answer the same questions for e (the base of natural logarithms), Euler's constant, $\sqrt{2}$, and $\log 2$. What are the highest powers you can find in the decimal expansions of these numbers?
3. Show there are no squarefree strings of length >3 over a two-letter alphabet.
4. Find necessary and sufficient conditions for a bordered word to equal a square.
5. Show that if x, w are strings, then xw cannot equal wx in all positions except one.
6. A morphism $h : \Sigma^* \to \Delta^*$ is *overlap-free* if for any overlap-free word $w \in \Sigma^*$, $h(w)$ is overlap-free. Prove that if $|\Sigma| > |\Delta|$, then the only overlap-free morphism h is the morphism defined by $h(a) = \epsilon$ for all $a \in \Sigma$.

7. Let $\mathbf{t} = (t_n)_{n \geq 0} = 01101001 \cdots$ be the Thue–Morse infinite word. Show that $\mathbf{t} = \mu(\mathbf{t})$, where μ is the Thue–Morse morphism introduced in Example 2.2.2.

8. Show that every finite nonempty prefix of the Thue–Morse word $01101001 \cdots$ is primitive.

9. Prove the following variation on Theorem 2.3.2: let $y \in \Sigma^*$, and $x, z \in \Sigma^+$. Then $xy = yz$ if and only if there exist $u, v \in \Sigma^*$, and an integer $e \geq 0$ such that $x = uv$, $z = vu$, and $y = (uv)^e u = u(vu)^e$.

10. Show that the relation $\sim$ ("is a conjugate of") is an equivalence relation.

11. Show that x and y are conjugates if and only if there exists a string t such that $xt = ty$.

12. Consider the equation $w^2 = x^2 y^2 z^2$ in nonempty words. Show that there exist solutions in which no pair of words chosen from $\{w, x, y, z\}$ commutes.

13. Let y, z be palindromes. Show that if at least one of $|y|, |z|$ is even, then some conjugate of yz is a palindrome. Show that if both $|y|, |z|$ are odd, then the result need not hold.

14. Find all solutions to the equation $(vu)^n = u^n v^n$ in nonempty words for $n \geq 1$.

15. Prove that every conjugate of $\mu^n(0)$ is overlap-free, for $n \geq 0$, where μ is the Thue–Morse morphism.

16. Let $x \in \{0, 1\}^*$. Define $\overline{x}$ to be the string obtained by changing every 0 in x to 1 and every 1 to 0. Define $X_0 = 0$ and $X_{n+1} = X_n \overline{X_n}$ for $n \geq 0$. Thus, $X_1 = 01$, $X_2 = 0110$, and so on. Show that $X_n = \mu^n(0)$, where μ is the Thue–Morse morphism of Section 2.2.

17. Prove the following "repetition theorem" for infinite words. Let $w = w_1 w_2 w_3 \cdots$, and suppose $w = w_{k+1} w_{k+2} w_{k+3} \cdots$ for some $k > 0$. Then $w = (w_1 w_2 \cdots w_k)^\omega$.

18. Suppose x, y are words with $xy \neq yx$. Show that, for all $n \geq 1$, at least one of $x^n y$ and $x^{n+1} y$ is primitive.

19. Let x, y, z be words. Show that $xyz = zyx$ if and only if there exist words u, v and integers $i, j, k \geq 0$ with $x = (uv)^i u$, $y = (vu)^j v$, and $z = (uv)^k u$.

20. Suppose xyz is a square and $xyyz$ is a square. Show that $xy^i z$ is a square for all $i \geq 0$.

21. Prove Theorem 2.6.2 by induction on N.

22. Let

$$w = a_1 a_2 a_3 \cdots$$

be an infinite squarefree word. Show that all the "shifts" of w (namely, the words $a_1 a_2 a_3 \cdots$, $a_2 a_3 a_4 \cdots$, $a_3 a_4 a_5 \cdots$, etc.) are distinct.

23. Call a word w *uneven* if every nonempty subword has the property that at least one letter appears an odd number of times. For example, abac is uneven.

    (a) Show that if w is an uneven word over an alphabet with k letters, then $|w| < 2^k$.

    (b) Prove that the bound in (a) is sharp, by exhibiting an uneven word of length $2^k - 1$ over every alphabet of size $k \geq 1$.

24. Let $\mathbf{w} = c_0 c_1 c_2 \cdots = 0010011010010110011 \cdots$ be the infinite sequence defined by $c_n =$ the number of 0s (mod 2) in the binary expansion of n. Prove or disprove that $\mathbf{w}$ is overlap-free.

    Note: $c_0 = 0$ because the binary expansion of 0 is understood to be ϵ, the empty string.

25. In this exercise we explore some alternative constructions of $\mathbf{c}$, the infinite squarefree word introduced in Section 2.5.

    (a) Let $t_0 t_1 t_2 \ldots$ be the Thue–Morse word. Define $b_n = \tau(t_n, t_{n+1})$, where

$$\tau(0, 0) = 1;$$

$$\tau(0, 1) = 2;$$

$$\tau(1, 0) = 0;$$

$$\tau(1, 1) = 1.$$

    Show that $\mathbf{c} = b_0 b_1 b_2 \cdots$.

    (b) Let f be the morphism that maps $2 \to 210$, $1 \to 20$, and $0 \to 1$. Show that $f(\mathbf{c}) = \mathbf{c}$.

    (c) Let g be the morphism that maps a $\to$ ab, b $\to$ ca, c $\to$ cd, d $\to$ ac, and let h be the coding that maps a $\to$ 2, b $\to$ 1, c $\to$ 0, d $\to$ 1. Show that $\mathbf{c} = h(g^\omega(\text{a}))$.

26. Is the Thue–Morse sequence *mirror invariant*, that is, if w is a finite subword of $\mathbf{t}$, need its reversal w^R also be a subword of $\mathbf{t}$?

*27. An infinite string $\mathbf{x}$ is said to be *recurrent* if every subword that occurs in $\mathbf{x}$ occurs infinitely often in $\mathbf{x}$.

    (a) Show that an infinite string is recurrent if and only if every subword that occurs in $\mathbf{x}$ occurs at least twice.

    (b) Show that if an infinite string is mirror invariant, then it is recurrent.

**28. Let x, y, z, w be finite strings. Find necessary and sufficient conditions for the following two equations to hold simultaneously: $xy = zw$ and $yx = wz$.

29. Recall the definition of the Möbius function,

$$\mu(n) = \begin{cases} 0, & \text{if } n \text{ is divisible by a square} > 1; \\ (-1)^j, & \text{if } n = p_1 p_2 \cdots p_j, \text{ where the } p_i \text{ are distinct primes.} \end{cases} \tag{2.3}$$

(Hopefully, there will be no confusion with the morphism μ defined in Section 2.2.)

Show that there are $\sum_{d \mid n} \mu(d) k^{n/d}$ distinct primitive strings of length n over a k-letter alphabet. (Here $\sum_{d \mid n}$ means that the sum is over the positive integer divisors d of n.)

30. Give an example of an infinite periodic group.

31. Give an example of a group G where each element has finite order but the group's exponent is ∞.

*32. It was once conjectured that if A and B are finite sets with $AB = BA$, then both A and B are a union of powers of some finite set E.

(a) Prove that this conjecture holds if $|A| = 1$ and $|B| = 2$.

(b) Prove that the conjecture does not hold in general.

33. Let $\mathbf{w} = a_1 a_2 a_3 \cdots$ be any infinite squarefree word over $\Sigma = \{0, 1, 2\}$. Show that the infinite word $a_1 a_1 a_2 a_2 a_3 a_3 \cdots$ contains no subword of the form ycy for $y \in \Sigma^+$ and $c \in \Sigma$.

34. Let $v, x \in \Sigma^+$ and $w \in \Sigma^*$. Show that the following two conditions are equivalent:

(a) There exist integers $k, l \geq 1$ such that $v^k w = w x^l$.

(b) There exist $r, s \in \Sigma^*$ and integers $m, n \geq 1$, $p \geq 0$ such that $v = (rs)^m$, $w = (rs)^p r$, and $x = (sr)^n$.

35. Find all solutions in words x_1, x_2, x_3 to the system of equations

$$x_1 x_2 x_3 = x_2 x_3 x_1 = x_3 x_1 x_2.$$

36. Let $\Sigma = \{0, 1\}$. Let $h : \Sigma^* \to \Sigma^*$ be the morphism defined by $h(0) = 0$, $h(1) = 10$, and let $k : \Sigma^* \to \Sigma^*$ be the morphism defined by $k(0) = 0$, $k(1) = 01$. Prove that $h(0w) = k(w0)$ for all finite words w.

37. Show that if $x, y \in \Sigma^*$ with $xy \neq yx$, then $xyxxy$ is primitive.

38. Show that for all words $w \in \{0, 1\}^*$, either $w0$ or $w1$ is primitive (or both).

39. Consider the equation in words $x \amalg y = z^2$. Describe all solutions to this equation. *Hint:* there are separate cases depending on whether $|x|$, $|y|$ are even or odd.

40. Let x, y, z be strings. In the Lyndon–Schützenberger theorems, we proved a necessary and sufficient condition for $xy = yx$ and $xy = yz$. Find similar necessary and sufficient conditions for
    (a) $xy = y^R x$;
    (b) $xy = y^R z$.

2.8 Projects

1. Investigate ω-languages, that is, those languages that consist of *infinite* words. Ordinary finite automata accept an ω-word if, according to one criterion, the path labeled by the word passes through an accepting state infinitely often. Start with the survey by Thomas [1991] and the book of Perrin and Pin [2003].
2. Look into efficient algorithms for determining if a word has repetitions of various kinds (overlaps, squares, cubes, etc.). Start with the papers of Crochemore [1981] and Kfoury [1988].
3. Find out more about the Burnside problem mentioned in Section 2.6 and how the Thue–Morse word $0110100110010110 \cdots$ played a role in its solution. Start with the book of Adian [1979] and the survey paper of Gupta [1989].

2.9 Research problems

1. An *abelian square* is a word of the form xx', $|x| = |x'| > 0$, with x' a permutation of x. An example in English is reappear. Similarly, an *abelian cube* is a word of the form $xx'x''$, $|x| = |x'| = |x''| > 0$, with x' and x'' both permutations of x. An example in English is deeded.
   (a) Does there exist an infinite word over a three-letter alphabet avoiding abelian squares xx' with $|x| = |x'| \geq 2$?
   (b) Does there exist an infinite word over a two-letter alphabet avoiding abelian cubes $xx'x''$ with $|x| = |x'| = |x''| \geq 2$?
2. Find a simple characterization of the lexicographically least squarefree word over a three-letter alphabet.

2.10 Notes on Chapter 2

Combinatorics on words is a vast subject that is becoming increasingly popular, especially in Europe. For an introduction to this area, see Lothaire [1983, 2002].

For the historical roots of combinatorics on words, see Berstel and Perrin [2007].

2.1 The book of Perrin and Pin [2003] is a very good source of information on infinite words.

2.2 Harju and Karhumäki [1997] is an excellent discussion of morphisms.

2.3 For Theorems 2.3.2 and 2.3.3, see Lyndon and Schützenberger [1962].

Theorems 2.3.5 is a new generalization of a classical theorem of Fine and Wilf [1965].

Theorem 2.3.6 is a new generalization of Theorem 2.3.3.

Some of the material of this section was taken essentially verbatim from Allouche and Shallit [2003], with permission of Cambridge University Press.

2.4 Theorem 2.4.2 is due to Shyr and Thierrin [1977].

Theorem 2.4.5 is from Lyndon and Schützenberger [1962]. Our proof is based on Harju and Nowotka [2004].

2.5 Much of the material of this section was taken essentially verbatim from Allouche and Shallit [2003], with permission of Cambridge University Press.

The area of repetitions on words is a huge one, with many dozens of papers; see Allouche and Shallit [2003] for an extensive annotated bibliography. Thue [1906] and Thue [1912] are the earliest papers on the subject. For an English translation of Thue's work, see Berstel [1995].

2.6 For more on the strange and wonderful properties of the Thue–Morse sequence, see the survey paper of Allouche and Shallit [1999].

For the Tarry–Escott problem, see Wright [1959] and Borwein and Ingalls [1994].

The infinite product (2.2) is due to Woods [1978]. The proof that it equals $\sqrt{2}/2$ is due to Jean-Paul Allouche and is from Allouche and Shallit [1999].

For the work of Max Euwe, see Euwe [1929] or the Web site www.maxeuwe.nl. For the official rules of chess, see the FIDE Web site,www.fide.com. For the Burnside problem, see Adian [1979].

3

Finite automata and regular languages

The finite automaton is one of the simplest and most fundamental computing models. You are almost certainly familiar with this model from your first course in the theory of computing, but if not, you may want to review the material in Sections 1.3–1.4.

In this chapter we reexamine the theory of finite automata from a more advanced standpoint. In particular, we prove the very important Myhill–Nerode theorem in Section 3.9.

We begin with some generalizations of the finite automaton model.

3.1 Moore and Mealy machines

In most introductory courses on automata theory, finite automata are viewed as language recognizers, not as computers of functions. A deterministic finite automaton (DFA), for example, takes a string as input and either accepts or rejects it. Of course, we can view a DFA as computing a function $f : \Sigma^* \to \{0, 1\}$, where 0 represents rejection and 1 acceptance, but there are other ways to associate outputs with machines.

In this section, we introduce two simple models of finite-state machines with output, called Moore and Mealy machines. A Moore machine has outputs associated with its states, while a Mealy machine has outputs associated with its transitions.

We can use transition diagrams to represent both Moore and Mealy machines. In a Moore machine, a state labeled q/b indicates that when state q is entered, the output b is produced. In a Mealy machine, a transition labeled a/b indicates that when this transition is taken on input symbol a, the output b is produced. The output corresponding to a given input string is the concatenation of all the outputs produced successively by the machine.

Let us consider some examples.

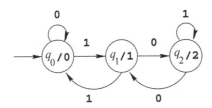

Figure 3.1: Example of a Moore machine

Example 3.1.1. Given n represented in base 2, the Moore machine in Figure 3.1 computes r mod 3 for all numbers r whose base-2 representation is a prefix of that for n.

On input 101001, which is the base-2 representation of the number 41, we successively enter states $q_0, q_1, q_2, q_2, q_1, q_2, q_2$ and output 0122122.

We now consider examples of Mealy machines.

Example 3.1.2. The simplest nontrivial Mealy machine is illustrated in Figure 3.2. It takes an input $w \in \{0, 1\}^*$ and complements it, changing each 0 to 1 and each 1 to 0.

Example 3.1.3. Our next example is a little less trivial. The Mealy machine in Figure 3.3 takes as input n expressed in base 2, starting with the *least significant digit*. The output is $n + 1$ in base 2. Note that if the input is all 1s, we must also include a trailing 0 to get the correct output. This is necessary because if $n = 2^k - 1$, then the binary representation of $n + 1$ is 1 bit longer than the binary representation of n.

We now turn to formal definitions of Moore and Mealy machines. Both machines are 6-tuples of the form $M = (Q, \Sigma, \Delta, \delta, \tau, q_0)$, where Δ is the nonempty output alphabet and τ is the output function. The difference is that in a Moore machine we have $\tau : Q \to \Delta$, while in a Mealy machine $\tau : Q \times \Sigma \to \Delta$.

On input $x = a_1 a_2 \cdots a_n$, a Moore machine M enters the states

$$q_0, \delta(q_0, a_1), \delta(q_0, a_1 a_2), \ldots, \delta(q_0, a_1 a_2 \cdots a_n)$$

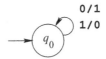

Figure 3.2: Example of a Mealy machine computing the complementary string

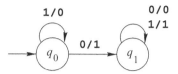

Figure 3.3: Example of a Mealy machine for incrementing in binary

and outputs

$$y = \tau(q_0)\, \tau(\delta(q_0, a_1))\, \tau(\delta(q_0, a_1a_2))\, \cdots\, \tau(\delta(q_0, a_1a_2 \cdots a_n)).$$

We write $T_M(x) = y$. A Mealy machine M outputs

$$z = \tau(q_0, a_1)\, \tau(\delta(q_0, a_1), a_2)\, \cdots\, \tau(\delta(q_0, a_1a_2 \cdots a_{n-1}), a_n).$$

We write $U_M(x) = z$. Note that on an input of length n, a Moore machine outputs a string of length $n + 1$ and a Mealy machine outputs a string of length n. This is because a Moore machine always provides an output associated with the initial state. In some sense, this output is not meaningful because it does not depend at all on the input.

Despite this difference, we can define a notion of equivalence for Moore and Mealy machines: we say a Moore machine M is equivalent to a Mealy machine M' if their input–output behavior is identical except that the first output of the Moore machine is disregarded. More formally, we say M is equivalent to M' if, for all $x \in \Sigma^*$, we have $T_M(x) = T_M(\epsilon)U_{M'}(x)$.

Theorem 3.1.4. *Let $M = (Q, \Sigma, \Delta, \delta, \tau, q_0)$ be a Moore machine. Then there exists an equivalent Mealy machine M' with the same number of states.*

Proof Idea. The idea is to define the output function τ' of a simulating machine so that its value depends on the output from the state that is reached *after* the transition is made.

Proof. Formally, let $M' = (Q, \Sigma, \Delta, \delta, \tau', q_0)$, where $\tau'(q, b) = \tau(\delta(q, b))$. If the input to M is $x = a_1a_2 \cdots a_n$, then M' outputs

$$\tau'(q_0, a_1)\, \tau'(\delta(q_0, a_1), a_2)\, \tau'(\delta(q_0, a_1a_2), a_3)\, \cdots\, \tau'(\delta(q_0, a_1a_2 \cdots a_{n-1}), a_n).$$

But by our definition of τ', this is

$$\tau(\delta(q_0, a_1))\, \tau(\delta(\delta(q_0, a_1), a_2))\, \cdots\, \tau(\delta(\delta(q_0, a_1a_2 \cdots a_{n-1}), a_n))$$

$$= \tau(\delta(q_0, a_1))\tau(\delta(q_0, a_1a_2)) \cdots \tau(\delta(q_0, a_1a_2 \cdots a_n)).$$

It follows that $T_M(x) = T_M(\epsilon)U_{M'}(x)$. ∎

Theorem 3.1.5. *Let* $M' = (Q', \Sigma, \Delta, \delta', \tau', q'_0)$ *be a Mealy machine. Then there exists an equivalent Moore machine M with* $|Q'||\Delta|$ *states.*

Proof Idea. The idea is to store in the state of the simulating Moore machine M both the state of the original Mealy machine M' and the symbol that M' would have output in its immediately previous transition. Thus states of M are chosen from $Q' \times \Delta$. (For the first state, there is no previous transition, so we simply arbitrarily choose an element c from Δ.)

Proof. Formally, let $M = (Q, \Sigma, \Delta, \delta, \tau, q_0)$, where

- $Q = Q' \times \Delta$;
- $\delta([q, b], a) = [\delta'(q, a), \tau'(q, a)]$ for all $q \in Q', b \in \Delta, a \in \Sigma$;
- $q_0 = [q'_0, c]$ for some arbitrary fixed $c \in \Delta$.
- $\tau([q, b]) = b$ for all $q \in Q', b \in \Delta$.

Now on input $x = a_1 a_2 \cdots a_n$, M' enters the states

$$q'_0, \delta'(q'_0, a_1), \ldots, \delta'(q'_0, a_1 a_2 \cdots a_n)$$

and outputs

$$\tau'(q'_0, a_1)\tau'(\delta'(q'_0, a_1), a_2) \cdots \tau'(\delta'(q'_0, a_1 \cdots a_{n-1}), a_n).$$

On the other hand, M enters the states

$$[q'_0, c], [\delta'(q'_0, a_1), \tau'(q'_0, a_1)], [\delta'(q'_0, a_1 a_2), \tau'(\delta'(q'_0, a_1), a_2)], \ldots,$$
$$[\delta'(q'_0, a_1 \cdots a_n), \tau'(\delta'(q'_0, a_1 \cdots a_{n-1}), a_n)]$$

and outputs

$$c\tau'(q'_0, a_1)\tau'(\delta'(q'_0, a_1), a_2) \cdots \tau'(\delta'(q'_0, a_1 \cdots a_{n-1}), a_n).$$

It follows that $T_M(x) = cU_{M'}(x)$. ∎

In Section 3.5 we consider a generalization of Mealy machines, the finite-state transducer.

3.2 Quotients

In this section we introduce a new operation on languages, the *quotient*. Let $L_1, L_2 \subseteq \Sigma^*$. We define

$$L_1/L_2 = \{x \in \Sigma^* : \text{ there exists } y \in L_2 \text{ such that } xy \in L_1\}.$$

Quotient is a kind of inverse to concatenation (but see Exercise 2).

Example 3.2.1. Let $L_1 = \text{a}^+\text{bc}^+$, $L_2 = \text{bc}^+$, and $L_3 = \text{c}^+$. Then $L_1/L_2 = \text{a}^+$ and $L_1/L_3 = \text{a}^+\text{bc}^*$.

Example 3.2.2. Let $L = \{\text{a}^{n^2} : n \geq 0\}$. Then $L/L = \text{a(aa)}^* + \text{(aaaa)}^*$. For we have

$$L/L = \{x : \text{there exists } y \in L \text{ such that } xy \in L\}$$
$$= \{\text{a}^t : \exists\, m, n \text{ with } t + m^2 = n^2\}$$
$$= \{\text{a}^{n^2-m^2} : 0 \leq m \leq n\}.$$

I now claim that t can be written in the form $n^2 - m^2$ for some $0 \leq m \leq n$ iff t is of the form $2k + 1$ or $4k$ for some $k \geq 0$. For if $t = n^2 - m^2$, then both n and m are of either the same parity, or different parity. If they are the same parity, then $t = (2n')^2 - (2m')^2 \equiv 0 \pmod 4$ or $t = (2n' + 1)^2 - (2m' + 1)^2 \equiv 0 \pmod 4$. If n and m are of different parity, then $t = (2n')^2 - (2m' + 1)^2 \equiv 1 \pmod 2$ or $t = (2n' + 1)^2 - (2m')^2 \equiv 1 \pmod 2$.

On the other hand, if $t = 2k + 1$, then we can choose $n = k + 1$, $m = k$ to get $t = n^2 - m^2$. If $t = 0$, then we choose $n = 0$, $k = 0$. Otherwise, if $t = 4k$ with $k \geq 1$, we choose $n = k + 1$, $m = k - 1$, so $n^2 - m^2 = t$.

Theorem 3.2.3. *Let $L, R \subseteq \Sigma^*$ and suppose R is regular. Then R/L is regular.*

Proof Idea. Let $R, L \subseteq \Sigma^*$ and let $M = (Q, \Sigma, \delta, q_0, F)$ be a DFA accepting R. Our goal is to create a machine M' accepting R/L. On input x, the machine M' must somehow determine if there exists a y such that if M were to process the symbols of y starting in the state $\delta(q_0, x)$, it would arrive in a final state.

Proof. Let $M' = (Q, \Sigma, \delta, q_0, F')$, where

$$F' = \{q \in Q : \text{there exists } y \in L \text{ such that } \delta(q, y) \in F\}.$$

Notice that M' is exactly the same as M, except that we have changed the set of final states. Now we have

$$x \in L(M') \iff \delta(q_0, x) \in F'$$
$$\iff \delta(q_0, x) = q \text{ and there exists } y \in L \text{ such that } \delta(q, y) \in F$$
$$\iff \text{there exists } y \in L \text{ such that } \delta(q_0, xy) \in F$$
$$\iff \text{there exists } y \in L \text{ such that } xy \in R$$
$$\iff x \in R/L. \qquad \blacksquare$$

Note that Theorem 3.2.3 is not constructive in the sense that no algorithm is provided to compute F'. In fact, no such algorithm is possible in general, since L is arbitrary, and could be nonrecursive. You should not let this bother you—much of mathematics is nonconstructive.

Under certain circumstances, M' becomes effectively constructible. For example, if L itself is specified by giving a DFA accepting it, then there is an easy algorithm for computing F' (see Exercise 36).

Now let us look at two applications of the quotient operation.

Example 3.2.4. We consider the effect of removing "trailing zeros" from words in a language. Let Σ be an alphabet containing the symbol 0, and let $L \subseteq \Sigma^*$.

By removing trailing zeros from words of L, we mean the language

$$\text{rtz}(L) = \{x \in \Sigma^*(\Sigma - \{0\}) \cup \{\epsilon\} \; : \; \text{there exists } i \geq 0 \text{ with } x0^i \in L\}.$$

If L is regular, must $\text{rtz}(L)$ necessarily be regular?

With quotient we can easily solve this problem. We claim that

$$\text{rtz}(L) = (L/0^*) \cap (\Sigma^*(\Sigma - \{0\}) \cup \{\epsilon\}).$$

Hence if L is regular, so is $\text{rtz}(L)$.

Similarly, we can remove leading zeros with

$$\text{rlz}(L) = \text{rtz}(L^R)^R.$$

Example 3.2.5. Recall the definition of the prefix language from Section 1.2:

$$\text{Pref}(L) = \{x \in \Sigma^* \; : \; \text{there exists } y \in L \text{ such that } x \text{ is a prefix of } y\}.$$

If L is regular, need $\text{Pref}(L)$ be regular? Noting that $\text{Pref}(L) = L/\Sigma^*$, the answer is yes.

3.3 Morphisms and substitutions

In this section we study two very useful transformations on languages, namely morphisms and substitutions.

Recall from Section 2.2 that a *homomorphism*, or just *morphism* for short, is a map that sends a letter to a string and is then extended to arbitrary strings by concatenation. Alternatively, we say that $h : \Sigma^* \to \Delta^*$ is a morphism if $h(xy) = h(x)h(y)$ for all $x, y \in \Sigma^*$. Note that $h(x\epsilon) = h(x)h(\epsilon)$, and so it follows that $h(\epsilon) = \epsilon$.

A morphism is then extended to a language L as follows: $h(L) := \bigcup_{x \in L} \{h(x)\}$.

Theorem 3.3.1. *For all languages* $L, L_1, L_2 \subseteq \Sigma^*$ *and morphisms* $h : \Sigma^* \to \Delta^*$, *we have*

(a) $h(L_1 L_2) = h(L_1)h(L_2)$;
(b) $h(L_1 \cup L_2) = h(L_1) \cup h(L_2)$;
(c) $h(L^*) = h(L)^*$.

Proof. We omit the proof as a more general result is proved in Theorem 3.3.5 later.

Example 3.3.2. Define $h(0) = $ a and $h(1) = $ ba. Then we have $h(010) = $ abaa and $h(0^*1) = $ a*ba.

Common Error 3.3.3. Students sometimes try to define "morphisms" as follows: $h(aa) = ab$. This is not a morphism, because for whatever choice of $h(a)$ we make, the identity $h(aa) = h(a)h(a)$ fails.

A *substitution* is a map $s : \Sigma^* \to 2^{\Delta^*}$ that sends each letter $a \in \Sigma$ to a language L_a and obeys the rules $s(\epsilon) = \{\epsilon\}$, and $s(xy) = s(x)s(y)$ for all $x, y \in \Sigma^*$. We extend s to languages as we did for morphisms: $s(L) := \bigcup_{x \in L} s(x)$.

Example 3.3.4. Define $s(0) = \{$a, ab$\}^*$ and $s(1) = ($cd$)^*$. Then $s(101) = ($cd$)^*($a $+$ ab$)^*($cd$)^*$.

The previous example is an example of *substitution by regular languages*, since each letter is mapped to a regular language.

Although, strictly speaking, a morphism is not a substitution (since a morphism is word-valued, whereas a substitution is language-valued), we may identify the word w with the language $\{w\}$. Thus if we prove that the class of regular languages is closed under substitution by regular languages, we will also have proved that this class is closed under morphism.

Theorem 3.3.5. *The class of regular languages is closed under substitution by regular languages.*

Proof. Let s be a substitution. We first prove that, for languages L_1, L_2, L, we have

(a) $s(L_1 \cup L_2) = s(L_1) \cup s(L_2)$;
(b) $s(L_1 L_2) = s(L_1)s(L_2)$;
(c) $s(L^*) = s(L)^*$.

For (a), we prove more generally that for any index set $\mathcal{I}$, finite or infinite, we have $s(\bigcup_{i\in\mathcal{I}} L_i) = \bigcup_{i\in\mathcal{I}} s(L_i)$. We have

$$s\left(\bigcup_{i\in\mathcal{I}} L_i\right) = \bigcup_{x\in\bigcup_{i\in\mathcal{I}} L_i} s(x)$$

$$= \bigcup_{i\in\mathcal{I}} \bigcup_{x\in L_i} s(x)$$

$$= \bigcup_{i\in\mathcal{I}} s(L_i).$$

For (b), we have

$$s(L_1 L_2) = s(\{xy \ : \ x \in L_1, \ y \in L_2\})$$

$$= \bigcup_{x\in L_1, \ y\in L_2} s(xy)$$

$$= \bigcup_{x\in L_1, \ y\in L_2} s(x)s(y)$$

$$= \left(\bigcup_{x\in L_1} s(x)\right)\left(\bigcup_{y\in L_2} s(y)\right)$$

$$= s(L_1)s(L_2).$$

For (c), we first show by induction on n that $s(L^n) = s(L)^n$. For $n = 0$, this follows since $L^0 = \{\epsilon\}$. Now assume that the result is true for $n < N$; we prove it for $n = N$. We then have

$$s(L^N) = s(L^{N-1}L) = s(L^{N-1})s(L)$$

by part (b). By induction $s(L^{N-1}) = s(L)^{N-1}$. Then $s(L^N) = s(L)^{N-1}s(L) = s(L)^N$, as was to be shown.

Now we have

$$s(L^*) = s\left(\bigcup_{i\geq0} L^i\right) = \bigcup_{i\geq0} s(L^i) = \bigcup_{i\geq0} s(L)^i = s(L)^*.$$

This completes the proof of part (c).

Now we can complete the proof of the theorem. If $L \subseteq \Sigma^*$ is regular, then it can be represented as a regular expression r. We prove by induction on n, the number of operators in r, that $s(L)$ is regular. (Here we count all occurrences of $+$, $*$, and implicit occurrences of concatenation.)

If r has no operators, then L equals either $\{a\}$ for some $a \in \Sigma$, or $\{\epsilon\}$, or $\emptyset$. It is easy to see that $s(L)$ is regular in each of these cases.

Now assume the result is true for all $n < N$; we prove it for $n = N$. Assume r has N operators. Then L can be written as $L_1 L_2$, or $L_1 \cup L_2$, or L_1^*, where L_1, L_2 are regular languages that can be represented by regular expressions with $\leq N - 1$ operators. Then $s(L_1 \cup L_2) = s(L_1) \cup s(L_2)$ by part (a), which proves regularity by induction. Similarly, $s(L_1 L_2) = s(L_1)s(L_2)$ by part (b), which is regular by induction. Finally, $s(L_1^*) = s(L_1)^*$ by part (c), which is regular by induction. ∎

Example 3.3.6. Suppose $L \subseteq \{a, b\}^*$ is a regular language. Let us show that the language formed by inserting the letter c in all possible ways into strings of L is still regular. Define the substitution $s(a) = c^*ac^*$ and $s(b) = c^*bc^*$. Then if L does not contain ϵ, then $s(L)$ is the desired language, while if L contains ϵ, then $s(L) \cup c^*$ is the desired language. In both cases the result is regular.

We now turn to a new type of transformation of languages, the *inverse morphism*. If $h : \Sigma^* \to \Delta^*$ is a morphism, and $L \subseteq \Delta^*$, then we define

$$h^{-1}(L) = \{x \in \Sigma^* : h(x) \in L\}.$$

The map h^{-1} can be viewed as a sort of inverse of h (see Exercise 6).

Example 3.3.7. In the previous example, we inserted the letter c in all possible ways into strings of L. We can accomplish the same result using inverse morphisms. Define $h(a) = a$, $h(b) = b$, and $h(c) = \epsilon$. Then $h^{-1}(L)$ achieves our goal. For example, $h^{-1}(\{aba\}) = c^*ac^*bc^*ac^*$.

Example 3.3.8. More generally, we can use inverse morphism to give a formal definition of a new operation on languages, the *shuffle*. The shuffle of two words x and w (not necessarily of the same length) consists of all words obtained by interleaving the letters as in shuffling a deck of cards. (Note this is not the same as the perfect shuffle defined in Section 1.2.) For example, shuff(ab, cd) = $\{abcd, acbd, acdb, cabd, cadb, cdab\}$. The shuffle of two languages L_1, and L_2 is defined to be

$$\text{shuff}(L_1, L_2) = \bigcup_{x \in L_1, \, y \in L_2} \text{shuff}(x, y).$$

We can define the operation shuff in terms of morphisms and inverse morphisms, as follows. Suppose $L_1, L_2 \subseteq \Sigma^*$ for some alphabet Σ. For each letter $a \in \Sigma$, construct a new letter a' and let $\Sigma' = \{a' : a \in \Sigma\}$. Define morphisms h by $h(a) = h(a') = a$ for each $a \in \Sigma$; $h_1(a) = a$ and $h_1(a') = \epsilon$ for each $a \in \Sigma$; and $h_2(a) = \epsilon$ and $h_2(a') = a$ for each $a \in \Sigma$. Then we have

$$\text{shuff}(L_1, L_2) = h(h_1^{-1}(L_1) \cap h_2^{-1}(L_2)).$$

We now prove that the class of regular languages is closed under inverse morphism.

Theorem 3.3.9. *If $L \subseteq \Delta^*$ is regular, and $h : \Sigma^* \to \Delta^*$ is a morphism, then $h^{-1}(L)$ is regular.*

Proof Idea. Consider trying to build a DFA M' for $h^{-1}(L)$, based on the DFA M for L. What must M' do? On input x, M' must compute $h(x)$ and determine if it is in L, accepting x if and only if M accepts $h(x)$. The easiest way to do that is to "rewire" the DFA M' so that on input x, M' simulates M on $h(x)$.

Think of it this way: L is a language of French words, and h is a map that takes an English word to its French translation. How can we accept $h^{-1}(L)$? On input an English word, we apply h to get the equivalent French word, and then see if the result is in L.

Proof. Let $M = (Q, \Delta, \delta, q_0, F)$ be a DFA accepting L. We create a DFA $M' = (Q', \Sigma, \delta', q_0', F')$, accepting $h^{-1}(L)$. We define

- $Q' := Q$;
- $\delta'(q, a) := \delta(q, h(a))$;
- $q_0' := q_0$;
- $F' := F$.

We now prove by induction on $|x|$ that $\delta'(q, x) = \delta(q, h(x))$. The base case is $|x| = 0$; that is, $x = \epsilon$. Then $\delta'(q, x) = q = \delta(q, h(x))$.

Otherwise, assume the result is true for all x with $|x| < n$; we prove it for $|x| = n$. Let $x = ya$, where $a \in \Sigma$. Then $\delta(q, h(x)) = \delta(q, h(ya)) = \delta(\delta(q, h(y)), h(a)) = \delta(\delta'(q, y), h(a)) = \delta'(\delta'(q, y), a) = \delta'(q, ya) = \delta'(q, x)$, as desired.

It now follows that $\delta'(q_0', x) \in F'$ if and only if $\delta(q_0, h(x)) \in F$; in other words, $x \in L(M')$ if and only if $h(x) \in L(M)$. Thus, $L(M') = h^{-1}(L(M))$. ■

3.4 Advanced closure properties of regular languages

In this section we introduce two new operations on regular languages and show that the class of regular languages is closed under them. In both cases, nondeterminism plays an essential role in the proofs.

We start with $\frac{1}{2}L$. If $L \subseteq \Sigma^*$, we define

$$\frac{1}{2}L = \{x \in \Sigma^* \; : \; \text{there exists } y \in \Sigma^* \text{ with } |y| = |x| \text{ such that } xy \in L\}.$$

Thus, $\frac{1}{2}L$ consists of the first halves of even-length strings of L.

Theorem 3.4.1. *If L is regular, then so is $\frac{1}{2}L$.*

Proof Idea. There are a number of different ways to approach the solution. Here is one. On input x, if we knew what state q we would be in after reading all the symbols of x, we could simply step forward in tandem from q and q_0. (From q, of course, we would have to move forward in all possible ways, because the only thing we demand about y is that $|x| = |y|$.) Then we would accept if we got from q_0 to q on x and from q to a state of F on the guessed symbols of y. Of course, we do not know q, but using nondeterminism we can guess it and check. The "there exists" in the definition of $\frac{1}{2}L$ is a hint that nondeterminism will be useful.

This suggests starting with a DFA $M = (Q, \Sigma, \delta, q_0, F)$ for L and converting it into a nondeterministic finite automaton with ϵ-transitions (NFA-ϵ) $M' = (Q', \Sigma, \delta', q_0', F')$ for $\frac{1}{2}L$. In M', states will be triples; the first element records the guessed state q and does not change once it is initially recorded, the second element records what state we are in after having processed some prefix of the input x, starting from state q_0, and the third element records what state we are in after having processed some prefix of the guessed y, starting from q.

Proof. Formally, we define $Q' = \{q_0'\} \cup Q \times Q \times Q$ and $F' = \{[q, q, p] : p \in F\}$. We also define

$$\delta'(q_0', \epsilon) = \{[q, q_0, q] : q \in Q\};$$
$$\delta'([q, p, r], a) = \{[q, \delta(p, a), \delta(r, b)] : b \in \Sigma\}.$$

An easy induction on $|x|$ now shows that $[q, p, r] \in \delta'(q_0', x)$ if and only if there exists $y \in \Sigma^*$, $|x| = |y|$, such that $\delta(q_0, x) = p$ and $\delta(q, y) = r$. Thus,

$$\delta'(q_0', x) \cap F' \neq \emptyset$$
$$\Updownarrow$$
$$\exists y \in \Sigma^*, |x| = |y|, \quad \text{with } \delta(q_0, x) = q, \ \delta(q, y) \in F$$
$$\Updownarrow$$
$$\exists y \in \Sigma^*, |x| = |y|, \quad \text{with } \delta(q_0, xy) \in F$$
$$\Updownarrow$$
$$\exists y \in \Sigma^*, |x| = |y|, \quad \text{with } xy \in L.$$

It follows that $L(M') = \frac{1}{2}L$. ∎

There is a different approach to the preceding proof. Instead of guessing q and moving forward from it, we could guess the appropriate final state and move backwards. This approach is left as Exercise 38.

Now, let us turn to another operation on formal languages, the cycle operation cyc. Roughly speaking, cyc sends every string to the set of all its cyclic shifts,

In M

In M'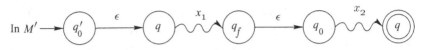

Figure 3.4: An NFA-ϵ for cyc(L)

or *conjugates*, as defined in Section 2.4. For a language L, we define

$$\text{cyc}(L) := \{x_1 x_2 \ : \ x_2 x_1 \in L\}.$$

Example 3.4.2. Suppose $L = 0^*1^*$. Then cyc(L) $= 0^*1^*0^* + 1^*0^*1^*$.

It turns out that the class of regular languages is closed under the cyc operation, as the following theorem shows.

Theorem 3.4.3. *If L is regular, then so is* cyc(L).

Proof Idea. Let $M = (Q, \Sigma, \delta, q_0, F)$ be a DFA accepting L. We construct an NFA-ϵ M' that accepts cyc(L). The idea is to "guess" the state the DFA M would be in after reading all the symbols of x_2, then process the symbols x_1, verify that a final state has been reached, and then continue with the symbols of x_2, returning to the first state. This is illustrated by Figure 3.4.

Figure 3.4 is a little misleading, because we will actually need the states of our machine for cyc(L) to be triples: if $[p, q, a] \in Q'$, then

- p records the current state in the simulation of M;
- q records the "guessed" initial state; and
- a records whether or not a final state has been reached.

Proof. More formally, let $M' = (Q', \Sigma, \delta', q_0', F')$, where

$$Q' = \{q_0'\} \ \cup \ Q \times Q \times \{y, n\}.$$

The transition function δ' is defined as follows:

$$\delta'(q_0', \epsilon) = \{[q, q, n] \ : \ q \in Q\} \quad \text{(get started)}$$
$$\delta'([p, q, n], a) = \{[\delta(p, a), q, n]\} \quad \text{(simulate moves of } M)$$
$$\delta'([p, q, n], \epsilon) = \{[q_0, q, y]\} \text{ for all } p \in F$$
$$\quad \text{(allow transition to } y \text{ if final state is encountered)}$$
$$\delta'([p, q, y], a) = \{[\delta(p, a), q, y]\} \quad \text{(simulate moves of } M).$$

Figure 3.5: An acceptance path for $x_2 x_1$

Finally, we define $F' = \{[q, q, y] : q \in Q\}$. We now claim that $L(M') =$ cyc(L).

First we show cyc(L) $\subseteq L(M')$. Suppose $x_2 x_1 \in L$. Then $x_2 x_1$ is accepted by M. Then, as in Figure 3.4, M starts in state q_0, reads the symbols of x_2 until it reaches a state q, and then reads the symbols of x_1 until it reaches a final state $q_f \in F$. In other words,

$$\delta(q_0, x_2) = q;$$

$$\delta(q, x_1) = q_f \in F.$$

How does M' behave on input $x_1 x_2$? First, it starts in state q_0'. Then there is an ϵ-transition to the state $[q, q, n]$. Then M' simulates M on input x_1, eventually reaching $[q_f, q, n]$. Since $q_f \in F$, there is an ϵ-transition to $[q_0, q, y]$. Now M' simulates M on input x_2, eventually reaching $[q, q, y]$ at which point M' accepts $x_1 x_2$.

Next we show $L(M') \subseteq$ cyc(L). If $x \in L(M')$, then there must be a path from q_0' to $[q, q, y]$ labeled with x. From q_0', the machine M' must enter a state of the form $[q, q, n]$ on an ϵ-transition. Since x is accepted, the path must look like as shown in Figure 3.5 for some x_1, x_2 with $x = x_2 x_1$. Hence, $\delta(q, x_2) = p$ for some $p \in F$ and $\delta(q_0, x_1) = q$. It follows that $\delta(q_0, x_1 x_2) \in F$. Hence, $x_1 x_2 \in L$. It follows that $x_2 x_1 \in$ cyc(L), as desired. ∎

3.5 Transducers

In Section 3.1, we studied the Mealy machine, which transformed inputs into outputs. We now study a useful generalization of this idea, called the *finite-state transducer*, or just *transducer* for short.

A finite-state transducer is similar to a Mealy machine, but differs in the following ways:

- It is nondeterministic,
- It has final states,
- Transitions are labeled with x/y, where x, y are strings, not necessarily just single symbols. Here x is an input string, and y is an output string.

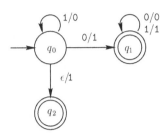

Figure 3.6: Transducer for incrementing in binary

Example 3.5.1. Recall Example 3.1.3, where we constructed a Mealy machine to compute the base-2 representation of $n + 1$, given the base-2 representation of n, starting with the least significant digit. That example was not completely satisfactory, because it did not behave properly if the input was of the form $11 \cdots 1$. With the transducer in Figure 3.6, however, we can correct this problem.

Example 3.5.2. Recall Example 3.2.4, where we showed how to remove leading zeros using a rather complicated expression involving quotient, intersection, and reversal. With the transducer in Figure 3.7, however, we can easily solve this problem (over the alphabet $\{0, 1\}$).

Now let us give the formal definition of a transducer. A finite-state transducer is a 6-tuple $T = (Q, \Sigma, \Delta, S, q_0, F)$, where Q is a finite nonempty set of states, Σ is the input alphabet, Δ is the output alphabet, q_0 is the start state, and F is the set of final states. The *transition set* S is a finite subset of $Q \times \Sigma^* \times \Delta^* \times Q$. The intent is that if $(p, x, y, q) \in S$, then if T is in state p, and reads the string x, it has the option of entering state q and outputting y. An accepting computation of T is a list of elements of S of the form

$$(p_0, x_0, y_0, p_1), (p_1, x_1, y_1, p_2), \ldots, (p_i, x_i, y_i, p_{i+1}),$$

where $p_0 = q_0$ and $p_{i+1} \in F$. In that case, the transducer maps the input string $x = x_0 x_1 \cdots x_i$ to $y = y_0 y_1 \cdots y_i$, and we write $x \to_T y$. By convention, there is always an implicit transition of the form $(p, \epsilon, \epsilon, p)$ for every state p. The

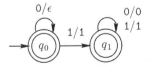

Figure 3.7: Transducer for removing leading zeros

set of all pairs $\{(x, y) : x \to_T y\}$ is called the *rational relation* computed by T.

Now we define how a transducer acts on a string x and a language L. We define

$$T(x) = \{y \in \Delta^* : x \to_T y\},$$

and

$$T(L) = \bigcup_{x \in L} T(x).$$

As we have seen, a transducer $T = (Q, \Sigma, \Delta, q_0, F, S)$ can be viewed as computing a *transduction*, that is, a function from 2^{Σ^*} to 2^{Δ^*}. The following theorem, sometimes called *Nivat's theorem*, precisely characterizes those functions.

Theorem 3.5.3 (Nivat). *Suppose f is a map from 2^{Σ^*} to 2^{Δ^*}. Then f is computed by a transducer $T = (Q, \Sigma, \Delta, q_0, F, S)$ iff there exist a finite alphabet Γ, a regular language $R \subseteq \Gamma^*$, and morphisms $g : \Gamma^* \to \Delta^*$ and $h : \Gamma^* \to \Sigma^*$ such that $f(z) = g(h^{-1}(z) \cap R)$ for all $z \in \Sigma^*$.*

Proof Idea. The basic idea is to replace each transition in T with a new symbol. We then mimic the reading of an input z by performing an inverse morphism (to factorize z into elements of Γ) and intersecting with a regular language R (to enforce the condition that the factorization correspond with a path through T). Finally, we get the output by applying another morphism. For the other direction, we just reverse this construction.

Proof. Suppose f is computed by the transducer T. Let Γ be a new alphabet with a letter $a_{x,y}$ for each transition labeled x/y in S. Now define R to be the language accepted by the NFA $M = (Q, \Gamma, \delta, q_0, F)$, where each transition in T, $(p, x, y, q) \in S$, is replaced with $\delta(p, a_{x,y}) = q$ in M. Finally, define the morphisms g, h by $g(a_{x,y}) = y$ and $h(a_{x,y}) = x$. We claim that for all $z \in \Sigma$, we have $T(z) = g(h^{-1}(z) \cap R)$.

To see this, let $w \in T(z)$. Then we can factor $z = z_0 z_1 \cdots z_i$, $w = w_0 w_1 \cdots w_i$, such that there is an accepting computation of T of the form $(p_0, z_0, w_0, p_1), (p_1, z_1, w_1, p_2), \ldots, (p_i, z_i, w_i, p_{i+1})$ with $p_{i+1} \in F$. Then $h^{-1}(z)$ and R both contain the string $a_{z_0,w_0} \cdots a_{z_i,w_i}$, so $g(h^{-1}(z) \cap R)$ contains w. The other direction is similar.

For the other direction, we are given g, h, and R. Since R is regular, there is a DFA $M = (Q, \Gamma, \delta, q_0, F)$ accepting R. Now create a transducer $T = (Q, \Sigma, \Gamma, q_0, F, S)$, where $S = \{(p, h(a), g(a), q) : \delta(p, a) = q\}$. We claim that $T(z) = g(h^{-1}(z) \cap R)$. The details are left to the reader. ∎

Example 3.5.4. Consider the transducer depicted in Figure 3.7 that removes leading zeroes. Define the new symbols b_1, b_2, b_3 as follows:

$$b_1 = a_{0,\epsilon}$$
$$b_2 = a_{0,0}$$
$$b_3 = a_{1,1}.$$

Then in the proof of Theorem 3.5.3 we get $R = b_1^* \cup b_1^* b_3 \{b_2, b_3\}^*$. Now define the morphisms g, h by

$$g(b_1) = \epsilon \qquad h(b_1) = 0$$
$$g(b_2) = 0 \qquad h(b_2) = 0$$
$$g(b_3) = 1 \qquad h(b_3) = 1.$$

Thus, to remove leading zeros from strings in a language L, we can use the expression

$$g(h^{-1}(L) \cap (b_1^* \cup b_1^* b_3 \{b_2, b_3\}^*)).$$

Corollary 3.5.5. *If L is regular, and T is a transducer, then $T(L)$ is regular.*

Proof. We know that regular languages are closed under intersection, morphism, and inverse morphism. ∎

For the last result of this section, we prove that the composition of two transductions is still a transduction.

Theorem 3.5.6. *Suppose $f : 2^{\Sigma^*} \to 2^{\Delta^*}$ and $g : 2^{\Delta^*} \to 2^{\Gamma^*}$ are two transductions. Then so is $f \circ g$.*

Proof. First we observe that any transducer can be rewritten in a so-called *normal form*, where every transition is of the form x/y with $|x|, |y| \le 1$. To see

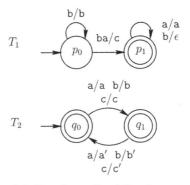

Figure 3.8: Transducers T_1 and T_2 to be composed

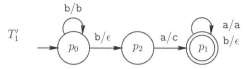

Figure 3.9: The normal form T_1' for transducer T_1

this, simply add extra states so that each transition inputs and outputs at most one letter. Do this for both transducers and then employ the usual cross-product construction for automata. If the first transducer has a transition labeled x/y, and the second has a transition labeled y/z, the new transducer has a transition labeled x/z. (Note we must take into account the implicit transitions labeled ϵ/ϵ from each state to itself.) ∎

Example 3.5.7. Consider Figure 3.8, where two transducers T_1 and T_2 are illustrated. Since T_1 is not in the normal form, we convert it to a transducer T_1' in Figure 3.9. Then the cross-product construction gives the transducer T for the composition of T_1' and T_2 in Figure 3.10.

3.6 Two-way finite automata

As is proved in nearly every first course on the theory of computation, the three computing models

- deterministic finite automata (DFA)
- nondeterministic finite automata (NFA)
- nondeterministic finite automata with ϵ-transitions (NFA-ϵ)

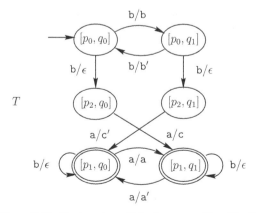

Figure 3.10: The transducer T for the composition $T_1' \circ T_2$

have equal computing power in the sense that they accept exactly the same class of languages: the regular languages. Another way to say this is that the class of regular languages is *robust*, by which we mean that small changes to the model (such as adding nondeterminism, or ϵ-transitions, etc.) do not affect the class of languages accepted.

In this section, we consider yet another variation on the computing model of the finite automaton: we give the automaton the extra capability of moving both left *and* right on its input tape. We call this new model a *two-way finite automaton*, or 2DFA for short. As we will see, this extra power does not enlarge the class of languages accepted.

A transition in a 2DFA is of the form $\delta(q, a) = (p, D)$, where $D \in \{L, R\}$. The meaning is that if the 2DFA is currently in state q scanning the symbol a, then it first changes to state p and then moves in direction D.

Recall that a DFA is said to accept an input string x if it is in a final state after processing the symbols of x. Similarly, we say a 2DFA accepts x if it eventually walks off the right edge of the tape while in a final state. However, a 2DFA can exhibit more complex behavior than a DFA, because its ability to move left and right means that it could

- walk off the *left* edge of the tape, which causes a crash; or
- enter an infinite loop (e.g., a nonterminating computation where the 2DFA never walks off either edge of the tape).

Formally, a 2DFA is a 5-tuple $(Q, \Sigma, \delta, q_0, F)$. Each of these components is exactly the same as for a DFA, with the exception of δ, which now maps $Q \times \Sigma \rightarrow Q \times \{L, R\}$. Here, L and R are codes that refer to a left and right move, respectively.

As in the case of a DFA, we can represent a 2DFA by a transition diagram. For example, consider a 2DFA

$$M = (\{q_0, q_1\}, \{0, 1\}, \delta, q_0, \{q_1\}),$$

where δ is given as follows:

δ	0	1
q_0	(q_0, R)	(q_1, R)
q_1	(q_1, L)	(q_0, L)

This 2DFA can be represented by a transition diagram as shown in Figure 3.11.

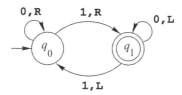

Figure 3.11: Example of a 2DFA

It is not hard to see that this 2DFA accepts the regular language 0^*1. You should verify that the following behaviors occur:

Input	Behavior
000	Walks off right edge in nonfinal state
001	Walks off right edge in final state
100	Walks off left edge
111	Enters an infinite loop

We now provide a way to record the current configuration of a 2DFA. A configuration describes the input string, the current state, and the current symbol being scanned. Formally, a configuration is an element of $\Sigma^* Q \Sigma^*$. The meaning of the configuration wqx is that the input to the 2DFA is wx and the machine is currently in state q and is scanning the first symbol of x (or has fallen off the right edge of the tape if $x = \epsilon$). (Using this convention, there is no way to represent having walked off the left edge of the tape.)

Now it is possible to formally define the moves of a 2DFA. If the current configuration is $wqax$ and there is a move $\delta(q, a) = (p, \text{R})$, then the next configuration is $wapx$. We write $wqax \vdash wapx$. If the current configuration is $waqbx$ and there is a move $\delta(q, b) = (p, \text{L})$, then the next configuration is $wpabx$. We write $waqbx \vdash wpabx$. If the current configuration is qbx and there is a move $\delta(q, b) = (p, \text{L})$, then the machine falls off the left edge of the tape and crashes.

For example, for the 2DFA in Figure 3.11, we have

$$q_0 111 \vdash 1q_1 11 \vdash q_0 111 \vdash 1q_1 11 \vdash \cdots$$

and

$$q_0 001 \vdash 0q_0 01 \vdash 00q_0 1 \vdash 001q_1.$$

We write $\overset{*}{\vdash}$ for the reflexive, transitive closure of $\vdash$. In other words, if $c \overset{*}{\vdash} c'$, then there exists a sequence of configurations $c_1, c_2, \ldots, c_r, r \geq 1$, such that

$$c = c_1 \vdash c_2 \vdash c_3 \vdash \cdots \vdash c_r = c'.$$

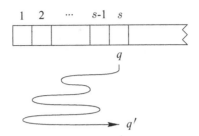

Figure 3.12: Path of a 2DFA

Finally, we are ready to give a formal definition of acceptance. We say a string w is accepted by a 2DFA $M = (Q, \Sigma, \delta, q_0, F)$ if $q_0 w \overset{*}{\vdash} wp$ for some $p \in F$. We define $L(M)$, the language accepted by the 2DFA M, as follows:

$$L(M) = \{w \in \Sigma^* : q_0 w \overset{*}{\vdash} wp \text{ for some } p \in F\}.$$

We now prove that the class of languages accepted by 2DFAs is exactly the regular languages. In other words, there is no gain in the ultimate computing power if we allow the tape head to move both right and left (but see Exercise 22).

The idea behind the proof is a simulation. Clearly, a 2DFA can simulate an ordinary DFA. Indeed, an ordinary DFA is a 2DFA in which every move is to the right. The other direction, the simulation of a 2DFA by a DFA, is more complicated.

Theorem 3.6.1. *We can simulate the computations of a 2DFA with a DFA.*

Proof Idea. The idea behind the simulation is to keep track of the possible behaviors of the 2DFA when it moves left from the current position. If the tape head is currently scanning cell number s of the input, the only way cells $1, 2, \ldots, s - 1$ can affect the computation is if the tape head moves left, moves around a bit, and exits back through cell s, having changed state. This is illustrated by Figure 3.12.

We can therefore simulate the 2DFA if we keep track of a table, which tells us for each state $q \in Q$ in what state we will eventually exit to the right. We also need to know whether the input we have seen so far is potentially acceptable.

We build these tables, one for each possible nonempty input w, as follows: the table τ_w is a map $Q \cup \{\overline{q}\} \to Q \cup \{0\}$. Here, $\overline{q}$ and 0 are two new symbols assumed not to be in Q. If $q \in Q$, then $\tau_w(q) := q'$ if M, when started in state q with w on the tape, scanning the *rightmost* symbol of w, ultimately falls off the right edge of the tape in state q', and 0 otherwise. We also define $\tau_w(\overline{q}) := q'$ if M, when started in state q_0 with w on the tape, scanning the *leftmost* symbol of w, ultimately falls off the right edge of the tape in state q', and 0 otherwise.

There are only finitely many distinct tables, so the automaton we create has finitely many states.

Proof. Define

$$\tau_w(q) := \begin{cases} q', & \text{if } w = w'a, a \in \Sigma, \text{ and } w'qa \overset{*}{\vdash} w'aq'; \\ 0, & \text{otherwise.} \end{cases}$$

$$\tau_w(\overline{q}) := \begin{cases} q', & \text{if } w \in \Sigma^+ \text{ and } q_0 w \overset{*}{\vdash} wq'; \\ 0, & \text{otherwise.} \end{cases}$$

We now prove the fundamental.

Lemma 3.6.2. *If w, x are nonempty strings, $a \in \Sigma$, and $\tau_w = \tau_x$, then $\tau_{wa} = \tau_{xa}$.*

Proof. Consider the behavior of the machine started in state q with tape contents wa and xa, reading the rightmost symbol of each. The movement of the machine depends only on $\delta(q, a)$, and so if we move right in either case, we move right in both. If we move left, and enter state p, we encounter the last symbol of w and x. Since $\tau_w = \tau_x$, we know when we reemerge, exiting to the right, the machine will be in the same state whether w or x was on the tape. If we do not reemerge, this must be due to falling off the left edge of the tape or entering an infinite loop, and $\tau_w(p) = \tau_x(p) = 0$. Then $\tau_{wa}(p) = \tau_{xa}(p) = 0$. Thus, $\tau_{wa}(q) = \tau_{xa}(q)$ for all $q \in Q$.

It remains to consider $\overline{q}$. If $\tau_w(\overline{q}) = \tau_x(\overline{q}) = q' \neq 0$, then on processing either w or x we eventually fall off the right edge of the tape in state q'. If in fact there is an a after either w or x, then if we move right on input a we will fall off the edge of the tape in the same state. If we move left then by the preceding argument we will have the same behavior for both inputs. If $\tau_w(\overline{q}) = \tau_x(\overline{q}) = 0$, then we either fall off the left edge of the tape or enter an infinite loop, and this behavior is the same for wa and xa. ∎

Now we build a simulating DFA for a 2DFA $M = (Q, \Sigma, \delta, q_0, F)$, where $\delta : Q \times \Sigma \to Q \times \{L, R\}$. Define $M' := (Q', \Sigma, \delta', q'_0, F')$, where

$$Q' := \{q'_0\} \cup \{\tau_w \ : \ w \in \Sigma^+\};$$
$$\delta'(q'_0, a) := \tau_a \text{ for each } a \in \Sigma;$$
$$\delta'(\tau_w, a) := \tau_{wa} \text{ for } w \in \Sigma^+, a \in \Sigma;$$
$$F' := \{\tau_w \ : \ \tau_w(\overline{q}) \in F\} \cup \{q'_0 \ : \ q_0 \in F\}.$$

By the lemma, our definition $\delta'(\tau_w, a) = \tau_{wa}$ is consistent. An easy induction now gives $\delta'(q'_0, w) = \tau_w$ for all $w \in \Sigma^+$.

Now $w \in L(M)$ if and only if there exists a state $p \in F$ such that $q_0 w \overset{*}{\vdash} wp$, if and only if $\tau_w(\overline{q}) \in F$, iff $\delta'(q_0', w) = \tau_w$ and $\tau_w \in F'$. It follows that $w \in L(M)$ if and only if $w \in L(M')$.   ∎

Remark. It may be worth noting that τ_w can be effectively computed. Simply simulate M starting in the various states on the last symbol of w. Within $|w| \|Q\|$ moves, one either falls off the left or right edge of the tape, or repeats a pair of the form (state, input position), and so M is in an infinite loop.

Remark. If M has n states, then M' has $\leq (n + 1)^{n+1} + 1$ states.

Let us look at an example of Theorem 3.6.1. Apply the construction to the 2DFA in Figure 3.11. We find

w	$\tau_w(q_0)$	$\tau_w(q_1)$	$\tau_w(\overline{q})$	State name
0	q_0	0	q_0	B
1	q_1	0	q_1	C
00	q_0	0	q_0	B
01	q_1	q_1	q_1	D
10	q_0	0	0	E
11	q_1	0	0	F
010	q_0	0	0	E
011	q_1	0	0	F
100	q_0	0	0	E
101	q_1	q_1	0	G
110	q_0	0	0	E
111	q_1	0	0	F
1010	q_0	0	0	E
1011	q_1	0	0	F

which corresponds to the DFA shown in Figure 3.13, where $A = q_0'$:

Sometimes 2DFAs are useful for showing that certain languages are regular. For example, define the following operation on languages:

$$\text{root}(L) := \{w \in \Sigma^* \ : \ \exists \, n \geq 1 \text{ such that } w^n \in L\}.$$

Theorem 3.6.3. *If L is regular, then so is* $\text{root}(L)$.

Proof. We build a 2DFA M' accepting $L' := \text{B root}(L) \text{ E}$, where B, E are new symbols not in the alphabet of L. The symbols B and E are delimiters representing the beginning and end, respectively, of the input.

On input B w E, the 2DFA scans the input from left to right, simulating the DFA M for L. If a final state of M is reached on reading the endmarker E, we

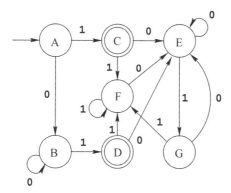

Figure 3.13: An equivalent DFA

move off the right edge. Otherwise, we store the current state q of M, rewind the read head to the start marker B, and continue processing the symbols of w again, starting from state q in M. We keep doing this. If $w^i \in L$ for some i, we eventually accept and walk off the right edge of the input tape. Otherwise we are in an infinite loop and hence do not accept. It follows that L' is regular. Now define a morphism h mapping the symbols B, E to ϵ and every element of Σ to itself. Then $h(L') = \text{root}(L)$, so $\text{root}(L)$ is regular. ∎

3.7 The transformation automaton

Given a DFA $M = (Q, \Sigma, \delta, q_0, F)$, there exists an associated automaton $M' = (Q', \Sigma, \delta', q'_0, -)$ with interesting properties. Echoing the construction of the previous section, the states of M' are *functions* with domain and range Q. The intent is that if M' reaches state f after processing the input string x, then $f(q)$ gives the state that M would be in, had it started in state q and processed x.

We call M' the *transformation automaton* of M. Note that we do not specify the set of final states, which means that we are, in effect, defining many different automata, one for each choice of final states.

Formally, here is the definition of the transformation automaton: the states Q' are Q^Q, which means all functions $f : Q \to Q$. The initial state q'_0 is the identity function i that maps each $q \in Q$ to itself. The transition function δ' is defined as follows: $\delta'(f, a) = g$ if $g(q) = \delta(f(q), a)$ for all $q \in Q$.

Theorem 3.7.1. *Let* $M = (Q, \Sigma, \delta, q_0, F)$ *be a DFA and* $M' = (Q', \Sigma, \delta', q'_0, -)$ *its transformation automaton. Suppose* $\delta'(q'_0, w) = f$. *Then for each* $q \in Q$, $f(q) = \delta(q, w)$.

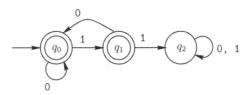

Figure 3.14: A DFA for the language $\{x \in \{0, 1\}^* \ : \ x$ contains no 11$\}$

Proof. By induction on $|w|$. If $|w| = 0$, then $w = \epsilon$. Then $\delta'(q_0', \epsilon) = q_0' = i$, the identity function. So $i(q) = q$ for all q, and $\delta(q, \epsilon) = q$.

Now assume the result is true for all $|w| < n$; we prove it for $w = n$. Write $w = xa$. Then $\delta'(q_0', xa) = \delta'(\delta'(q_0', x), a)$. By induction if $f = \delta'(q_0', x)$, then $f(q) = \delta(q, x)$. By definition if $g = \delta'(f, a)$, then $g(q) = \delta(f(q), a)$. So $g(q) = \delta(f(q), a) = \delta(\delta(q, x), a) = \delta(q, xa) = \delta(q, w)$.   ∎

One property of the transformation automaton that makes it useful is the following.

Theorem 3.7.2. *If* $\delta'(q_0', x) = f$ *and* $\delta'(q_0', y) = g$, *then* $\delta'(q_0', xy) = g \circ f$.

Proof. We have $\delta(q, x) = f(q)$ for all $q \in Q$ and $\delta(r, y) = g(r)$ for all $r \in Q$. Now let $r = f(q)$ to get $\delta(q, xy) = \delta(\delta(q, x), y) = \delta(f(q), y) = \delta(r, y) = g(r) = g(f(q))$.   ∎

Corollary 3.7.3. *Let* $g = \delta'(q_0', x^n)$. *Then* $g = f^n$, *where* $f = \delta'(q_0', x)$.

Example 3.7.4. An example may make this clearer. Figure 3.14 illustrates a DFA that accepts the language of strings over $\{0, 1\}^*$ that contain no occurrence of the subword 11, and Figure 3.15 illustrates the associated transformation automaton (with only the states reachable from the start state shown).

The transformation automaton can be used to solve many problems that would otherwise be difficult. The following example illustrates this.

Example 3.7.5. Consider the following transformation on languages. Given a language $L \subseteq \Sigma^*$, consider the language

$$T(L) = \{x \in \Sigma^* \ : \ x^* \subseteq L\}.$$

Suppose L is regular. Then must $T(L)$ be regular?

Using our familiar techniques, this might seem a difficult problem, since it would seem to require simulating a DFA for L on infinitely many different powers of x and ensuring that all are accepted. Using the transformation

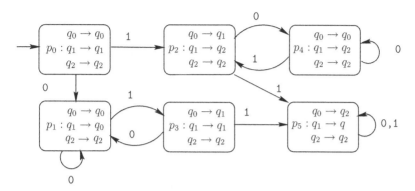

Figure 3.15: The corresponding transformation automaton

automaton, however, the solution is easy. Given a DFA M for L, create its transformation automaton M'. Now let the set of final states of M' be

$$F' = \{f \in Q' \ : \ f^n(q_0) \in F \text{ for all } n \geq 0\}.$$

Using Corollary 3.7.3, we see that M' accepts $T(L)$.

In Figure 3.15, for example, we would make the states p_0, p_1, p_3, and p_4 final.

3.8 Automata, graphs, and Boolean matrices

In the previous section, we showed how to compute a function $f_w(q)$ that, for each state q, determined the state a DFA A would be in after reading the input word w. Now imagine that A is, instead, an NFA. Instead of being in a single state after reading w, the NFA A could be in a set of states. How can we handle this more complicated situation?

The transition diagram of an NFA or DFA can be viewed as a directed graph, with a distinguished source vertex, the start state, and a set of distinguished sink vertices, the final states. Directed graphs, in turn, can be viewed as Boolean matrices—that is, matrices with entries in $\{0, 1\}$—and doing so allows us to easily solve problems that would otherwise be hard.

Boolean matrices are multiplied like ordinary matrices, except that instead of addition and multiplication as the operations, we instead use the Boolean operators $\vee$ (or) and $\wedge$ (and).

Let us assume that the states of our automaton are $\{q_0, q_1, \ldots, q_{n-1}\}$ for some integer $n \geq 1$ and that q_0 is the start state. Given an NFA $A = (Q, \Sigma, \delta, q_0, F)$, we can form the Boolean *incidence matrix* M_a for each $a \in \Sigma$ as follows: the entry in row i and column j is 1 if $q_j \in \delta(q_i, a)$, and 0 otherwise. To put it another way, $(M_a)_{i,j} = 1$ if and only if in A's transition diagram there is a directed edge labeled a from state q_i to state q_j.

We can generalize this definition as follows: for a word w, the entry in row i and column j of M_w is 1 if $q_j \in \delta(q_i, w)$, and 0 otherwise. The next theorem shows why matrices are useful.

Theorem 3.8.1. *Let* $w = a_1 a_2 \cdots a_i$, $i \geq 0$. *Then* $M_w = M_{a_1} M_{a_2} \cdots M_{a_i}$.

Proof. By induction on i. (As usual, if $w = \epsilon$, then M_w is the $n \times n$ identity matrix.) The theorem is clearly true for $i = 0, 1$. Now assume that it is true for i; we prove it for $i + 1$. Write $w = xa$ with $|w| = i + 1$. Then $|x| = i$, and we have $M_w = M_{xa}$. The entry in row i and column j of M_{xa} is, by definition, 1 if and only if $q_j \in \delta(q_i, xa)$. But $q_j \in \delta(q_i, xa)$ if and only if there exists a state q_k such that $q_k \in \delta(q_i, x)$ and $q_j \in \delta(q_k, a)$. This occurs iff there exists k with a 1 in row i, column k of M_x, and a 1 in row k, column j of M_a. But this occurs if and only if $M_x M_a$ has a 1 in row i and column j. It follows that $M_{xa} = M_x M_a$. By induction, $M_x = M_{a_1} M_{a_2} \cdots M_{a_i}$. Since $a = a_{i+1}$, we get $M_w = M_{a_1} M_{a_2} \cdots M_{a_i} M_{a_{i+1}}$, as desired. ∎

Corollary 3.8.2.

(a) For all words w, x, we have $M_{wx} = M_w M_x$.
(b) For all words w and integers $n \geq 0$, we have $M_{w^n} = M_w^n$.

With Boolean incidence matrices, we can turn the computations of an NFA into an algebraic problem.

Theorem 3.8.3. *Let* $A = (Q, \Sigma, \delta, q_0, F)$ *be an NFA with n states, and let M_a be its associated matrices. Let u be the vector* $[1 \ \overbrace{0 \ 0 \cdots \ 0}^{n-1}]$ *and let v be the vector where the ith entry is 1 if $q_i \in F$ and 0 otherwise. Then A accepts w if and only if $u M_w v = 1$.*

Proof. The NFA A accepts w if and only if $q_j \in \delta(q_0, w)$ for some $q_j \in F$, if and only if M_w has 1 entry in row 0 and column j for some $q_j \in F$, if and only if $u M_w v = 1$. ∎

Now let us look at an application of this approach. Consider an n-state NFA A. Given a word w, how can we efficiently decide if A accepts w^r for very large r? We could, of course, simply simulate A on w^r, but this would take $O(n^2 r |w|)$ steps by the usual approach. Can we do this more efficiently?

Using the incidence matrix approach solves this problem. Given $w = a_1 a_2 \cdots a_i$, we first form the matrix $M = M_w$ by multiplying together the matrices $M_{a_1}, \ldots, M_{a_i}$. Next, we raise M to the r power using the usual "binary method." In this approach, we use the identities $M^{2i} = (M^i)^2$ and $M^{2i+1} = M^{2i} M$ to raise M to the r power using only $O(\log r)$ matrix multiplications. Each multiplication uses $O(n^e)$ steps, where e is the optimal exponent for matrix multiplication. (Currently, $e = 2.376$.) Finally, we look in row 0 to see if there are any 1 entries in columns corresponding to final states. Thus we have shown

Theorem 3.8.4. *For a word w, we can decide if an n-state NFA accepts w^r in $O(n^e(|w| + \log r))$ steps, where e is the exponent for matrix multiplication.*

Here is another application of the matrix approach. Suppose we are given a unary NFA A that accepts a finite language, and we want to enumerate all the elements of $L(A)$. How efficiently can we do this? The naive approach would be to maintain a list L of the states of A, perhaps represented as a bit vector, and update this list as we read additional symbols of input. If A has n states, then the longest word accepted is of length $\leq n - 1$. To update L after reading each new symbol potentially requires a union of n sets, each with at most n elements. Thus, the total cost is $O(n^3)$.

We can improve this using the incidence matrix approach. Suppose A has n states. Take 2^k to be the smallest power of 2 that is $\geq n$.

Now add 2^k new states to A, labeled $p_0, p_1, \ldots, p_{2^k-1}$. Let p_0 be the new initial state and add transitions from p_i to p_{i+1} for $0 \leq i < p_{2^k-1}$ and from p_{2^k-1} to q_0. Call the result A', and let M be the incidence matrix of A.

Now A accepts a word of length i if and only if there is a path of length i from q_0 to a final state of A, if and only if there is a path of length 2^k from p_i to a final state of A'. So compute M^{2^k} through repeated squaring and check the entry corresponding to the row for p_i and the columns for the final states of A'. We must do this for each possible length, 0 through $n - 1$, and so the total cost is $O(n^e \log n + n^2)$.

We have proved

Theorem 3.8.5. *If M is a unary NFA that accepts a finite language L, we can enumerate the elements of L in $O(n^e \log n)$ steps, where e is the optimal exponent for matrix multiplication.*

Up to now we have been considering Boolean matrix multiplication. But ordinary matrix multiplication can also be useful, as the following theorem shows.

Theorem 3.8.6. *Let A be a DFA and M_a be the associated incidence matrix corresponding to transitions on the symbol a. Let $M = \sum_{a \in \Sigma} M_a$. Then the*

(ordinary) matrix power M^n has the property that the element in row i and column j is the number of strings of length n that take A from state q_i to state q_j.

Proof. Similar to the proof of Theorem 3.8.1.   ∎

Example 3.8.7. Consider the DFA from Figure 3.14. The associated matrices M_0, M_1, and $M = M_0 + M_1$ are then

$$M_0 = \begin{bmatrix} 1 & 0 & 0 \\ 1 & 0 & 0 \\ 0 & 0 & 1 \end{bmatrix} \qquad M_1 = \begin{bmatrix} 0 & 1 & 0 \\ 0 & 0 & 1 \\ 0 & 0 & 1 \end{bmatrix} \qquad M = \begin{bmatrix} 1 & 1 & 0 \\ 1 & 0 & 1 \\ 0 & 0 & 2 \end{bmatrix}.$$

Thus, for example, to count the number of strings of length 4 accepted by this DFA, we square M twice:

$$M^2 = \begin{bmatrix} 2 & 1 & 1 \\ 1 & 1 & 2 \\ 0 & 0 & 4 \end{bmatrix} \qquad M^4 = \begin{bmatrix} 5 & 3 & 8 \\ 3 & 2 & 11 \\ 0 & 0 & 16 \end{bmatrix}.$$

Thus, there are five strings of length four that take the DFA from state q_0 to q_0 (namely, $\{0000, 0010, 0100, 1000, 1010\}$) and three strings from q_0 to q_1 (namely, $\{0001, 0101, 1001\}$) for a total of eight strings.

Let's look at one more application of the Boolean matrix approach. Recall that in Theorem 3.4.1, we proved that if L is regular, then so is

$$\frac{1}{2}L = \{x \in \Sigma^* \ : \ \text{there exists } y \in \Sigma^* \text{ with } |y| = |x| \text{ such that } xy \in L\}.$$

Given a language L, define the analogous transformation $\log(L)$ as follows:

$$\log(L) = \{x \in \Sigma^* \ : \ \text{there exists } y \in \Sigma^* \text{ with } |y| = 2^{|x|} \text{ such that } xy \in L\}.$$

We now prove

Proposition 3.8.8. If L is regular, then so is $\log(L)$.

Proof. Given a DFA $A = (Q, \Sigma, \delta, q_0, F)$ for L, let M_a be the incidence matrix corresponding to the input symbol a. Let $M = \bigvee_{a \in \Sigma} M_a$, the Boolean "or" of all the matrices M_a. Then M has the property that there is an entry in row i and column j if and only if there is a transition in A on some symbol from q_i to q_j.

We now make a DFA $A' = (Q', \Sigma, \delta', q'_0, F')$ for $\log(L)$. Here

$$Q' = \{[B, C] \ : \ B, C \text{ are } n \times n \text{ Boolean matrices}\},$$

where n is the number of states in Q. The basic idea is that if on input x we arrive at the state $[B, C]$, then $B = M_x$ and $C = M^{2^{|x|}}$. To enforce this, we set

$q_0' = [I, M]$, where I is the $n \times n$ identity matrix and define $\delta'([B, C], a) = [BM_a, C^2]$. We also set

$$F' = \{[B, C] : BC \text{ has a 1 in row 0 and column } j \text{ such that } q_j \in F\}.$$

Then x is accepted by A' if and only if $M_x M^{2^{|x|}}$ has a 1 in row 0 and a column corresponding to a final state, which occurs if and only if there exists y, $|y| = 2^{|x|}$, such that $xy \in L(M)$. ∎

3.9 The Myhill–Nerode theorem

The Myhill–Nerode theorem is probably the single most important characterization of regular languages.

To begin, let us recall the definition of equivalence relation. A *relation* R over a nonempty set S is a subset $R \subseteq S \times S$. We write $x R y$ if $(x, y) \in R$. A relation R is said to be an *equivalence relation* if it obeys the following three properties:

(a) *Reflexive property.* For all x, we have $x R x$.
(b) *Symmetric property.* If $x R y$, then $y R x$.
(c) *Transitive property.* If $x R y$, and $y R z$ then $x R z$.

An equivalence relation partitions S into a number of disjoint *equivalence classes*. An equivalence class E with representative x is $E = \{y \in S : x R y\}$. We sometimes write $E = [x]$. The number of distinct equivalence classes is called the *index* of the equivalence relation; it may be infinite. If the index is finite, we say that R is of *finite index*.

If we have two equivalence relations R_1 and R_2 over S, we say that R_1 is a *refinement* of R_2 if $R_1 \subseteq R_2$, that is, if $x R_1 y \Rightarrow x R_2 y$ for all $x, y \in S$. If R_1 is a refinement of R_2, then each equivalence class of R_2 is a union of some of the equivalence classes of R_1.

Example 3.9.1. Let us consider some equivalence relations over $\mathbb{Z}$, the integers. For a positive integer n, define E_n as follows: $x E_n y$ means $x \equiv y$ (mod n). Then the index of E_n equals n, as E_n partitions $\mathbb{Z}$ into equivalence classes corresponding to each of the residue classes, mod n.

We have $x \equiv y$ (mod 6) implies that $x \equiv y$ (mod 3), and so E_6 is a refinement of E_3. In fact, each equivalence class of E_3 is a union of two of the equivalence classes of E_6.

Now let us consider two equivalence relations on Σ^*. For a DFA $M = (Q, \Sigma, \delta, q_0, F)$, define R_M by $x R_M y$ means $\delta(q_0, x) = \delta(q_0, y)$. The index of this equivalence relation is at most $|Q|$, the number of states, and hence is finite.

This particular equivalence relation has a very nice property: namely, it is *right invariant*. We say that an equivalence relation R is right invariant if xRy implies that for all $z \in \Sigma^*$, we have $xzRyz$. Suppose xR_My. Then

$$\delta(q_0, xz) = \delta(\delta(q_0, x), z)$$

$$= \delta(\delta(q_0, y), z)$$

$$= \delta(q_0, yz),$$

so xzR_Myz and hence R_M is right invariant.

Another property of R_M is that $L(M)$ is the union of some of R_M's equivalence classes, namely, those classes corresponding to final states of M.

Now let us turn to another equivalence relation. Consider any language (not necessarily regular) $L \subseteq \Sigma^*$. With L we associate the equivalence relation R_L defined by xR_Ly means that for all $z \in \Sigma^*$, we have $xz \in L$ if and only if $yz \in L$. This equivalence relation is sometimes called the *Myhill–Nerode equivalence relation*. Once again, we have that R_L is right-invariant: suppose xR_Ly. Then $xu \in L$ if and only if $yu \in L$. Take $u = zv$ to get

$$(xz)v \in L \iff x(zv) \in L \iff y(zv) \in L \iff (yz)v \in L.$$

Now L is the union of some of the equivalence classes of R_L: namely, those equivalence classes corresponding to elements of L.

Common Error 3.9.2. One very common error that students make when first exposed to the Myhill–Nerode equivalence relation is to think that it only deals with strings in L. In fact, this equivalence relation can be used to compare any pair of strings chosen from Σ^*. Of course, not all pairs are necessarily related.

Now we are ready for the fundamental observation about the Myhill–Nerode equivalence relation:

Lemma 3.9.3. *Let $L \subseteq \Sigma^*$, and let E be any right-invariant equivalence relation on Σ^* such that L is the union of some of E's equivalence classes. Then E is a refinement of R_L, the Myhill–Nerode equivalence relation.*

Proof. Suppose xEy. Then $xzEyz$ for all $z \in \Sigma^*$. Since L is the union of some of E's equivalence classes, this gives that $xz \in L$ if and only if $yz \in L$. Hence, xR_Ly. ∎

Example 3.9.4. It is worthwhile pointing out that Lemma 3.9.3 holds even if E or R_L has infinite index. For example, consider $\Sigma = \{a, b\}$, $L = (\{a, b\}^3)^*$, and let E be the equivalence relation $x E y$ if $|x| = |y|$. Then each of the three equivalence classes of R_L is the union of infinitely many equivalence classes of E. For example, L itself is the union of the equivalence classes $[\epsilon], [a^3], [a^6], \ldots$ of E.

Now we are ready for the Myhill–Nerode theorem:

Theorem 3.9.5. *Let $L \subseteq \Sigma^*$ be a language. The following statements are equivalent:*

(a) L is regular.

(b) L can be written as the union of some of the equivalence classes of E, where E is a right-invariant equivalence relation of finite index.

(c) Let R_L be the Myhill–Nerode equivalence relation. Then R_L is of finite index.

Proof. (a) $\Rightarrow$ (b): If L is regular, it is accepted by some DFA M. By the preceding discussion L is the union of some of the equivalence classes of R_M, and R_M is right-invariant and of finite index.

(b) $\Rightarrow$ (c): By Lemma 3.9.3, E is a refinement of R_L. Then the index of R_L must be $\leq$ the index of E. But E is of finite index, so R_L is of finite index.

(c) $\Rightarrow$ (a): We construct a DFA $M' = (Q', \Sigma, \delta', q_0', F')$ accepting L. To do so we let $Q' = \{[x] : x \in \Sigma^*\}$, $q_0' = [\epsilon]$, $F' = \{[x] : x \in L\}$, and $\delta'([x], a) = [xa]$.

As usual when dealing with equivalence relations, we must see that the definition is meaningful. In other words, we need to see that if we pick a different representative from the equivalence class $[x]$, say y, then $[xa] = [ya]$. But this is just what it means to be right-invariant.

Now a simple induction on $|y|$ gives that $\delta'([\epsilon], y) = [y]$ for all $y \in \Sigma^*$. It follows that $L(M) = L$. ∎

We now consider some applications of the Myhill–Nerode theorem. By Theorem 1.4.1, we know that every NFA with n states can be simulated by a DFA with at most 2^n states. But is this bound of 2^n best possible? The Myhill–Nerode theorem allows us to prove that 2^n is best possible for alphabets of size ≥ 2.

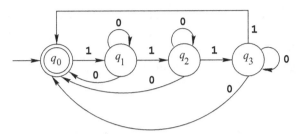

Figure 3.16: The NFA M_4

Theorem 3.9.6. *Let* $M_n = (Q_n, \Sigma, \delta_n, q_0, \{q_0\})$ *be the NFA defined as follows:*

- $Q_n = \{q_0, q_1, \ldots, q_{n-1}\}$;
- $\Sigma = \{0, 1\}$;
- $\delta_n(q_i, 0) = \{q_0, q_i\}$ *for* $1 \leq i < n$;
- $\delta_n(q_0, 0) = \emptyset$;
- $\delta_n(q_i, 1) = \{q_{(i+1) \bmod n}\}$.

Then any DFA for M_n *has at least* 2^n *states.*

For example, Figure 3.16 illustrates M_4.

Proof Idea. Our plan is to generate 2^n inequivalent strings, one corresponding to each of the 2^n possible subsets of states of M_n. By the Myhill–Nerode theorem, it will then follow that any DFA for M_n must have at least 2^n states.

To generate these strings, we use the structure of the NFA M_n. Note that processing an input of 1 increments the subscript number of the state, modulo n, and processing an input of 0 has the effect of both staying in the same state and resetting the state to q_0 (unless the machine is already in q_0).

Proof. For each subset $S \subseteq Q_n$, we define a string $w(S)$ such that $\delta(q_0, w(S)) = S$, as follows: if $S = \{q_{e_1}, q_{e_2}, \ldots, q_{e_k}\}$ with $e_1 < e_2 < \cdots < e_k$, then

$$
w(S) = \begin{cases} 0, & \text{if } S = \emptyset; \\ 1^i, & \text{if } S = \{q_i\}; \\ 1^{e_k - e_{k-1}} 0 1^{e_{k-1} - e_{k-2}} 0 \cdots 1^{e_2 - e_1} 0 1^{e_1}, & \text{otherwise.} \end{cases}
$$

To see that $\delta(q_0, w(S)) = S$ for $|S| \geq 2$, note that successively reading the blocks of 1s separated by single 0s gives the following sequence of states encountered:

$1^{e_k-e_{k-1}}$	$q_{e_k-e_{k-1}}$
0	$q_0, q_{e_k-e_{k-1}}$
$1^{e_{k-1}-e_{k-2}}$	$q_{e_{k-1}-e_{k-2}}, q_{e_k-e_{k-1}}$
0	$q_0, q_{e_{k-1}-e_{k-2}}, q_{e_k-e_{k-1}}$
$1^{e_{k-2}-e_{k-3}}$	$q_{e_{k-2}-e_{k-3}}, q_{e_{k-1}-e_{k-3}}, q_{e_k-e_{k-3}}$
$\vdots$	$\vdots$
$1^{e_2-e_1}$	$q_{e_2-e_1}, q_{e_3-e_1}, \ldots, q_{e_k-e_1}$
0	$q_0, q_{e_2-e_1}, q_{e_3-e_1}, \ldots, q_{e_k-e_1}$
1^{e_1}	$q_{e_1}, q_{e_2}, \ldots, q_{e_k}$

We now show that if $S, T \subseteq Q_n$ with $S \neq T$, then the strings $w(S)$ and $w(T)$ are inequivalent under the Myhill–Nerode equivalence relation. If $S \neq T$, then one of S, T contains an element q_s not contained in the other. Without loss of generality, assume $q_s \in S$ and $q_s \notin T$. Then $w(S)1^{n-s} \in L(M_n)$ but $w(T)1^{n-s} \notin L(M_n)$. Since there are 2^n subsets of Q_n, the result follows. ∎

The Myhill–Nerode theorem can even be used to generate the "minimal" *infinite* automaton for nonregular languages, as the following example shows.

Example 3.9.7. Let $L = \{0^n1^n : n \geq 0\}$ and let us compute the equivalence classes for the Myhill–Nerode equivalence relation. The equivalence classes are

$$\{[\epsilon], [0], [00], \ldots, \} \cup \{[1], [01], [001], \ldots\}.$$

To see that these classes are pairwise distinct, consider $w = 0^m$ and $x = 0^n$ for $m < n$. By choosing $z = 1^m$ we see $wz \in L$ but $xz \notin L$. Similarly, given $w = 0^m1$ and $x = 0^n1$ with $m < n$, choose $z = 1^{n-1}$ to get $wz \notin L$ but $xz \in L$. Finally, if $w = 0^m$ and $x = 0^n1$, choose $z = 01^{m+1}$ to get $wz \in L$ and $xz \notin L$.

We leave it to the reader to verify that these are all the equivalence classes. We can generate an infinite automaton from the equivalence classes, as in Figure 3.17.

3.10 Minimization of finite automata

One of the important consequences of the Myhill–Nerode theorem is that the automaton constructed from the equivalence relation R_L is actually the smallest possible for the regular language L.

Theorem 3.10.1. *The automaton M' in Theorem 3.9.5 is the unique minimal automaton for L, up to renaming of the states.*

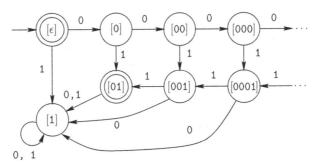

Figure 3.17: Minimal infinite automaton for $\{0^n 1^n \; : \; n \geq 0\}$

Proof. Let $M = (Q, \Sigma, \delta, q_0, F)$ be a minimal DFA for L, and consider the equivalence relation R_M. From Lemma 3.9.3 we have that R_M is a refinement of R_L and hence the index of R_M is $\geq$ the index of R_L. It follows that M has at least as many states as M', where M' is the DFA constructed in the proof of Theorem 3.9.5.

Assume M has the same number of states as M'. We now show how to create an isomorphism between Q and Q'. Let q be a state of M. Then q must be reachable from q_0; that is, there must be an x such that $\delta(q_0, x) = q$. For if not, we could remove q from M and hence obtain a smaller DFA. Now associate $q \in Q$ with $[x]$ in M'. This is consistent, since both R_M and R_L are right-invariant. ∎

Furthermore, we can use the Myhill–Nerode theorem as the basis of an algorithm for minimizing a finite automaton. Suppose we are given a DFA $M = (Q, \Sigma, \delta, q_0, F)$ for a regular language L. From the results given before, we know that R_M is a refinement of R_L, the Myhill–Nerode equivalence relation. It follows that if M is not minimal, then there must be at least two distinct states $p, q \in Q$ such that both $\{x \in \Sigma^* : \delta(q_0, x) = p\}$ and $\{y \in \Sigma^* : \delta(q_0, y) = q\}$ are contained in some equivalence class of R_L. In other words, for all z, we have $\delta(p, z) \in F$ if and only if $\delta(q, z) \in F$. We call the states p and q *indistinguishable* if this is the case, and we write $p \equiv q$. It is easy to see that $\equiv$ is actually an equivalence relation.

One way to minimize a DFA is to determine the distinguishable states. Once they have been determined, we can construct a minimal equivalent automaton in two steps: first, discard all states not reachable from the start state q_0, and second, collapse any maximal set of mutually indistinguishable states into a single state. The states of M reachable from q_0 can be determined in $O(kn)$ time through depth-first or breadth-first search if M is over a k-letter input alphabet and has n states. This time is dominated by the time for the rest of the algorithm, so we do not discuss it further in this section.

Algorithm	Worst-case complexity	In practice	Implementation
NAIVE-MINIMIZE	$O(n^3)$	Reasonable	Easy
MINIMIZE	$O(n^2)$	Good	Moderately easy
FAST-MINIMIZE	$O(n \log n)$	Very good	Quite difficult
BRZOZOWSKI	$O(n2^{2n})$	Often good	Easy

Figure 3.18: Four different minimization algorithms compared

There are several different minimization algorithms known. The properties of some of the most important algorithms are listed in Figure 3.18. The running times given assume a fixed alphabet size.

We now present the algorithm NAIVE-MINIMIZE:

NAIVE-MINIMIZE(M)

0. For all unordered pairs $\{p, q\}$, $p \neq q$, set $U(\{p, q\}) := 0$
1. For all unordered pairs $\{p, q\}$ with $p \in F$ and $q \in Q - F$,
   set $U(\{p, q\}) := 1$
2. Set done := false
3. while not(done) do
       4. done := true
       5. $T := U$
       6. for each unordered pair $\{p, q\}$ with $T(\{p, q\}) = 0$, do
           7. For each $a \in \Sigma$ do
               8. If $T(\{\delta(p, a), \delta(q, a)\}) = 1$ then set $U(\{p, q\}) := 1$
               and set done := false
9. return(U)

If we set $U(\{p, q\})$ to 1 in the algorithm, then we say the pair $\{p, q\}$ is marked.

Theorem 3.10.2. *Algorithm* NAIVE-MINIMIZE *terminates and correctly returns an array*

$$U(\{p, q\}) = \begin{cases} 1, & \text{if } p \not\equiv q; \\ 0, & \text{if } p \equiv q. \end{cases}$$

Furthermore, the pair $\{p, q\}$ is marked at the nth iteration of the while loop if and only if the shortest string distinguishing p from q is of length n.

Proof. Clearly, the algorithm terminates, since there are a finite number of pairs and so eventually we make it through the while loop starting on line 3 without marking any new pairs.

We claim that the pair $\{p, q\}$ is marked by the algorithm at iteration n iff $p \not\equiv q$ and the shortest string distinguishing p from q is of length n.

Suppose $\{p, q\}$ is marked. We prove by induction on the number of iterations n of the loop on line 3 that $p \not\equiv q$ and, further, that p is distinguished from q by a string of length n. The base case is 0 iterations; that is, $\{p, q\}$ is marked on line 1. Then $p \in F$ and $q \in Q - F$, so $p \not\equiv q$. So ϵ distinguishes p from q. Now suppose the claim is true for those pairs marked in some iteration $< n$; we prove it for iteration n.

Pairs are marked in step 8, and this occurs only if $\{\delta(p, a), \delta(q, a)\}$ was marked on some previous iteration. In fact, this marking must have occurred at iteration $n - 1$; otherwise we would have considered $\{p, q\}$ at an earlier iteration. Let $r = \delta(p, a)$ and $s = \delta(q, a)$. If $\{r, s\}$ was marked, then by induction $r \not\equiv s$ and r is distinguished from s by a string t of length $n - 1$. Then the string at distinguishes p from q and $|at| = n$.

For the converse, suppose $p \not\equiv q$, and x is a shortest string distinguishing p from q, and $n = |x|$. We will prove by induction on n that the pair $\{p, q\}$ gets marked at iteration n. If $|x| = 0$, then $\{p, q\}$ gets marked on line 1 of the algorithm, at iteration 0 of the while loop. Now assume the claim is true for all x with $|x| < n$. We prove the claim for $|x| = n$. Write $x = ay$ with $|y| = k$, $a \in \Sigma$. Consider $\{p', q'\}$, where $p' = \delta(p, a)$ and $q' = \delta(q, a)$. Now $p' \not\equiv q'$ since the string y distinguishes them. Let z be a shortest string distinguishing p' from q'. Then by induction $\{p', q'\}$ gets marked at iteration $|z|$. Then the flag done gets set in line 8, and $\{p, q\}$ gets marked at the next iteration. It follows that $n = |z| + 1 = |ay|$. ∎

To estimate the running time of NAIVE-MINIMIZE, we need the following theorem.

Theorem 3.10.3. *If M has $n \geq 2$ states, then the while loop of NAIVE-MINIMIZE is performed at most $n - 1$ times, and in the last iteration, no new pairs are marked.*

Proof. Define a relation $\underset{k}{\equiv}$ on states of M as follows: $p \underset{k}{\equiv} q$ if there is no string x of length $\leq k$ that distinguishes state p from state q. Then it is not hard to see that $\underset{k}{\equiv}$ is an equivalence relation. Also, if p and q cannot be distinguished with a string of length $\leq k + 1$, they cannot be distinguished with a string of length $\leq k$. Thus, $\underset{k+1}{\equiv}$ is a refinement of $\underset{k}{\equiv}$.

Now from the argument of the previous theorem, $p \underset{k}{\equiv} q$ if and only if after k iterations of NAIVE-MINIMIZE, we have failed to distinguish p from q. We also have

(i) If $p \underset{k}{\equiv} q$, then $p \underset{k+1}{\equiv} q$ if and only if $\delta(p, a) \underset{k}{\equiv} \delta(q, a)$ for all $a \in \Sigma$.

(ii) If the relations $\underset{k}{\equiv}$ and $\underset{k+1}{\equiv}$ are identical, then $\underset{k+a}{\equiv}$ equals $\underset{k}{\equiv}$ for all $a \geq 0$.

Now $\underset{0}{\equiv}$ has two equivalence classes, and $\underset{i}{\equiv}$ is the same as $\underset{i}{\equiv}$ for some i; without loss of generality, assume i is as small as possible. But either $\underset{k+a}{\equiv}$ coincides with $\underset{k}{\equiv}$ for all $a \geq 1$ or $\underset{k+1}{\equiv}$ defines at least one more equivalence class than $\underset{k}{\equiv}$; hence, $\underset{i}{\equiv}$ defines at least $i + 2$ equivalence classes. But $i + 2 \leq n$, and so $i \leq n - 2$. ∎

Corollary 3.10.4. *The algorithm* `NAIVE-MINIMIZE` *uses* $O(kn^3)$ *steps, where* $k = |\Sigma|$ *and* $n = |Q|$.

Proof. The while loop is performed at most $n - 1$ times by Theorem 3.10.3. Line 6 takes $O(n^2)$ time and line 7 takes $O(k)$ time. ∎

The next corollary to Theorem 3.10.3 is both surprising and useful. Basically, it states that if we are given two DFAs that accept different languages, then there is a relatively short string that is accepted by one but rejected by the other. If the DFAs have m and n states, it is not difficult to obtain a bound of mn for this problem, but the following theorem says that we can do much better.

Theorem 3.10.5. *Let L_1, L_2 be regular languages accepted by DFAs with m and n states, respectively, with $L_1 \neq L_2$. Then there exists a string x of length $\leq m + n - 2$ that is in $(L_1 - L_2) \cup (L_2 - L_1)$.*

Proof. Take the DFA $M_1 = (Q_1, \Sigma, \delta_1, q_1, F_1)$ and form the "direct sum" with $M_2 = (Q_2, \Sigma, \delta_2, q_2, F_2)$. That is, create the DFA $M = (Q, \Sigma, \delta, q, F)$ as follows:

$$Q = Q_1 \cup Q_2$$

$$\delta(p, a) = \begin{cases} \delta_1(p, a), & \text{if } p \in Q_1; \\ \delta_2(p, a), & \text{if } p \in Q_2; \end{cases}$$

$$q = q_1$$

$$F = F_1 \cup F_2.$$

Then if $L_1 \neq L_2$, $q_1 \not\equiv q_2$, and furthermore by Theorem 3.10.3 these two states can be distinguished by a string of length $\leq |Q| - 2 = m + n - 2$, where $m = |Q_1|, n = |Q_2|$. ∎

In fact, as the following theorem shows, the bound of $m + n - 2$ is best possible:

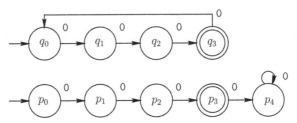

Figure 3.19: The construction for $m = 4, n = 5$

Theorem 3.10.6. *For all integers $m, n \geq 1$, there exist DFAs M_1 and M_2 over a unary alphabet with m and n states, respectively, such that the shortest string accepted by one DFA but not the other is of length $m + n - 2$.*

Proof. Without loss of generality we may assume $m \leq n$. If $m = 1$, the result is easy. Otherwise assume $m \geq 2$. Let $M_1 = (Q_1, \Sigma, \delta_1, q_0, F_1)$ be the DFA given as follows:

$$Q_1 = \{q_0, q_1, q_2, \ldots, q_{m-1}\}$$
$$\Sigma = \{0\}$$
$$\delta_1(q_i, 0) = q_{(i+1) \bmod m}$$
$$F_1 = \{q_j \ : \ j \equiv n - 2 \ (\bmod m)\}.$$

Let $M_2 = (Q_2, \Sigma, \delta_2, p_0, F_2)$ be the DFA given as follows:

$$Q_2 = \{p_0, p_1, p_2, \ldots, p_{n-1}\}$$
$$\Sigma = \{0\}$$
$$\delta_2(p_i, 0) = \begin{cases} p_{i+1}, & \text{if } i < n - 1; \\ p_{n-1}, & \text{if } i = n - 1; \end{cases}$$
$$F_2 = \{p_j \ : \ j \equiv n - 2 \ (\bmod m)\}.$$

For example, Figure 3.19 illustrates this construction for $m = 4, n = 5$.

Then it is easy to verify that 0^{m+n-2} is the shortest string accepted by one machine but rejected by the other. We see that M_1 and M_2 behave identically on all strings of length up to $n - 2$. For lengths $n - 1, n, \ldots, n + m - 3$, M_1 rejects (since the next largest string accepted after 0^{n-2} is 0^{m+n-2}) and so does M_2. But M_1 accepts 0^{m+n-2} while M_2 rejects this string. ∎

We now discuss how to modify NAIVE-MINIMIZE to improve the running time to $O(kn^2)$. The main difference in MINIMIZE is that for each pair of states $\{p, q\}$, we maintain a list of pairs. Recall that if $U(\{p, q\}) = 1$, we say $\{p, q\}$ is marked.

MINIMIZE(M)
0. For all unordered pairs $\{p, q\}$, $p \neq q$, set $U(\{p, q\}) := 0$
1. For all unordered pairs $\{p, q\}$ with $p \in F$ and $q \in Q - F$,
   set $U(\{p, q\}) := 1$
2. For each unordered pair $\{p, q\}$ with either $p, q \in F$ or $p, q \notin F$ do
   3. If $U(\{\delta(p, a), \delta(q, a)\}) = 1$ for some symbol $a \in \Sigma$ then
      4. $U(\{p, q\}) := 1$
      5. Recursively set $U(\{p', q'\}) := 1$ for all unmarked pairs $\{p', q'\}$ on the
         list for $\{p, q\}$, and all pairs on those lists, etc.
   6. Else
      7. For all $a \in \Sigma$ do
         8. If $\delta(p, a) \neq \delta(q, a)$, put $\{p, q\}$ on the list for $\{\delta(p, a), \delta(q, a)\}$
9. return(U)

The proof that MINIMIZE is correct is very similar to that for NAIVE-MINIMIZE, and we leave it as Exercise 17.

Theorem 3.10.7. *The algorithm* MINIMIZE *uses* $O(kn^2)$ *steps.*

Proof. Line 1 uses $O(n^2)$ steps. The loop in line 2 uses $O(kn^2)$ steps, not including the time to do the recursion in step 5. To count the number of steps in line 5, we must think about it not during one step of the loop, but over the entire algorithm. There are at most kn^2 entries over all lists during the running of the algorithm, so step 5 uses at most $O(kn^2)$ steps. ∎

We mention that there exists a refinement of the algorithm MINIMIZE that runs in $O(kn \log n)$ steps. For more details, see the notes.

We now turn to another minimization algorithm originally due to Brzozowski. This algorithm has the property that it is excellent for hand computation and often works well in practice. However, its worst-case running time is exponential.

Given a DFA $M = (Q, \Sigma, \delta, q_0, F)$, define M^R to be the machine obtained by reversing the arrows in M's transition diagram. Formally, define $M^R = (Q, \Sigma, \delta^R, F, \{q_0\})$, where

$$\delta^R(q', a) = \{q \in Q \ : \ \delta(q, a) = q'\}.$$

Note that M^R is not strictly an NFA, since it may have more than one initial state. Nevertheless it should be clear how to treat acceptance in such a generalized NFA, and furthermore we can easily perform the subset construction on M^R

to obtain an equivalent DFA; the only significant difference is that the initial state in the corresponding DFA is the set of initial states of the generalized NFA.

For such a generalized NFA A, define $S(A)$ to be the DFA that arises from the subset construction, *using only states reachable from the start state(s)*.

Theorem 3.10.8 (Brzozowski). *The machine given by $S((S(M^R))^R)$ is a minimal DFA equivalent to M.*

Proof. We first prove the following lemma. Our theorem will then follow by applying the lemma twice.

Lemma 3.10.9. *Suppose $M = (Q, \Sigma, \delta, q_0, F)$ is a DFA accepting the regular language L, and suppose that every state of Q is reachable from q_0. Then $N = S(M^R)$ is a minimal DFA for L^R.*

Proof. Let $M^R = (Q, \Sigma, \delta^R, q_0', F')$, where δ^R is defined as earlier, and $q_0' = F$, $F' = \{q_0\}$. Let $S(M^R) = N = (Q'', \Sigma, \delta'', q_0'', F'')$. To show N is minimal, it suffices to show that no two states of N are equivalent. Let $A, B \in Q''$ be states of N, so that A and B represent sets of states of M. Suppose A is equivalent to B. We show $A = B$.

Let $p \in A$. Since every state of M is reachable from the start state, there exists $w \in \Sigma^*$ such that $\delta(q_0, w) = p$. Hence, $q_0 \in \delta^R(p, w^R)$ in M^R. Thus, $\delta''(A, w^R) \in F''$ in N.

If A is equivalent to B, then $\delta''(B, w^R) \in F''$ in N. Thus, there exists $p' \in B$ such that $q_0 \in \delta^R(p', w^R)$ in M^R. Hence, $p' = \delta(q_0, w)$. But then $p = p'$, since M is a DFA. Thus, $p \in B$.

We have now shown $A \subseteq B$ and, by symmetry, $B \subseteq A$. Hence, $A = B$.

This completes the proof of correctness of Brzozowski's algorithm. ∎

Figure 3.20 illustrates Brzozowski's algorithm on a simple automaton.

We now estimate the worst-case running time of Brzozowski's algorithm.

Theorem 3.10.10. *Brzozowski's algorithm can be made to run in $O(kn2^{2n})$ time.*

Proof. The cost of reversals is negligible compared to the cost of the two subset constructions, so we estimate those.

Using Exercise 1.31, we can perform the initial subset construction in $O(kn2^n)$ time. The resulting DFA has at most 2^n states. When we reverse and perform another subset construction, we may have to perform as many as n rounds of 2^n unions of 2^n states. ∎

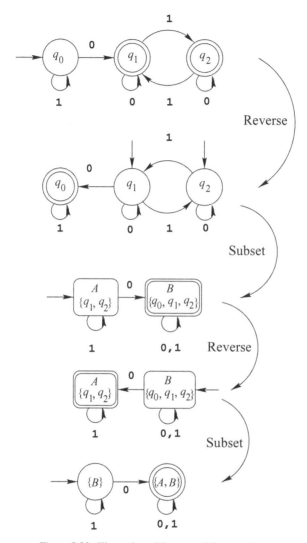

Figure 3.20: Illustration of Brzozowski's algorithm

3.11 State complexity

Some regular languages, such as $\{0, 1\}^*$, can be accepted by DFAs with very few states, while others, such as $\{0, 1\}^*1\{0, 1\}^n$, require many states. The *state complexity* of a regular language L, denoted by $\mathrm{sc}(L)$, is the smallest number of states in any DFA accepting L or, equivalently, the number of states in the minimal DFA accepting L.

Similarly, we can study the *nondeterministic state complexity* of L, denoted $nsc(L)$, which is the smallest number of states in any NFA accepting L.

Theorem 3.11.1. *Let $L, L' \subseteq \Sigma^*$ be regular languages. Then $sc(L \cap L') \leq sc(L)sc(L')$.*

Proof Idea. The idea is to use the "direct-product" construction for automata. The states of the new automaton consist of pairs, with the first component simulating the automaton for L and the second component simulating the automaton for L'.

Proof. Let L be accepted by the DFA $(Q, \Sigma, \delta, q_0, F)$ and L' be accepted by the DFA $(Q', \Sigma, \delta', q_0', F')$. Then $L \cap L'$ can be accepted by a DFA

$$(Q'', \Sigma, \delta'', q_0'', F''),$$

where

- $Q'' := Q \times Q'$;
- $q_0'' := [q_0, q_0']$;
- $F'' := F \times F'$; and
- $\delta''([p, q], a) = [\delta(p, a), \delta(q, a)]$.

This DFA has $|Q||Q'|$ states. ∎

We now show that the upper bound of the previous theorem is tight.

Theorem 3.11.2. *If $|\Sigma| \geq 2$, then for all $m, n \geq 1$, there exist regular languages L, L' such that $sc(L) = m$, $sc(L') = n$, and $sc(L \cap L') = mn$.*

Proof. Let Σ be an alphabet containing the letters a, b. Define

$$L := \{x \in \Sigma^* : |x|_a \equiv 0 \ (\mathrm{mod}\ m)\};$$

$$L' := \{y \in \Sigma^* : |y|_b \equiv 0 \ (\mathrm{mod}\ n)\}.$$

Then it is easy to see that $sc(L) = m$ and $sc(L') = n$. We claim $sc(L \cap L') = mn$. To see this, note that

$$L \cap L' = \{x \in \Sigma^* : |x|_a \equiv 0 \ (\mathrm{mod}\ m), |x|_b \equiv 0 \ (\mathrm{mod}\ n)\}.$$

We claim that for $0 \leq i < m, 0 \leq j < n$, each string $a^i b^j$ lies in a distinct equivalence class of the Myhill–Nerode equivalence relation. For choose $w = a^i b^j$ and $x = a^{i'} b^{j'}$ for $0 \leq i, i' < m$, $0 \leq j, j' < n$. If $w \neq x$, then either $i \neq i'$ or $j \neq j'$. Without loss of generality, assume the former case holds. Then $w a^{m-i} b^{n-j} \in L \cap L'$, but $x a^{m-i} b^{n-j} \notin L$, since $i' + m - i \not\equiv 0 \ (\mathrm{mod}\ m)$. It follows that the minimal DFA for $L \cap L'$ has $\geq mn$ states, and by Theorem 3.11.1, it must have exactly mn states. ∎

Similar but more complicated theorems can be proved for the deterministic state complexity of other operations (see Exercise 49).

Now we turn to nondeterministic state complexity. Here the situation is more challenging, since a minimal NFA for a given regular language is not necessarily unique (see Exercise 18). Furthermore, it is known that the following decision problem is PSPACE-hard:

Instance: a DFA M and an integer k.
Question: Is there an NFA with $\leq k$ states accepting $L(M)$?

However, there are two simple theorems that can often be used to give lower bounds on $nsc(L)$.

Theorem 3.11.3. *Let L be a nonempty regular language, and let n be the length of a shortest string in L. Then $nsc(L) \geq n + 1$.*

Proof. Let $M = (Q, \Sigma, \delta, q_0, F)$ be an NFA accepting L, and let x be a shortest string in L with $|x| = n$. Suppose M has $\leq n$ states. Now consider the states encountered on an accepting computation for x. Since $|x| = n$, some state must be encountered at least twice. We can now cut out this loop to find a shorter string accepted by M, a contradiction. ∎

Theorem 3.11.4. *Let $L \subseteq \Sigma^*$ be a regular language, and let $M = (Q, \Sigma, \delta, q_0, F)$ be an NFA accepting L.*

Suppose there exists a set of pairs of words $P = \{(x_i, w_i) : 1 \leq i \leq n\}$ such that

(a) For all i with $1 \leq i \leq n$, we have $x_i w_i \in L$.
(b) For all i, j with $1 \leq i, j \leq n$, and $i \neq j$, at least one of $x_j w_i \notin L$ and $x_i w_j \notin L$ holds.

Then $nsc(L) \geq n$.

Proof. We can define a function $f : \{1, 2 \ldots, n\} \to Q$ as follows: for each i, since $x_i w_i \in L$, there must be a state $q \in \delta(q_0, x_i)$ such that $\delta(q, w_i) \cap F \neq \emptyset$. Define $f(i) = q$. Note that $\delta(f(i), w_i) \cap F \neq \emptyset$.

Now we claim that this map is an injection; that is, if $i \neq j$, then $f(i) \neq f(j)$. For suppose $i \neq j$ but $f(i) = f(j)$. Then $x_i w_j \in L$ since $f(j) = f(i) \in \delta(q_0, x_i)$. Similarly, $x_j w_i \in L$ since $f(i) = f(j) \in \delta(q_0, x_j)$. This contradiction proves that f is an injection.

Since the domain of f has cardinality n and f is an injection, Q has cardinality $\geq n$ and $\text{nsc}(L) \geq n$.   ∎

Example 3.11.5. Let $k \geq 1$ be an integer and consider the language $L_k = \{0^i 1^i 2^i : 0 \leq i < k\}$. Take the set of pairs P to be the set

$$P = \{(0^i 1^j, 1^{i-j} 2^i) : 0 \leq j \leq i < k\}.$$

Let $(x, w) = (0^i 1^j, 1^{i-j} 2^i)$ and $(x', w') = (0^{i'} 1^{j'}, 1^{i'-j'} 2^{i'})$ be two such distinct pairs. Then $xw, x'w' \in L$ but $xw' = 0^i 1^{i'+j-j'} 2^{i'}$ cannot be in L unless $i = i'$ and $j = j'$. Hence there are at least $|P| = k(k+1)/2$ states in any NFA that accepts L_k.

3.12 Partial orders and regular languages

A *partial order* is a binary relation R on a set S that behaves like the usual relation $\leq$ on real numbers. More precisely, it must be

 (i) *reflexive*, that is, $a R a$ for all $a \in S$;
 (ii) *antisymmetric*, that is, $a R b$ and $b R a \Rightarrow a = b$;
(iii) *transitive*, that is, $a R b$ and $b R c \Rightarrow a R c$.

Given any two real numbers x and y, they are *comparable* in the sense that either $x \leq y$ or $y \leq x$. However, this is not the case for a general partial order. If xRy or yRx, we say x and y are comparable; otherwise we say they are incomparable.

There are two natural partial orders associated with strings. The first is the *subword ordering*: we write $x S y$ if x is a subword of y, that is, if there exist strings w, z such that $y = wxz$. The second is the *subsequence ordering*: we write $x \mid y$ if x is a *subsequence* of y, that is, if we can obtain x from y by striking out 0 or more symbols from y. More precisely, $x \mid y$ if there exist an integer $n \geq 0$ and strings $x_i, y_j \in \Sigma^*$, $1 \leq i \leq n$, $1 \leq j \leq n+1$ such that $x = x_1 x_2 \cdots x_n$ and $y = y_1 x_1 y_2 x_2 \cdots y_n x_n y_{n+1}$. You should now verify that both of these relations are partial orders.

For the subword ordering it is possible to find an infinite set of pairwise incomparable strings. For example, $\{ab^n a : n \geq 1\}$ forms such a set. However, the following theorem shows the somewhat surprising fact that the corresponding situation cannot occur for the subsequence ordering.

Theorem 3.12.1. *Let Σ be a finite alphabet. Every set of strings over Σ that are pairwise incomparable for the subsequence ordering is finite.*

Proof. Assume there exists an infinite set of pairwise incomparable strings. Then there is certainly an infinite *division-free sequence* of strings $(f_i)_{i \geq 1}$, that is, a sequence of strings $f_1, f_2, \ldots$ such that $i < j \Rightarrow f_i \nmid f_j$.

Now iteratively choose a minimal such sequence, as follows:

- let f_1 be a shortest word beginning an infinite division-free sequence;
- let f_2 be a shortest word such that f_1, f_2 begins an infinite division-free sequence;
- let f_3 be a shortest word such that f_1, f_2, f_3 begins an infinite division-free sequence; and so on.

By the pigeonhole principle, there exists an infinite subsequence of the f_i, say $f_{i_1}, f_{i_2}, f_{i_3}, \ldots$, such that each of the strings in this subsequence starts with the same letter, say a. Define x_j for $j \geq 1$ by $f_{i_j} = a x_j$. Then we claim that

$$f_1, f_2, f_3, \ldots, f_{i_1 - 1}, x_1, x_2, x_3, \ldots$$

is an infinite division-free sequence that precedes $(f_i)_{i \geq 1}$, contradicting the supposed minimality of $(f_i)_{i \geq 1}$.

To see that the constructed sequence is indeed division-free, note that $f_i \nmid f_j$ for $1 \leq i < j < i_1$ by assumption. Next, if $f_i \mid x_j$ for some i with $1 \leq i < i_1$ and $j \geq 1$, then $f_i \mid a x_j = f_{i_j}$, a contradiction. Finally, if $x_j \mid x_k$, then $a x_j \mid a x_k$, and hence $f_{i_j} \mid f_{i_k}$, a contradiction. ∎

Notice that although we have proved that there are no infinite pairwise incomparable sets for the subsequence ordering, there are arbitrarily large such sets. For example, the language $\{0, 1\}^n$ consists of 2^n strings that are pairwise incomparable.

We now introduce two operations on languages, the *subsequence* and *supersequence* operations. Let $L \subseteq \Sigma^*$. We define

$$\sup(L) = \{x \in \Sigma^* \ : \ \text{there exists } y \in L \text{ such that } y \mid x\};$$

$$\mathrm{sub}(L) = \{x \in \Sigma^* \ : \ \text{there exists } y \in L \text{ such that } x \mid y\}.$$

Our goal is to prove that if L is a language, then $\mathrm{sub}(L)$ and $\sup(L)$ is regular. First, though, we need some lemmas.

Lemma 3.12.2. *Let $L \subseteq \Sigma^*$. Then*

(a) $L \subseteq \sup(L)$;
(b) $L \subseteq \mathrm{sub}(L)$;
(c) $\mathrm{sub}(L) = \mathrm{sub}(\mathrm{sub}(L))$.

Proof. Left to the reader. ∎

We now introduce some terminology. Let R be a partial order on a set S. Then we say $x \in S$ is *minimal* if $yRx \Rightarrow y = x$ for $y \in S$. Let $D(y)$ be the set $\{x \in S : xRy\}$.

Lemma 3.12.3. *Let R be a partial order on a set S.*

(a) If x, y are distinct minimal elements, then x, y are incomparable.
(b) Suppose the set $D(y)$ is finite. Then there exists a minimal y' such that $y'Ry$.

Proof.   (a) Suppose yRx . Then $x = y$ since x is minimal. But x, y were assumed distinct, a contradiction. A similar argument applies if xRy.

(b) If $D(y) = \{y\}$, then we may take $y' = y$. Otherwise let z be an element in $D(y) - \{y\}$. Then $D(z) \subset D(y)$, and $D(z) \neq D(y)$. If $D(z) = \{z\}$, we may take $y' = z$. Continue in this fashion. Since $D(y)$ is finite, we eventually terminate and the last element chosen can be taken as y'.   ■

Lemma 3.12.4. *Let $L \subseteq \Sigma^*$. Then*

(a) there exists a finite subset $M \subseteq L$ such that $\mathrm{sup}(L) = \mathrm{sup}(M)$.
(b) there exists a finite subset $G \subseteq \Sigma^*$ such that $\mathrm{sub}(L) = \Sigma^* - \mathrm{sup}(G)$.

Proof.

(a): Let M be the set of minimal elements of L. By Lemma 3.12.3 the elements of M are pairwise incomparable. By Theorem 3.12.1, M is finite. It remains to see that $\mathrm{sup}(L) = \mathrm{sup}(M)$.

Proof that $\mathrm{sup}(M) \subseteq \mathrm{sup}(L)$: suppose $x \in \mathrm{sup}(M)$. Then there exists $y \in M \subseteq L$ such that $y \mid x$. Thus, $x \in \mathrm{sup}(L)$.

Proof that $\mathrm{sup}(L) \subseteq \mathrm{sup}(M)$: suppose $x \in \mathrm{sup}(L)$. Then there exists $y \in L$ such that $y \mid x$. By Lemma 3.12.3 (b), there exists $y' \in M$ such that $y' \mid y$. Then $y' \mid y \mid x$, and so $x \in \mathrm{sup}(M)$.

(b) Let $T = \Sigma^* - \mathrm{sub}(L)$. I claim that $T = \mathrm{sup}(T)$. The inclusion $T \subseteq \mathrm{sup}(T)$ follows from Lemma 3.12.2(a). Suppose $\mathrm{sup}(T) \not\subseteq T$; then there exists an $x \in \mathrm{sup}(T)$ with $x \notin T$. Since $T = \Sigma^* - \mathrm{sub}(L)$, this means $x \in \mathrm{sub}(L)$. Since $x \in \mathrm{sup}(T)$, there exists $y \in T$ such that $y \mid x$. Hence, by Lemma 3.12.2(c), we have $y \in \mathrm{sub}(L)$. But then $y \notin T$, a contradiction.

Finally, by part (a), there exists a finite subset G such that $\mathrm{sup}(G) = \mathrm{sup}(T)$. Then $\mathrm{sup}(G) = \mathrm{sup}(T) = T = \Sigma^* - \mathrm{sub}(L)$, and so $\mathrm{sub}(L) = \Sigma^* - \mathrm{sup}(G)$.   ■

We are now ready to prove the main result of this section.

Theorem 3.12.5. *Let L be a language (not necessarily regular). Then both* sub(L) *and* sup(L) *are regular.*

Proof. Clearly, sup(L) is regular if $L = \{w\}$ for some single word w. This is because if $w = a_1 a_2 \cdots a_k$, then

$$\text{sup}(\{w\}) = \Sigma^* a_1 \Sigma^* a_2 \Sigma^* \cdots \Sigma^* a_k \Sigma^*.$$

Similarly, for any finite language $F \subseteq \Sigma^*$, sup(F) is regular because

$$\text{sup}(F) = \bigcup_{w \in F} \text{sup}(\{w\}).$$

Now let $L \subseteq \Sigma^*$, and let M and G be defined as in the proof of Lemma 3.12.4. Then sup(L) = sup(M), and so sup(L) is regular, since M is finite. Also, sub(L) = $\Sigma^* - $ sup(G), and so sub(L) is regular since G is finite. ∎

Example 3.12.6. Consider the language

$$P_3 = \{2, 10, 12, 21, 102, 111, 122, 201, 212, 1002, \ldots\},$$

which represents the primes in base 3. I claim that the minimal elements of P_3 are $\{2, 10, 111\}$. Clearly, each of these are in P_3 and no proper subsequence is in P_3. Now let $x \in P_3$. If $2 \nmid x$, then $x \in \{0, 1\}^*$. If further $10 \nmid x$, then $x \in 0^* 1^*$. Since x represents a number, x cannot have leading zeros. It follows that $x \in 1^*$. But the numbers represented by the strings 1 and 11 are not primes. However, 111 represents 13, which is prime.

It now follows that

$$\text{sup}(P_3) = \Sigma^* 2 \Sigma^* \cup \Sigma^* 1 \Sigma^* 0 \Sigma^* \cup \Sigma^* 1 \Sigma^* 1 \Sigma^* 1 \Sigma^*,$$

where $\Sigma = \{0, 1, 2\}$.

On the other hand, sub(P_3) = Σ^*. This follows from Dirichlet's theorem on primes in arithmetic progressions, which states that every arithmetic progression of the form $(a + nb)_{n \geq 0}$, $\gcd(a, b) = 1$, contains infinitely many primes.

For base 10, you can use the card shown in Figure 3.21. Photocopy it on thick cardboard stock and take it to a bar sometime.

3.13 Exercises

1. (a) Prove or disprove that $\overline{L_1}/L_2 = \overline{(L_1/L_2)}$ for all languages L_1, L_2.
   (b) Prove or disprove that $\overline{L}/\{x\} = \overline{(L/\{x\})}$ for all languages L and all finite strings x.

THE PRIME GAME

Ask a friend to write down a prime number.
Bet them that you can always strike out 0 or
more digits to get a prime on this card.

2, 3, 5, 7, 11, 19, 41, 61, 89, 409, 449, 499, 881, 991,
6469, 6949, 9001, 9049, 9649, 9949, 60649,
666649, 946669, 60000049, 66000049, 66600049

©2007—shallit@cs.uwaterloo.ca

Figure 3.21: The prime game

2. Which of the following is true for all languages L_1, L_2?
   (a) $(L_1/L_2)L_2 \subseteq L_1$,
   (b) $L_1 \subseteq (L_1/L_2)L_2$.

3. Suppose $L \subseteq \Sigma^*$ is regular. Prove that the language

$$2L := \{a_1a_1a_2a_2 \cdots a_ka_k \ : \ \text{each } a_i \in \Sigma \text{ and } a_1a_2 \cdots a_k \in L\}$$

   is regular.

4. Generalizing the previous exercise, suppose $x \in \Sigma_k^* = \{0, 1, \ldots, k-1\}$ and $y \in \Delta^*$ for some alphabet Δ. If $|x| = |y|$, and $x = a_1 \cdots a_n$, $y = b_1 \cdots b_n$, we define rep(x, y) to be the string $b_1^{a_1} b_2^{a_2} \cdots b_n^{a_n}$. If $|x| \neq |y|$, we define rep(x, y) = $\emptyset$. Thus, for example, rep(234, abc) = aabbbccccc. Extend this definition to languages, as follows: if $L_1 \subseteq \Sigma_k^*$ and $L_2 \subseteq \Delta^*$, then rep(L_1, L_2) = $\bigcup_{x \in L_1, y \in L_2}$ rep(x, y). Thus, for example, rep($1^*, L$) = L for all languages L and rep($2^*, L$) is just the language $2L$ of the previous exercise. Show that if L_1 and L_2 are both regular, then so is rep(L_1, L_2).

5. Let $L_1 \subseteq L_2$ be regular languages with $L_2 - L_1$ infinite. Show that there exists a regular language L such that $L_1 \subseteq L \subseteq L_2$ and $L_2 - L$ and $L - L_1$ are both infinite.

6. Let L be a language and h a morphism. Show that
   (a) $L \subseteq h^{-1}(h(L))$;
   (b) $h(h^{-1}(L)) \subseteq L$.
   Also give examples where $L \neq h^{-1}(h(L))$ and $h(h^{-1}(L)) \neq L$.

7. Recall the definition of Pref(L) from Example 3.2.5. Give another proof of the fact that if L is regular, so is Pref(L), by directly modifying the DFA for L.

*8. Let $L \subseteq \Sigma^*$ be a language. For an integer $n \geq 0$, define

$$L^{1/n} = \{x \in \Sigma^* : x^n \in L\}.$$

Note that

$$\mathrm{root}(L) := \bigcup_{i \geq 1} L^{1/i}.$$

   (a) Show that if L is regular, so is $L^{1/n}$ for each $n \geq 1$.
   (b) Show that if L is accepted by a DFA with n states, then $\mathrm{root}(L) = \bigcup_{1 \leq i \leq n} L^{1/i}$.

**9. Show that if L is a regular language, then so is

$$\mathrm{ROOT}(L) := \{w : w^{|w|} \in L\}.$$

10. Define the perfect shuffle of languages as follows:

$$L_1 \, \mathrm{III} \, L_2 = \{x \, \mathrm{III} \, y : x \in L_1, y \in L_2, \text{ and } |x| = |y|\}.$$

Show how to modify Example 3.3.8 to give a formal definition of the perfect shuffle in terms of morphisms, inverse morphisms, and intersection.

11. If $\mathrm{shuff}(L, \{0\})$ is regular, need L be regular?

12. If L is regular, then must

$$\mathrm{pow}(L) := \{u^k : u \in L, k \geq 0\}$$

also be regular?

13. Define the operation perm on strings as follows: $\mathrm{perm}(x)$ is the set of all permutations of the letters of x. For example,

$$\mathrm{perm}(0121) = \{0112, 0121, 0211, 1012, 1021, 1102, 1120, 1201,$$
$$1210, 2011, 2101, 2110\}.$$

Extend perm to languages as follows: $\mathrm{perm}(L) = \bigcup_{x \in L} \mathrm{perm}(x)$.
If L is regular, need $\mathrm{perm}(L)$ be regular?

14. Show that any DFA accepting the language

$$L_n := \{x \in \{0, 1\}^* : \text{ the } n\text{th symbol from the right is } 1\},$$

introduced in Section 1.4, must have at least 2^n states.

*15. Is the class of regular languages closed under inverse substitution? That is, let L be a regular language and s be a substitution that maps each letter a to a regular language L_a. Define

$$s^{-1}(L) = \{x : s(x) \subseteq L\}.$$

Must $s^{-1}(L)$ be regular?

16. Consider replacing the definition for inverse substitution given in the previous exercise with a new definition:

$$s^{[-1]}(L) := \{x \ : \ s(x) \cap L \neq \emptyset\}.$$

Suppose s maps letters to regular languages, and L is regular. Must $s^{[-1]}(L)$ be regular?

17. Using the proof of Theorem 3.10.2 as a guide, prove the correctness of algorithm MINIMIZE.

18. Theorem 3.10.1 says that if M_1, M_2 are minimal DFAs accepting a regular language L, then M_1 and M_2 are isomorphic. (*Isomorphic* means that the machines are identical, up to renaming the states.) Show, by means of an example, that this result is not true if "DFA" is replaced by "NFA."

19. Let L be a regular language, and let M be the minimal DFA accepting L. Suppose M has n final states. Show that *any* DFA accepting L must have at least n final states.

20. Let $\Sigma = \{0, 1\}$. Give an example of a language $L \subseteq \Sigma^*$ for which the Myhill–Nerode equivalence relation R_L has the property that every string in Σ^* is an equivalence class by itself.

21. Let L be a regular language, and let $M = (Q, \Sigma, \delta, q_0, F)$ be its minimal DFA. Let $M' = (Q', \Sigma, \delta', q_0', -)$ be the transformation automaton of M, as described in Section 3.7, but with all states not reachable from q_0' discarded. Let $R_{M'}$ be the equivalence relation based on M', where x and y are equivalent iff $\delta'(q_0', x) = \delta'(q_0', y)$.

    Now consider the equivalence relation $x \equiv y$, where "$x \equiv y$" means "for all $u, v \in \Sigma^*$, $uxv \in L$ iff $uyv \in L$." Show that the equivalence relation $\equiv$ is the same as $R_{M'}$.

*22. The point of this exercise is to show that 2DFAs can be exponentially more concise than DFAs in accepting certain languages.

    Let n be an integer ≥ 1, and let $F_n \subseteq \{0, 1, 2, 3, 4\}^*$ be defined as follows:

$$F_n = \{3 \ 0^{i_1} \ 1 \ 0^{i_2} \ 1 \cdots 1 \ 0^{i_n} \ 2^k \ 0^{i_k} \ 4 \ : \ 1 \leq k, j, i_j \leq n\}.$$

    For example,

$$F_2 = \{3010204, 30102204, 300102004, 300102204,$$
$$30100204, 3010022004, 3001002004, 30010022004\}.$$

    (a) Show that F_n can be accepted by a 2DFA using $O(n)$ states.
    (b) Using the Myhill–Nerode theorem, show that the smallest DFA accepting F_n has at least n^n states.

**23. For a word w, define $SD(w)$, the *subword-doubling* map, as follows:

$$SD(w) = \{u \in \Sigma^* \; : \; \text{there exist } x, y, z \in \Sigma^* \text{ such that } u = xyyz$$
$$\text{and } w = xyz\}.$$

In other words, $SD(w)$ is the language of all strings obtainable from w by doubling some subword.

For a language L, define

$$SD(L) = \bigcup_{w \in L} SD(w).$$

Define $SD^0(w) = \{w\}$ and $SD^i(w) = SD(SD^{i-1}(w))$ for $i \geq 1$.

Finally, for a word w, define $SDC(w)$, the *subword-doubling closure* of w, as follows:

$$SDC(w) = \bigcup_{i \geq 0} SD^i(w).$$

Prove that $SDC(012)$ is not regular.

24. Let L_1, L_2 be languages with $L_1 \subseteq \Sigma^*$, $L_2 \subseteq \Delta^*$, and let $h : \Sigma^* \to \Delta^*$ be a morphism. Prove or disprove that

$$h(L_1) - L_2 \subseteq h(L_1 - h^{-1}(L_2)).$$

Note: $A - B$ means $\{x \in A \; : \; x \notin B\}$.

25. The *star height* of a regular expression is the maximum number of nested occurrences of the $*$ operator. The star height of a regular language L is the minimum of the star heights of all regular expressions representing L.

Show that the star height of any regular language over a one-letter alphabet is ≤ 1.

26. Consider an alternate definition of quotient, defined as follows for $L_1, L_2 \subseteq \Sigma^*$:

$$L_1 \div L_2 = \{x \in \Sigma^* \; : \; xy \in L_1 \text{ for all } y \in L_2\}.$$

If R is regular and L is any language, must $R \div L$ be regular?

27. Characterize all regular languages $L \subseteq \Sigma^*$ with the following property: there exists a constant c, depending on L, such that for all $n \geq 0$, we have $|L \cap \Sigma^n| \leq c$.

28. Fix an alphabet Σ. Give good upper and lower bounds on the number of distinct languages that can be accepted by some DFA with n states.

29. Let L_1, L_2 be languages. Consider the equation $X = L_1 X + L_2$. Assuming L_1 does not contain the empty string, find a solution X of this equation and prove it is unique. What if L_1 contains ϵ?

30. Let $\Sigma_k = \{0, 1, \ldots, k - 1\}$. Let $L \subseteq \Sigma_k^*$, and consider the set $\mathcal{L}(L)$ of *lexicographically largest strings* of each length in L. Thus, for example, in $\mathcal{L}(\{0, 1\}^*) = 1^*$ and $\mathcal{L}(\epsilon + 1(0 + 01)^*) = (10)^*(\epsilon+1)$.

    Show that if L is regular, so is $\mathcal{L}(L)$.

31. (Continuation.) Instead of taking the lexicographically largest strings of each length, consider taking the lexicographically median string of each length. (That is, if there are r strings of length n, take string number $\lceil r/2 \rceil$.) Show that if the original language is regular, the resulting language need not be regular.

32. In analogy with Example 3.12, compute the minimal elements for the language

$$\{2, 3, 5, 6, 7, 8, 10, 11, 12, 13, 14, 15, \ldots\}$$

of those strings that do not represent squares in base 10.

33. (a) A finite string $x = a_1 a_2 a_3 \cdots a_n \in \Sigma^*$ is said to possess the *Friedman property* if for all i, j with $1 \le i < j \le n/2$, we have $a_i \cdots a_{2i} \nmid a_j \cdots a_{2j}$. (Recall that $w \mid x$ means w is a subsequence of x.) Prove that for each Σ, there is a longest finite string with the Friedman property.

    (b) By analogy with (a), an infinite string $\mathbf{x} = a_1 a_2 a_3 \cdots \in \Sigma^\omega$ is said to possess the Friedman property if for all i, j with $1 \le i < j$, we have $a_i \cdots a_{2i} \nmid a_j \cdots a_{2j}$. Prove that no infinite string possesses the Friedman property.

*34. Recall the operation $\mathrm{cyc}(L)$ from Section 3.4. Give an example of a language L such that $\mathrm{cyc}(L)$ is regular, but L is not.

*35. Let n be a positive integer and let $L_n = (0 + (0\,1^*)^{n-1} 0)^*$. Show that L_n can be accepted by an NFA with n states, but no DFA with less than 2^n states accepts L_n.

36. Show that if R and L are regular languages given by DFAs, then there is an algorithm to construct a DFA for R/L.

37. Consider the language $A_k = \{w \in \{0, 1\}^k : w = w^R\}$. Show that any NFA accepting A_k has at least $2^{\lfloor k/2 \rfloor + 1} + 2^{\lfloor (k+1)/2 \rfloor} - 2$ states. Also show that this bound is tight.

38. Give a different proof of Theorem 3.4.1, based on the suggestion following the proof.

39. Find the equivalence classes for the Myhill–Nerode equivalence relation for

(a) $L = \{w \in \{0, 1\}^* : |w|_0 = |w|_1\}$.

(b) $L = \{a^n b^n c^n : n \geq 1\}$.

**40. Let Σ be a finite alphabet with at least two letters. A language $L \subseteq \Sigma^*$ is said to be *sparse* if

$$\lim_{n \to \infty} \frac{|L \cap \Sigma^n|}{|\Sigma^n|} = 0.$$

Prove or disprove that there exists a sparse language L such that $LL = \Sigma^*$.

41. Describe a family of DFAs M_n for which Brzozowski's algorithm takes exponential time.

42. Show that for any word $w \in \Sigma^+$, there exists a regular expression r_w for the language of all prefixes of w, such that $|r_w| \leq 4|w|$.

43. Show that there exists a constant c such that for any word $w \in \Sigma^+$, there exists a regular expression for $\Sigma^* - \{w\}$ of length $\leq c|w|$.

*44. Construct a family of regular expressions r_n such that

(a) $L(r_n) \subseteq 0^*$.

(b) There exists a constant c such that $|r_n| = O(n^c)$.

(c) There exists a constant d such that the shortest regular expression for $\overline{L(r_n)}$ is of length $> 2^{dn}$.

45. For each $k \geq 0$, show how to construct a regular language L_k over a finite alphabet Σ_k such that L_k has exactly n^k words of length n, for all $n \geq 0$. (Note that $0^0 = 1$.)

**46. Describe a family of NFAs $(M_n)_{n \geq 1}$ over a finite alphabet Σ satisfying the following three conditions:

(a) M_n has $O(n)$ states.

(b) $L(M_n) \neq \Sigma^*$.

(c) the shortest string not accepted by M_n is of length $\geq 2^n$.

47. Give a proof of Theorem 1.4.2, (b) $\Rightarrow$ (a), along the following lines. Let $M = (Q, \Sigma, \delta, q_1, F)$ be a DFA, where $Q = \{q_1, q_2, \ldots, q_n\}$. Define $R_{i,j,k}$ to be the language of all strings that take us from state i to state j without passing through a state numbered higher than k. Now give a recursion formula that allows you to compute $R_{i,j,k}$.

48. (Continuation.) Using the previous exercise, prove that if M is a DFA with $n = |Q|$ and $k = |\Sigma|$, then $L(M)$ is specified by a regular expression of length $O(kn4^n)$.

*49. Show that if M_1 is a DFA with $m \geq 1$ states and M_2 is a DFA with $n \geq 2$ states, then there is a DFA with $\leq m2^n - 2^{n-1}$ states accepting $L(M_1)L(M_2)$. Furthermore, show that this bound is tight.

50. We can consider the input–output behavior of a finite-state transducer on an *infinitely long* input. Now think about real numbers expressed in base-3 notation. Every real number between 0 and 1 has a base-3 expansion of the form

$$.a_1 a_2 a_3 \cdots ,$$

where $a_i \in \{0, 1, 2\}$; this expansion represents the number $\sum_{i \geq 1} a_i 3^{-i}$. (You should think of the period as representing a "ternary point," not a decimal point.) Provided that the expansion does not end in infinitely many 2s, this expansion is unique.

The *Cantor set* C is defined to be the set of all real numbers between 0 and 1 whose base-3 expansion contains only 0s and 2s. Prove that every real number x between 0 and 1 can be written as the sum of two numbers y and z chosen from C by giving a finite state transducer that, on input $a_1 a_2 a_3 \cdots$, outputs the string $[b_1, c_1][b_2, c_2][b_3, c_3] \cdots$, where $x = .a_1 a_2 a_3 \cdots$, $y = .b_1 b_2 b_3 \cdots$, $z = .c_1 c_2 c_3 \cdots$, $y, z \in C$, and $x = y + z$.

51. (J. Buss) For each integer $n \geq 1$, compute the deterministic state complexity of the language $L_n = \{x \in \{0, 1\}^* : [x]_2 \equiv 0 \pmod{n}\}$, where by $[x]_2$ we mean the integer represented in base 2 by the string x.

52. Give a short regular expression for the language $L(M_n)$ in Theorem 3.9.6. By *short* we mean having $O(n)$ symbols.

53. In an extended regular expression, intersection and complement may be used. Give a short extended regular expression for the language $L(w, x) = \{y : \text{every occurrence of } w \text{ in } y \text{ is followed by } x\}$.

54. Let $\Sigma = \{1, 2, \ldots, n\}$, and define

$$L_n = \{w \in \Sigma^* : |w|_i = 1 \text{ for all } i\}.$$

For example, $L_3 = \{123, 132, 213, 231, 312, 321\}$.

(a) Prove that no regular expression of length $< 2^{n-1}$ can specify L_n.

(b) Prove that there exists a regular expression of length $O(n^2)$ specifying $\overline{L_n}$.

*55. Let $\Sigma = \{1, 2, \ldots, n\}$. Consider the language L_n consisting of all strings over Σ such that there exists a way to partition the symbols of the string into two multisets whose sum is equal. For example, $1122 \in L_2$, but $11221 \notin L_2$. Show that each L_n is regular for $n \geq 1$.

56. Let $M = (Q, \Sigma, \delta, q_0, F)$ be a DFA. Show that the language of strings x that cause M to visit every state of Q while processing x is a regular language.

57. An NFA $M = (Q, \Sigma, \delta, q_0, F)$ is *ambiguous* if there exists at least one string w that M accepts via at least two distinct computation paths.

(a) Show that an n-state NFA M is ambiguous if and only if it is ambiguous on an input of length $<n^2 + n$.

(b) Is this bound tight?

58. Let M be a DFA with n states, and suppose $L(M)$ contains at least one palindrome. Show that $L(M)$ contains a palindrome of length $<2n^2$.

59. Let E be a regular expression such that $\epsilon \notin L(E)$. Show that there exists a regular expression using only the operators union, concatenation, and positive closure that specifies $L(E)$.

60. Show that the Myhill–Nerode equivalence classes for a language L are the same as those for $\overline{L}$.

61. Define the map $r : \Sigma^* \to \Sigma^*$ as follows: if $w = a_1 a_2 \cdots a_n$ with each $a_i \in \Sigma$, then $r(w) = a_1^n a_2^n \cdots a_n^n$. For example, $r(\text{abc}) = \text{aaabbbccc}$. Note that r is *not* a morphism. Now extend r in the obvious way to languages as follows: $r(L) = \bigcup_{x \in L} r(x)$.

(a) Let $L = (a + ba)^*(\epsilon + b)$, the language of words not containing bb as a subword. What is $r^{-1}(L)$?

(b) Show by means of an example that if L is regular then $r(L)$ need not be regular.

(c) Define $r^{-1}(L) = \{x : r(x) \in L\}$. Prove that if L is regular then so is $r^{-1}(L)$.

*62. Let $M = (Q, \Sigma, \delta, q_0, F)$ be an NFA, and let $a \in \Sigma$. Let $t \geq 0, c \geq 1$ be the smallest integers such that $\delta(q_0, a^t) = \delta(q_0, a^{t+c})$. Show that $t \leq (n-1)^2 + 1$ and c divides $\text{lcm}(1, 2, \ldots, n)$.

63. Call a language L *commutative* if for all $x, y \in L$, we have $xy = yx$. Show that L is commutative if and only if there exists a word w such that $L \subseteq w^*$.

64. In this exercise you will develop an efficient algorithm to determine if a regular language specified by an NFA M is palindromic, that is, if $x = x^R$ for all $x \in L(M)$. Your algorithm should run in time bounded by a polynomial in the number of states of M.

(a) First, prove the following lemma: Let $x, u, v, w, y, x', u', v', w', y'$ be words. If

(i) $y'x' = xy$

(ii) $y'u'x' = xuy$

(iii) $y'v'x' = xvy$

(iv) $y'w'x' = xwy$

(v) $y'v'u'x' = xuvy$

(vi) $y'w'v'x' = xvwy$

all hold, then $y'w'v'u'x' = xuvwy$.

(b) Using the previous lemma, show that $L(M)$ is palindromic if and only if $\{x \in L(M) : |x| < 3n\}$ is palindromic.

(c) Show that there exists an NFA M' with $O(r)$ states that accepts only nonpalindromes and accepts all the nonpalindromes of length $<r$.

(d) Complete the proof of the algorithm by forming the cross-product of M with M' to compute $L(M) \cap L(M')$. Finally, show that one can efficiently determine if the resulting NFA accepts any word.

65. Show that for all $n \geq 2$, there exists an NFA with n states such that the shortest nonpalindrome accepted is of length $3n - 1$.

66. Show that if L is regular, then $L' = \{u \in \Sigma^+ : \text{there exists } v \in \Sigma^* \text{ such that } uvu \in L\}$ is regular.

67. A word $w \in \Sigma^*$ is said to be *bordered* if it can be written in the form uvu with $u \in \Sigma^+$, $v \in \Sigma^*$. Show that the following problem is solvable in polynomial time: given an NFA M, does M accept a bordered word?

68. For a word $w \in \Sigma^*$, we define palc(w) to be the *palindromic closure* of w, that is, the (unique) shortest palindrome x such that w is a prefix of x. Define palc$(L) = \bigcap_{w \in L} \{\text{palc}(w)\}$.

(a) Show that palc$(w) = wt^{-1}w^R$, where t is the longest palindromic suffix of w.

(b) If L is regular, need palc(L) be regular?

(c) If L is regular, need palc$^{-1}(L) = \{x \in \Sigma^* : \text{palc}(x) \in L\}$ be regular?

69. Let $x_1, x_2, \ldots, x_k \in \Sigma^*$. Show that $\Sigma^* - x_1^* x_2^* \cdots x_k^*$ is finite if and only if $|\Sigma| = 1$ and $\gcd(|x_1|, |x_2|, \ldots, |x_k|) = 1$.

70. Let Σ, Δ be alphabets. We say a word *pattern* $p \in \Sigma^*$ matches a word $z \in \Delta^*$ if there exists a nonerasing morphism h such that $h(p) = z$. (By nonerasing, we mean that $h(a) \neq \epsilon$ for all $a \in \Sigma$.) For example, xx is a pattern for the English word murmur. Define Pat(L) to be the language of all patterns that match words in L.

(a) Give an example of a nonregular language L such that Pat$(L) = L$.

(b) Give an example of a nonregular language L such that Pat(L) is regular.

(c) Prove that if $L \subseteq \Delta^*$ is regular, then the language
Pat$(L) = \{y \in \Sigma^* : \text{there exists } z \in L \text{ such that } y \text{ is a pattern for } z\}$
is regular.

71. Let $h : \Sigma^* \to \Sigma^*$ be a morphism, and let $L \subset \Sigma^*$ be a language. Define

$$h^{-*}(L) = \bigcup_{i \geq 0} h^{-i}(L),$$

where by $h^{-i}(L)$, we mean $\overbrace{h^{-1}(h^{-1}(\cdots h^{-1}(L)))}^{i \text{ times}}$. Show that if L is regular, so is $h^{-*}(L)$.

72. Let L be a language, and define $q(L) = \{z \in L : xy \neq z \text{ for all } x, y \in L\}$. Show that if L is regular, so is $q(L)$.

73. Let us say that a language L' is an nth-order approximation to L if $L \cap \Sigma^{\le n} = L' \cap \Sigma^{\le n}$.

(a) Define $A_L(n)$, the *automaticity function* of L, to be the smallest number of states in any DFA M such that $L(M)$ is an nth-order approximation to L. Find good upper and lower bounds for $A_L(n)$.

(b) Prove that if L is not regular, then $A_L(n) \ge (n+3)/2$ infinitely often.

3.14 Projects

1. Find out more about applications of automata theory to game theory and economics ("bounded rationality"). You could start with Axelrod [1984], Rubinstein [1986], and Linster [1992].

2. Find out more about the connections between finite automata and number theory. You can start with the book of Allouche and Shallit [2003].

3. Look into how regular languages can be efficiently learned. The paper of Angluin [1987] is a good place to start. Also see Ibarra and Jiang [1991].

4. Look into the relationship between cellular automata and regular languages. Start with Wolfram [1984]. The book of Wolfram [2002] also has some useful information, but at a much less technical level.

5. Look into generalizations of Theorem 3.4.1 and Theorem 3.8.8, the class of *regularity-preserving transformations*. Start with the papers of Stearns and Hartmanis [1963], Seiferas and McNaughton [1976], and Kozen [1996].

6. Look into the star-height problem, which asks for the minimum number of nested stars needed in a regular expression for a given language. Start with the papers of Eggan [1963] and Hashiguchi [1982, 1988].

3.15 Research problems

1. A DFA is called *synchronizing* if there exists a finite word w and a state q such that reading w starting in any state leads to q. Cerny's conjecture asks if the length of the shortest synchronizing word for an automaton with n states is $\le (n-1)^2$. The best starting point is the Web page of Pin, http://www.liafa.jussieu.fr/~jep/Problemes/Cerny.html.

2. Suppose you are given two distinct words u, v with $|u|, |v| \le n$. What is the size of the smallest DFA that accepts u but rejects v, or vice versa? If u and v are of different lengths then a simple argument gives a $O(\log n)$ upper bound. How about if u and v are of the same length? Robson [1989] showed that in this case a machine of size $O(n^{2/5}(\log n)^{3/5})$ exists. Can this bound be improved?

3.16 Notes on Chapter 3

A good survey on regular languages is Yu [1997].

3.1 For Moore machines, see Moore [1956]. For Mealy machines, see Mealy [1955].

3.2 Quotients were introduced by Ginsburg and Spanier [1963]. In the literature, L_1/L_2 is sometimes denoted $L_1 L_2^{-1}$ and is called the *right quotient*. There is a corresponding notion of *left quotient*, written $L_1^{-1} L_2$.

3.3 For more on morphisms, see Harju and Karhumäki [1997].

3.4 For generalizations of Theorem 3.4.1, see Seiferas and McNaughton [1976].

3.5 Transducers are covered extensively in the book of Berstel [1979].

The particular kind of transducer we have studied in this section is the most powerful finite-state version. Other, weaker, types of transducers include the *generalized sequential machine* or GSM, the *sequential transducer* (in left and right versions), and the *subsequential transducer*.

3.6 The material in this section is from Shepherdson [1959]. In the literature, 2DFAs are often equipped with distinguished symbols that serve as endmarkers for the input.

3.7 The transformation automaton can be found, in somewhat disguised form, in McNaughton and Papert [1968]. Also see Lawson [2004, chapters 8 and 9].

3.8 For more about the applications of Boolean matrices, see Zhang [1999].

The current record for efficient $n \times n$ matrix multiplication is held by Coppersmith and Winograd; it can be done in $O(n^{2.376})$ steps.

3.9 The Myhill–Nerode theorem is due to Nerode [1958]. Myhill [1957] proved a similar result.

3.10 Theorem 3.10.5 can be considered with "NFA" replacing "DFA." See Nozaki [1979].

The algorithm MINIMIZE can be found in Hopcroft and Ullman [1979].

For fast algorithms for DFA minimization, see, for example, Hopcroft [1971], Gries [1973], and Blum [1996].

For Brzozowski's algorithm, see Brzozowski [1962a]. This simple algorithm has been rediscovered several times, for example, see Brauer [1988] and Brzozowski [1989]. Our treatment of the equivalence relation $\equiv_k$ is based on Wood [1987].

3.11 Theorem 3.11.1 is due to Maslov [1970] and Yu, Zhuang, and Salomaa [1994].

The PSPACE-completeness result is due to Jiang and Ravikumar [1993, theorem 3.2].

Theorem 3.11.4 is due to Birget [1992] and was rediscovered in a weaker form by Glaister and Shallit [1996], which is the source of Example 3.11.5.

3.12 The material in this section is based on the treatment in Lothaire [1983, §6.1] and Harrison [1978, §6.6]. Also see Haines [1969].

4

Context-free grammars and languages

In this chapter we consider some advanced topics on context-free grammars and languages. We start with closure properties.

4.1 Closure properties

You may recall from a first course on formal languages that the class of context-free languages (CFLs) is closed under the operations of union, concatenation, and Kleene $*$. (This follows easily from an argument using the representation of a CFL by a grammar.)

Also recall that the class of CFLs is not closed under the operations of intersection and complement. For example,

$$L_1 = \{a^i b^i c^j \; : \; i, j \geq 0\}$$

and

$$L_2 = \{a^i b^j c^j \; : \; i, j \geq 0\}$$

provide examples of two CFLs such that their intersection is not context-free. Similarly, $L = \{a^n b^n c^n \; : \; n \geq 0\}$ is a non-CFL, but $\overline{L}$ is context-free (see Exercise 1).

In this section we consider some of the operations we introduced in Sections 3.3–3.4, but for CFLs.

Theorem 4.1.1. *The class of CFLs is closed under substitution by context-free languages.*

Proof. Let Σ, Δ be alphabets, let $L \subseteq \Sigma^*$ be a CFL, and suppose s is a substitution such that $s(a) = L_a \subseteq \Delta^*$ is a CFL for each $a \in \Sigma$. We wish to show that $s(L)$ is context-free.

To see this, let $G = (V, \Sigma, P, S)$ be a context-free grammar generating L, and for each $a \in \Sigma$, let $G_a = (V_a, \Delta, P_a, S_a)$ be a context-free grammar generating L_a. By renaming variables, if necessary, we may assume that the sets V and V_a for $a \in \Sigma$ are pairwise disjoint.

Now we construct a grammar for $s(L)$. First, replace every occurrence of a in G with S_a, the start symbol for the grammar G_a, and call the resulting set of productions P'. Now form the grammar

$$G' = (V \cup \bigcup_{a \in \Sigma} V_a, \Delta, P' \cup \bigcup_{a \in \Sigma} P_a, S).$$

Clearly, $L(G') = s(L)$. ∎

Corollary 4.1.2. *The class of CFLs is closed under morphism.*

Example 4.1.3. Theorem 4.1.1 and Corollary 4.1.2 are useful to prove that certain languages are not context-free. For example, consider the language

$$\mathtt{ODD} := \{\mathtt{a}^1\mathtt{b}^3\mathtt{a}^5\mathtt{b}^7 \cdots \mathtt{b}^{4n-1} : n \geq 1\}.$$

To see that ODD is not context-free, let $h(\mathtt{a}) = h(\mathtt{b}) = \mathtt{c}$. Assume ODD is context-free. Then by Corollary 4.1.2, $h(\mathtt{ODD})$ would be context-free, too. But $h(\mathtt{ODD}) = \{\mathtt{c}^{4n^2} : n \geq 1\}$. This last language is easily seen not to be context-free using the pumping lemma.

Theorem 4.1.4. *The class of CFLs is closed under inverse morphism.*

Proof Idea. Let $L \subseteq \Delta^*$ be a CFL and $h : \Sigma^* \to \Delta^*$ be a morphism. We want to show that $h^{-1}(L)$ is context-free.

First, recall how the analogous property for regular languages was proved. We took a deterministic finite automaton (DFA) $M = (Q, \Delta, \delta, q_0, F)$ for L and changed the "wiring," defining $\delta'(q, a) = \delta(q, h(a))$. By analogy we could start with a pushdown automaton (PDA) $M = (Q, \Delta, \Gamma, \delta, q_0, Z_0, F)$ accepting by final state and modify it in a similar way. Unfortunately, this approach does not work directly for PDAs, since $h(a)$ is a string, and on processing a string a PDA may make many moves, including multiple pops of the stack. In our PDA model there is no way to pop multiple symbols from a stack in one move.

The solution is as follows: we read a symbol a from the input, compute $h(a)$, and then process the symbols of $h(a)$ one by one. When we are done with the symbols of $h(a)$ we read another symbol from the input. The easiest way to accomplish this is to store the as-yet-unprocessed symbols of $h(a)$ in the state of the PDA.

Proof. More precisely, given $M = (Q, \Delta, \Gamma, \delta, q_0, Z_0, F)$ we create a PDA

$$M' = (Q', \Sigma, \Gamma, \delta', q_0', Z_0, F'),$$

where $Q' = Q \times T$ and

$$T = \{x \; : \; \text{there exists } a \in \Sigma \text{ such that } x \text{ is a suffix of } h(a)\}.$$

Since Σ is finite, so is T. Also, we define $q_0' = [q_0, \epsilon]$ and $F' = F \times \{\epsilon\}$.

The transition function δ' is defined as follows: there are Type 1 transitions of the form

$$\delta'([q, \epsilon], a, X) = \{([q, h(a)], X)\}$$

for all $q \in Q, a \in \Sigma, X \in \Gamma$, and Type 2 transitions of the form

$$\delta'([q, bx], \epsilon, X) = \{([p, x], \gamma) \; : \; (p, \gamma) \in \delta(q, b, X)\}$$

for all $q \in Q, b \in \Sigma \cup \{\epsilon\}, X \in \Gamma$, and $bx \in T$.

To see that this actually works, we must prove by induction on $|x|$ that $(q, h(x), \alpha) \overset{*}{\vdash} (p, \epsilon, \beta)$ iff $([q, \epsilon], x, \alpha) \overset{*}{\vdash} ([p, \epsilon], \epsilon, \beta)$. The details are left to the reader. ∎

Theorem 4.1.5. *Let $T = (Q, \Sigma, \Delta, q_0, F, S)$ be a finite-state transducer and let $L \subseteq \Sigma^*$ be a CFL. Then $T(L)$ is context-free.*

Proof. From Theorem 3.5.3 we know that the action of T on L can be represented as $g(h^{-1}(L) \cap R)$, where g and h are morphisms and R is a regular language. But the context-free languages are closed under these operations. ∎

Theorem 4.1.6. *The class of CFLs is not closed under quotient.*

Proof. Let $L = \{a^{2n}ba^n \; : \; n \geq 1\}$. Then L is easily seen to be context-free. Define

$$L_1 = (Lb)^+ab$$

and

$$L_2 = b(Lb)^+.$$

Then both L_1 and L_2 are CFLs, since the class of CFLs is closed under the operations of concatenation and Kleene $*$. If the CFLs were closed under quotient then

$$L_1/L_2 = \{x \; : \; \exists y \in L_2 \text{ such that } xy \in L_1\}$$

would be a CFL. If $xy \in L_1$ then

$$xy = a^{c_1} b a^{c_2} b \cdots a^{c_{2k-1}} b a^{c_{2k}} b a^{c_{2k+1}} b$$

for some positive integers $c_1, c_2, \ldots, c_{2k+1}$ with $c_{2i-1} = 2c_{2i}$ for $1 \leq i \leq k$ and $c_{2k+1} = 1$. If $y \in L_2$ then

$$y = b a^{c_{2j}} b a^{c_{2j+1}} b \cdots a^{c_{2k}} b a^{c_{2k+1}} b$$

for some j, $1 \leq j \leq k$ with $c_{2t} = 2c_{2t+1}$ for $j \leq t \leq k$ and $c_{2k+1} = 1$. Now $c_{2k} = 2$, $c_{2k-1} = 4$, and so on, so it follows that

$$x = a^{c_1} b a^{c_2} b \cdots b a^{c_{2j-1}}$$

with $c_{2j-1} = 4^{k+1-j}$. Hence,

$$(L_1/L_2) \cap a^* = \{a^{4^n} : n \geq 1\},$$

and this language would also be context-free by Theorem 1.5.8. But $\{a^{4^n} : n \geq 1\}$ is easily seen not to be context-free using the pumping lemma, a contradiction. ∎

However, if L is a CFL and R is a regular language, then L/R is a CFL (see Exercise 18).

4.2 Unary context-free languages

Consider CFLs over an alphabet consisting of a single symbol. In this section we prove the following.

Theorem 4.2.1. *A unary language is context-free if and only if it is regular.*

Proof. If L is regular then it is context-free by Corollary 1.5.9.

For the converse, let L be a CFL with $L \subseteq 0^*$, and let n be the constant in the pumping lemma for CFLs. For each $m \geq n$ with $0^m \in L$, the pumping lemma applied to the string $z = 0^m$ says that there is some decomposition $0^m = uvwxy$, where $|vx| \geq 1$ and $|vwx| \leq n$, such that $uv^i wx^i y \in L$ for all $i \geq 0$. Now let $a_m = |uwy|$ and $b_m = |vx|$. Then $1 \leq b_m \leq n$, $m = a_m + b_m$, and $0^{a_m + i b_m} \in L$ for all $i \geq 0$.

Let $M = \{m \geq n : 0^m \in L\}$, and let $L' = L \cap \{\epsilon, 0, 0^2, \ldots, 0^{n-1}\}$. Then

$$L = L' \cup \{0^m : m \in M\} \subseteq L' \cup \bigcup_{m \in M} 0^{a_m} (0^{b_m})^* \subseteq L,$$

so $L = L' \cup \bigcup_{m \in M} 0^{a_m} (0^{b_m})^*$.

Now each language $0^{a_m}(0^{b_m})^*$ is a subset of $0^a(0^{b_m})^*$ with $a = a_m \bmod b_m$. So define the finite set

$A = \{(a, b) : 1 \leq b \leq n,\ 0 \leq a < b,$ and there exists $m \in M$ with $b_m = b$ and $a_m \equiv a \ (\bmod\ b_m)\},$

and, for all pairs $(a, b) \in A$, define

$$q_{a,b} = \min\{a_m \ :\ m \in M \text{ and } b_m = b \text{ and } a_m \equiv a \ (\bmod\ b_m)\}.$$

Then

$$\bigcup_{\substack{m \in M \\ b_m = b \\ a_m \equiv a \ (\bmod\ b_m)}} 0^{a_m}(0^{b_m})^* = \bigcup_{(a,b) \in A} 0^{q_{a,b}}(0^b)^*,$$

so

$$L = L' \cup \bigcup_{(a,b) \in A} 0^{q_{a,b}}(0^b)^*.$$

Thus we have written L as the union of a finite set (L') and at most n^2 regular languages, so L is regular. ∎

4.3 Ogden's lemma

The pumping lemma is one of the most important tools we have for proving languages not context-free (see Theorem 1.5.5). In this section we state and prove a more powerful version of the pumping lemma known as Ogden's lemma.

Recall that the statement of the ordinary pumping lemma refers to a sufficiently long string z, which we write as $z = uvwxy$ with $|vwx| \leq n$ and $|vx| \geq 1$. By contrast, Ogden's lemma permits us to identify certain symbols in the string z as "marked" and consider only repetitions involving these symbols.

Lemma 4.3.1. *Let L be a CFL generated by a grammar G with k variables, where the right-hand side of every production is of length $\leq d$. Set $n = d^{k+1}$. Then for all $z \in L$ with $|z| \geq n$, if n or more symbols of z are marked arbitrarily, there exists a decomposition $z = uvwxy$ such that*

(a) vx has at least one marked symbol.
(b) vwx has at most n marked symbols.
(c) There exists a variable A in G such that $S \Longrightarrow^* uAy$, $A \Longrightarrow^* vAx$, and $A \Longrightarrow^* w$.

Hence, $uv^i wx^i y \in L$ for all $i \geq 0$.

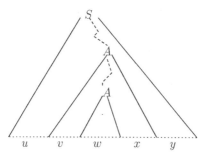

Figure 4.1: Proof of Ogden's lemma

Note that by marking every symbol of z, we obtain the ordinary pumping lemma for CFLs as a special case of Ogden's lemma.

Proof. Let $z \in L$ with $|z| \geq n = d^{k+1}$, and let T be a derivation tree for z. For each vertex γ in T, we let $m(\gamma)$ be the number of marked descendants of γ. We iteratively construct a path P in T having the property that for all vertices α in P, we have $m(\alpha) > 0$.

First, we add the root of T to P. If α is the last vertex added to P, we consider the children of α. If α has no children, we stop. If α has only one child β with $m(\beta) > 0$, add β to P and continue the construction starting with β. Otherwise, if two or more children of α have marked descendants, call α a *branch point*, pick a child β that maximizes the number of marked descendants, add β to P, and continue the construction starting with β.

Now let the branch points on P, from top to bottom, be $\alpha_0, \alpha_1, \alpha_2, \ldots, \alpha_j$. By our construction, $m(\alpha_{i+1}) \geq \frac{1}{d} m(\alpha_i)$ for $0 \leq i < j$. Now $m(\alpha_0) \geq d^{k+1}$ (since z has $\geq n$ marked descendants) and so inductively we get $m(\alpha_1) \geq \frac{1}{d} m(\alpha_0) \geq d^k$, $m(\alpha_2) \geq \frac{1}{d} m(\alpha_1) \geq d^{k-1}$, and so forth, until $m(\alpha_j) \geq d^{k-j+1}$. But $m(\alpha_j) \leq d$ (since otherwise α_j could not be the last branch point). It follows that $d \geq d^{k+1-j}$, and so $1 \geq k + 1 - j$. Thus, $j \geq k$.

Hence there are at least $k + 1$ branch points. Each branch point is labeled with a variable, and there are only k variables, so among the last $k + 1$ branch points there are two labeled with the same variable, say A. Thus we have a situation like that depicted in Figure 4.1.

It follows that there exist strings $u, v, w, x, y \in \Sigma^*$ such that $S \overset{*}{\Longrightarrow} uAy$, $A \overset{*}{\Longrightarrow} vAx$, and $A \overset{*}{\Longrightarrow} w$. Furthermore, vwx is the yield of the subtree of T rooted at the branch point p labeled with the higher occurrence of A, and this branch point has at most k other branch points below it in the path P. So $p = \alpha_i$ for $i \geq j - k$. Now α_j has at most d marked descendants; α_{j-1} has at most d^2 marked descendants, and so on, so α_i has at most d^{k+1} marked descendants. Hence, vwx has no more than $d^{k+1} = n$ marked symbols. Since the higher occurrence of A is a branch point, we know it has at least two children, say β and γ, with marked descendants. Now w is the yield of one of these children, so the other child with marked descendants yields at least one symbol in vx.

By induction on i we get $S \overset{*}{\Longrightarrow} uAy \overset{*}{\Longrightarrow} uv^i Ax^i y \overset{*}{\Longrightarrow} uv^i wx^i y$ and so $uv^i wx^i y \in L(G)$. This completes the proof of Ogden's lemma.   ∎

Example 4.3.2. Let us prove that

$$L = \{a^i b^j c^k \ : \ i = j \text{ or } j = k \text{ but not both}\}$$

is not context-free. Note that the ordinary pumping lemma does not suffice to prove L not context-free, since, for example, if we choose $z = a^n b^n c^r$, $r \neq n$, we cannot rule out the possibility that vx contains nothing but c's, so by pumping we cannot force the number of b's to equal the number of c's.

However with Ogden's lemma and $z = a^n b^n c^{n+n!}$, we can mark the a's. (This idea is sometimes called the $n!$ *trick*.) Let $z = uvwxy$ be the resulting decomposition. Since vx must have at least one marked symbol, either (a) $v = \epsilon$ and x contains an a or (b) v contains an a. In case (a), x cannot contain any b's or c's, for otherwise $uv^2 wx^2 y \notin L$. Hence, x consists only of a's, say $x = a^l$ for some $l \geq 1$. Then $uv^2 wx^2 y = a^{n+l} b^n c^{n+n!} \notin L$.

In case (b), v cannot contain any b's or c's, for otherwise $uv^2 wx^2 y \notin L$. Hence, v consists only of a's, say $v = a^l$ for some l with $1 \leq l \leq n$. Now x cannot contain two types of letters, for if it did, $uv^2 wx^2 y \notin L$. So either $x = a^m$, or $x = b^m$, or $x = c^m$ for some m. If $x = a^m$ or c^m, then $uv^2 wx^2 y \notin L$. If $x = b^m$, then either $m \neq l$ or $m = l$. If $m \neq l$, then, by choosing $i = 0$, we get that uwy has unequal numbers of a's and b's, so it is not in L. If $m = l$, then choosing $i = n!/l + 1$ we get $uv^{(n!/l)+1} wx^{(n!/l)+1} y = a^{n+n!} b^{n+n!} c^{n+n!} \notin L$.

Common Error 4.3.3. Note that Ogden's lemma does not restrict the length of v, w, or x other than the restriction implied by the number of marked symbols. In particular, Ogden's lemma does not necessarily imply that $|v|, |w|, |x| \leq n$.

4.4 Applications of Ogden's lemma

In this section we look at two additional applications of Ogden's lemma. The first concerns inherent ambiguity, while the second concerns the optimality of a common construction for converting from a PDA to a CFG.

As we have seen in Section 1.5, a context-free grammar can be ambiguous; that is, at least one word in the language generated has at least two different leftmost derivations. Often it is possible to generate the language using a different grammar that is unambiguous. However, this is not always the case:

there exist CFLs for which every grammar is ambiguous. Such languages are called *inherently ambiguous*. Note that inherent ambiguity is a property of languages, while ambiguity is a property of grammars. It is notoriously difficult to prove that a given language is inherently ambiguous.

Theorem 4.4.1. *Let*

$$L_a = \{a^i b^j c^k : i = j \ or \ j = k\}.$$

Then L_a is a CFL that is inherently ambiguous.

The reason why this theorem is difficult to prove is that we have to show that, no matter what context-free grammar is chosen to generate L_a, some string with at least two different derivations exists. While this is believable—intuitively we will need some variable that derives strings of the form $a^i b^i c^j$ and another that derives strings of the form $a^i b^j c^j$, and hence some string of the form $a^i b^i c^i$ will be derived by both variables—note that it is *not* true that the same string be derived ambiguously for all grammars. For every string you pick, there is a CFG that generates L_a and generates that particular string in only one way.

Proof. Clearly, L_a is context-free, as it is the union of $\{a^i b^i : i \geq 0\}c^*$ and $a^*\{b^i c^i : i \geq 0\}$, both of which are CFLs.

Let n be the constant in Ogden's lemma. Consider the string $z = a^m b^m c^{m+m!}$, where $m = \max(n, 3)$, and mark the a's. By Ogden's lemma there exists a factorization $z = uvwxy$ and a variable A such that $S \Longrightarrow^* uAy$, $A \Longrightarrow^* vAx$, and $A \Longrightarrow^* w$. Thus, $uv^i wx^i y \in L_a$ for all $i \geq 0$; take $i = 2$ to get $\alpha := uv^2 wx^2 y \in L_a$. Also, vx has at most m b's, because that is the total number of b's in z. Since $m \geq 3$, we have $m < m!$, and so $|\alpha|_b \leq 2m < m + m! \leq |\alpha|_c$. Thus, $|\alpha|_a = |\alpha|_b$. Thus, vx contains the same number of a's as b's and must contain at least one a since vx contains at least one marked symbol. Now v and x can each contain only one type of symbol, for otherwise $\alpha \notin L_a$. Thus, $v = a^j$, $x = b^j$, for $1 \leq j \leq m$. Now let $i = \frac{m!}{j} + 1$ to get a derivation of

$$\beta = uv^i wx^i y = a^{m+m!} b^{m+m!} c^{m+m!}$$

by using the production $A \Longrightarrow^* vAx$ i times.

Now play exactly the same game starting with the string $z' = a^{m+m!} b^m c^m$, but this time, mark the c's. Once again, we get a factorization $z' = u'v'w'x'y'$ and a variable A' such that $S \Longrightarrow^* u'A'y'$, $A' \Longrightarrow^* v'A'x'$, and $A' \Longrightarrow^* w'$. And once again, we get that $v' = b^{j'}$, $x' = c^{j'}$ for some j', $1 \leq j' \leq m$. Now let $i' = \frac{m!}{j'} + 1$ to get a derivation of

$$\beta = u'v'^{i'}w'x'^{i'}y' = a^{m+m!}b^{m+m!}c^{m+m!}.$$

I claim these two derivations are different. To see this, observe that first obtains all but $m - j$ of its b's through the production $A \Longrightarrow^* a^j Ab^j$, while the second obtains all but $m - j'$ of its b's through the production $A' \Longrightarrow^* b^{j'} A'b^{j'}$. ∎

Now let us turn to our second application of Ogden's lemma.

In Section 1.5 we examined a well-known construction for finding a context-free grammar that generates the same language as that accepted by a given PDA (accepting by empty stack). Students seeing this construction for the first time are often surprised at how difficult it seems. After all, the construction is not particularly obvious. This leads to the following natural question: can the triple construction be simplified? Perhaps surprisingly, the answer is no, at least with respect to the number of variables, as the following theorem shows. As a bonus, we get a nice application of Ogden's lemma.

Theorem 4.4.2. *For all integers $n, p \geq 1$, there exists a PDA $M = M(n, p)$ with n states and p stack symbols such that every context-free grammar G generating $L_e(M)$ uses at least $n^2 p$ variables.*

Proof. Let $M = (Q, \Sigma, \Gamma, \delta, q_1, Z_1, \emptyset)$, where

- $Q = \{q_i \ : \ 1 \leq i \leq n\}$;
- $\Gamma = \{Z_j \ : \ 1 \leq j \leq p\}$;
- $\Sigma = \{a_{i,j}, t_{i,j} \ : \ 1 \leq i \leq n, 1 \leq j \leq p\} \cup \{b_k, d_k \ : \ 1 \leq k \leq n\}$;

and δ is defined as follows:

$$\delta(q_1, a_{i,j}, Z_1) = \{(q_i, Z_j)\}$$

$$\delta(q_i, t_{i,j}, Z_j) = \{(q_i, Z_j Z_j)\}$$

$$\delta(q_i, b_k, Z_j) = \{(q_k, Z_j)\}$$

$$\delta(q_k, d_k, Z_j) = \{(q_k, \epsilon)\}.$$

Let $L = L_e(M)$ and let $G = (V, \Sigma, P, S)$ be a context-free grammar such that $L(G) = L$. Let m be the constant in Ogden's lemma applied to G. For every triple (i, j, k) such that $1 \leq i, k \leq n, 1 \leq j \leq p$, let

$$z = z(i, j, k) = a_{i,j} t_{i,j}^m b_k d_k^{m+1}.$$

We claim that M accepts z for we have the accepting computation

$$(q_1, z, Z_1) \vdash (q_i, t_{i,j}^m b_k d_k^{m+1}, Z_j)$$

$$\overset{*}{\vdash} (q_i, b_k d_k^{m+1}, Z_j^{m+1})$$

$$\overset{*}{\vdash} (q_k, d_k^{m+1}, Z_j^{m+1})$$

$$\overset{*}{\vdash} (q_k, \epsilon, \epsilon).$$

Now, using Ogden's lemma, mark all the symbols $t_{i,j}$ and d_k; hence, $2m + 1 \geq m$ symbols are marked. By Ogden's lemma we can write $z = uvwxy$ such that

$$vx \quad \text{has at least one marked letter}$$

$$vwx \quad \text{has} \leq m \text{ marked letters},$$

and there exists a variable $A_{i,j,k} \in V$ such that

$$S \overset{*}{\Longrightarrow} uA_{i,j,k}y \overset{*}{\Longrightarrow} uv^r A_{i,j,k}x^r y \overset{*}{\Longrightarrow} uv^r wx^r y$$

for all $r \geq 0$. This gives $n^2 p$ variables. Now we must show they are all distinct.

If $uwy \in L_e(M)$, it must contain one more d letter than t letter, so vx must contain the same number of t's as d's. By Ogden's lemma, vx contains at least one t or d, so it must contain both a t and a d. Since vwx has $\leq m$ t's and d's, u and y must be nonempty. Hence there exist integers $s, \sigma \geq 1$ with $s + \sigma \leq m$ and

$$u = a_{i,j} t_{i,j}^{m-s};$$

$$vwx = t_{i,j}^s b_k d_k^\sigma;$$

$$y = d_k^{m+1-\sigma}.$$

Let $A_{i,j,k}$ be a variable in G associated with $z(i, j, k) = uvwxy$. Let $A_{i',j',k'}$ be a variable in G associated with $z(i', j', k') = u'v'w'x'y'$. Suppose $A_{i,j,k} = A_{i',j',k'}$. Then we have

$$S \overset{*}{\Longrightarrow} uA_{i,j,k}y = uA_{i',j',k'}y$$

$$\overset{*}{\Longrightarrow} uv'w'x'y = a_{i,j} t_{i,j}^{m-s} t_{i',j'}^{s'} b_{k'} d_{k'}^{\sigma'} d_k^{m+1-\sigma} \in L.$$

But after reading $a_{i,j} t_{i,j}^{m-s}$, the configuration of M is of the form $(q_i, -, Z_j^{m-s+1})$, and it will now crash on reading $t_{i',j'}$ unless $i' = i$ and $j' = j$. Similarly, after having read $uv'w'x'$, the configuration of M is of the form $(q_{k'}, -, Z_j^{m+1-s+s'-\sigma'})$ and will crash on reading d_k unless $k = k'$. Thus, $A_{i,j,k} = A_{i',j',k'}$ implies that $(i, j, k) = (i', j', k')$. ∎

4.5 The interchange lemma

There are not many tools known to prove that a given language is not a CFL. In this section we examine another tool: the interchange lemma. Roughly speaking, the interchange lemma says that if a language is context-free, then there is a large subset of the words of length n such that one can take two strings from this subset, and interchange the subwords appearing at the same position, and still get strings in the language. We then use this tool to prove that the language of square-containing words is not a CFL.

Lemma 4.5.1. *Let L be a CFL. Then there is a constant $c > 0$, depending on L, such that for all integers $n \geq 2$, all subsets $R \subseteq L \cap \Sigma^n$, and all integers with $2 \leq m \leq n$, there exists a subset $Z \subseteq R$, $Z = \{z_1, z_2, \ldots, z_k\}$ such that $k \geq \frac{|R|}{c(n+1)^2}$ and there exist decompositions $z_i = w_i x_i y_i$, $1 \leq i \leq k$, such that*

(a) $|w_1| = |w_2| = \cdots = |w_k|$;
(b) $|y_1| = |y_2| = \cdots = |y_k|$;
(c) $\frac{m}{2} < |x_1| = |x_2| = \cdots = |x_k| \leq m$; and
(d) $w_i x_j y_i \in L$ for all i, j, $1 \leq i, j \leq k$.

First, we prove two technical lemmas.

Lemma 4.5.2. *Let $G = (V, \Sigma, P, S)$ be a context-free grammar in Chomsky normal form generating L. Let m be an integer with $m \geq 2$. Then for all strings $z \in L$ with $|z| \geq m$, there exists a variable $A \in V$ and a derivation*

$$S \stackrel{*}{\Longrightarrow} wAy \stackrel{*}{\Longrightarrow} wxy = z$$

with $\frac{m}{2} < |x| \leq m$.

Proof. Let p be root of T, a parse tree for z. Clearly, p has $\geq m$ descendants that are terminal symbols. If p has exactly m descendants that are terminals, take $w = y = \epsilon$, $A = S$, and $x = z$. So assume p has $>m$ descendants. Now repeatedly replace p with the child that has the larger number of terminal descendants, until p has $\leq m$ descendants. Since the parent of p had $>m$ descendants, p must have $>m/2$ descendants. Let A be the label of p. Then there exist strings w, y with $S \stackrel{*}{\Longrightarrow} wAy$ and $A \stackrel{*}{\Longrightarrow} x$ with $\frac{m}{2} < |x| \leq m$. ∎

We now define certain sets involving derivations. Choose a subset $R \subseteq L \cap \Sigma^n$. For integers n_1, n_2 with $0 \leq n_1, n_2 \leq n$ define

$$Q_{n,R}(n_1, A, n_2) := \{z \in R \; : \; \text{there exists a derivation } S \stackrel{*}{\Longrightarrow} wAy \stackrel{*}{\Longrightarrow}$$
$$wxy = z, \; |w| = n_1, |y| = n_2\}.$$

Lemma 4.5.3. *Let* $G = (V, \Sigma, P, S)$ *be a context-free grammar in Chomsky normal form generating* L. *Let* $2 \leq m \leq n$. *Then for all subsets* $R \subseteq L \cap \Sigma^n$, *there exist integers* $0 \leq n_1, n_2 \leq n$ *such that*

$$\frac{m}{2} < n - n_1 - n_2 \leq m$$

and a variable $A \in V$ *such that*

$$|Q_{n,R}(n_1, A, n_2)| \geq \frac{|R|}{|V|(n+1)^2}.$$

Proof. We have

$$R = \bigcup_{\substack{A \in V \\ 0 \leq n_1, n_2 \leq n}} Q_{n,R}(n_1, A, n_2) = \bigcup_{\substack{A \in V \\ 0 \leq n_1, n_2 \leq n \\ \frac{m}{2} < n - n_1 - n_2 \leq m}} Q_{n,R}(n_1, A, n_2),$$

where in the last line we used Lemma 4.5.2. Thus we have written R as the union of at most $(n+1)^2|V|$ sets, so at least one of these sets has $\frac{|R|}{|V|(n+1)^2}$ elements. ∎

We can now prove the interchange lemma.

Proof. Let $G = (V, \Sigma, P, S)$ be a context-free grammar in Chomsky normal form generating $L - \{\epsilon\}$. Let $c = |V|$, and choose a subset $R \subseteq L \cap \Sigma^n$. Then by Lemma 4.5.3 there exist integers $0 \leq n_1, n_2 \leq n$ with $\frac{m}{2} < n - n_1 - n_2 \leq m$ and a variable A such that $|Q_{n,R}(n_1, A, n_2)| \geq \frac{|R|}{|V|(n+1)^2}$. Take $Z = Q_{n,R}(n_1, A, n_2)$. Every string $z_i \in Z$ has a derivation of the form

$$S \overset{*}{\Longrightarrow} w_i A y_i \overset{*}{\Longrightarrow} w_i x_i y_i = z_i$$

with $|w_i| = n_1$ and $|y_i| = n_2$. Thus,

$$S \overset{*}{\Longrightarrow} w_i A y_i \overset{*}{\Longrightarrow} w_i x_j y_i \in L.$$

The proof of the interchange lemma is now complete. ∎

We now give an application of the interchange lemma. Let L_i be the language

$$\{xyyz \ : \ x, z \in \Sigma^*, y \in \Sigma^+\},$$

where $\Sigma = \{0, 1, \ldots, i-1\}$. Thus, L_i is the language of all words containing (nontrivial) squares over an alphabet of i letters. It is not hard to see that L_1 and L_2 are context-free. (In fact, they are regular, by Exercise 2.3.) We will use the interchange lemma to prove the following theorem.

Theorem 4.5.4. *The language* L_i *is not a CFL for* $i \geq 3$.

Proof. First we prove the result for $i = 6$. At the end we explain how to get the result for all $i \geq 3$.

Assume that L_6 is context-free. Let c be the constant in the interchange lemma and choose n sufficiently large so that it is divisible by 8 and

$$\frac{2^{n/4}}{c(n+1)^2} > 2^{n/8}.$$

(The reason for this choice will be clear in a moment.)

By Theorem 2.5.2 there exists a squarefree string of every length over a three-letter alphabet. Choose such a string r' of length $\frac{n}{4} - 1$ over $\{0, 1, 2\}$ and define $r = 3r'$. Define

$$A_n := \{rr\amalg s \;:\; s \in \{4, 5\}^{n/2}\},$$

where $\amalg$ is the perfect shuffle introduced in Section 1.2. Thus, every string in A_n is of length n.

The strings in A_n have the following useful properties:

1. If $z_1 = w_1 x_1 y_1$, and $z_2 = w_2 x_2 y_2$ are strings in A_n with $|w_1| = |w_2|$, $|x_1| = |x_2|$, and $|y_1| = |y_2|$, then $w_1 x_2 y_1$ and $w_2 x_1 y_2$ are both in A_n, too. For $z_1 = rr\amalg s$, $z_2 = rr\amalg s'$, and substituting x_2 for x_1 leaves the symbols corresponding to rr the same, while possibly changing the symbols corresponding to s. But since any s is permissible, this change does not affect membership in A_n.

2. If $z \in A_n$, then z contains a square if and only if z is a square. For if z contained a square, then considering only the symbols of z in $\{0, 1, 2, 3\}$, we would still have a square. But this is impossible, since r is squarefree.

Now define the following subset of A_n:

$$B_n := L_6 \cap A_n$$
$$= \{rr\amalg ss \;:\; s \in \{4, 5\}^{n/4}\}.$$

Clearly, $|B_n| = 2^{\frac{n}{4}}$. Since $B_n \subseteq L_6$, the interchange lemma applies with $m = n/2$ and $R = B_n$. Then there is a subset $Z \subseteq B_n$, $Z = \{z_1, z_2, \ldots, z_k\}$ with $z_i = w_i x_i y_i$ satisfying the conclusions of that lemma. In particular, $k = |Z| \geq \frac{2^{n/4}}{c(n+1)^2} > 2^{n/8}$.

There are now two cases to consider, and each will lead to a contradiction.

Case 1: There exist indices g, h such that $x_g \neq x_h$.

Case 2: There do not exist such indices.

In Case 1, we know from the interchange lemma that $w_g x_h y_g \in L$. Since $x_g \neq x_h$, there must be a 4 or 5 in one-half of z_g that is changed. But since $|x_h| \leq n/2$, the corresponding symbol is not changed in the other half of the string. So $w_g x_h y_g$ cannot be a square. Since $w_g x_h y_g \in A_n$, by observation (2) given before see that $w_g x_h y_g$ cannot contain a square, either. Thus, $w_g x_h y_g \notin L$, a contradiction.

In Case 2, all the x_i must be the same. So there are at least $n/4$ positions in which all the z_i agree. This set of $n/4$ positions contains at least $n/8$ 4's and 5's. There are only at most $n/8$ positions where we are free to make a choice between 4 and 5. Thus, $|Z| \leq 2^{n/8}$, a contradiction.

It now follows that L_6 is not a CFL.

We now show how to get the result for L_i, $i \geq 3$. In Exercise 34 you are asked to show that the following morphism h is *squarefree-preserving*; that is, x is squarefree if and only if $h(x)$ is squarefree.

$$0 \to 0102012022012102010212$$
$$1 \to 0102012022201210120212$$
$$2 \to 0102012101202101210212$$
$$3 \to 0102012101202120121012$$
$$4 \to 0102012102010210120212$$
$$5 \to 0102012102120210120212.$$

Now suppose L_3 is context-free. Then, by Theorem 4.1.4, the language $h^{-1}(L_3)$ is context-free. But since h is squarefree-preserving, $h^{-1}(L_3)$ is the language of all square-containing words over a six-letter alphabet, that is, L_6, which we have just proved non-context-free, a contradiction.

Finally, suppose L_i is context-free for some $i \geq 3$. Then $L_i \cap \{0, 1, 2\}^*$ is context-free by Theorem 1.5.8. But this is L_3, a contradiction. ∎

4.6 Parikh's theorem

In Section 4.2 we saw that every CFL over a unary alphabet is regular. In this section we consider a beautiful generalization of this result, called Parikh's theorem. Parikh's theorem has been described as "among the most fundamental, yet subtly difficult to prove, in the theory [of context-free languages]."

If $L \subseteq a^*$ is a unary language, then we can consider the associated set

$$\text{lengths}(L) = \{i \ : \ a^i \in L\}.$$

As we have seen in the proof of Theorem 4.2.1, if L is context-free, then $\text{lengths}(L)$ has the property that it is the union of finitely many *arithmetic progressions*, that is, sets of the form $\{k + it \ : \ i \geq 0\}$. It is natural to wonder if this observation can be generalized to languages over larger alphabets.

It can. To do so, we need to introduce the concepts of linear and semilinear sets. Let k be an integer ≥ 1. A subset A of $\mathbb{N}^k$ is said to be *linear* if there exist $u_0, u_1, \ldots, u_r \in \mathbb{N}^k$ such that

$$A = \{u_0 + a_1 u_1 + \cdots + a_r u_r \; : \; a_1, a_2, \ldots, a_r \in \mathbb{N}\}. \tag{4.1}$$

The right-hand side of Eq. (4.1) is sometimes written as $u_0 + \langle u_1, u_2, \ldots, u_r \rangle$. A subset A of $\mathbb{N}^k$ is said to be *semilinear* if it is the union of finitely many linear sets.

Next, we introduce the *Parikh map* ψ. We start with an ordered alphabet $\Sigma = \{a_1, a_2, \ldots, a_k\}$. Then $\psi : \Sigma^* \to \mathbb{N}^k$ maps a word $w \in \Sigma^*$ to the vector of length k given by

$$(|w|_{a_1}, |w|_{a_2}, \ldots, |w|_{a_k}).$$

For example, if $\Sigma = \{\mathsf{a, b, c, d, e}\}$ and is ordered by alphabetic order, then $\psi(\mathsf{beaded}) = (1, 1, 0, 2, 2)$. The map ψ can be extended to languages L as follows:

$$\psi(L) = \bigcup_{w \in L} \{\psi(w)\}.$$

Note that the Parikh map is essentially the commutative image of a word and that $\psi(xy) = \psi(x) + \psi(y)$ for all strings $x, y \in \Sigma^*$.

A very useful result about semilinear sets is the following:

Theorem 4.6.1. *For any $k \geq 1$, the class of semilinear sets of $\mathbb{N}^k$ is closed under union, intersection, and complement.*

Proof. The result about union is clear. Unfortunately, the proof for intersection and complement is quite difficult and we omit it. A proof can be found in the references at the end of this chapter. ∎

Now, Parikh's theorem says that if L is a CFL, then $\psi(L)$ is semilinear. Note that the converse does not hold (see Example 4.6.2(d)).

Example 4.6.2. Let us look at some examples:

(a) $L_0 = \{0, 01\}^*$. Then $\psi(L_1) = \langle (1, 0), (1, 1) \rangle$.
(b) $L_1 = \{0, 1\}^2$. Then $\psi(L_1) = \{(0, 2), (1, 1), (2, 0)\}$. (This can be written as $((0, 2) + \langle (0, 0) \rangle) \cup ((1, 1) + \langle (0, 0) \rangle) \cup ((2, 0) + \langle (0, 0) \rangle)$.)
(c) $L_2 = \{0^n 1^n \; : \; n \geq 1\}$. Then $\psi(L_2) = (1, 1) + \langle (1, 1) \rangle$.
(d) $L_3 = \{0^n 1^n 2^n \; : \; n \geq 1\}$. Then $\psi(L_3) = (1, 1, 1) + \langle (1, 1, 1) \rangle$.
(e) $L_4 = \mathrm{PAL} = \{w \in \{0, 1\}^* \; : \; w = w^R\}$. Then

$$\psi(L_4) = \langle (0, 2), (2, 0) \rangle \cup ((0, 1) + \langle (0, 2), (2, 0) \rangle) \cup ((1, 0) + \langle (0, 2), (2, 0) \rangle).$$

To see this, note that we can generate a palindrome with any given Parikh image, except the case where both coordinates are odd.

(f) $L_5 = \{0^m 1^m 2^n 3^n : m, n \geq 1\}$. Then $\psi(L_5) = (1, 1, 1, 1) + \langle(1, 1, 0, 0),$ $(0, 0, 1, 1)\rangle$.

(g) $L_6 = \text{EQ} = \{w \in \{0, 1\}^* : |w|_0 = |w|_1\}$. Then $\psi(L_6) = \langle(1, 1)\rangle$.

(h) $L_7 = \{x \in \{0, 1\}^* : x \text{ is not of the form } ww\}$. Then

$$\psi(L_7) = ((0, 1) + X) \cup ((1, 0) + X) \cup ((1, 1) + X) \cup ((2, 2) + X),$$

where $X = \langle(0, 2), (2, 0)\rangle$. The proof is left as Exercise 31.

The next theorem gives a relationship between semilinear sets and regular languages.

Theorem 4.6.3. *Let $X \subseteq \mathbb{N}^k$ be a semilinear set. Then there exists a regular language $L \subseteq \Sigma^*$, where $\Sigma = \{a_1, a_2, \ldots, a_k\}$, such that $\psi(L) = X$.*

Proof. A semilinear set is a union of a finite number of linear sets. So it suffices to show the result for a linear set T.

Let $T = u_0 + \langle u_1, u_2, \ldots, u_t \rangle$, where $u_i = (v_{i,1}, v_{i,2}, \ldots, v_{i,k})$. Now let

$$L = a_1^{v_{0,1}} a_2^{v_{0,2}} \cdots a_k^{v_{0,k}} \left(\sum_{1 \leq i \leq t} a_1^{v_{i,1}} a_2^{v_{i,2}} \ldots a_k^{v_{i,k}} \right)^*.$$

Then L is regular and $\psi(L) = T$. ∎

Now let us prove Parikh's theorem. First, we need a lemma.

Lemma 4.6.4. *Let $G = (V, \Sigma, P, S)$ be a context-free grammar with k variables in Chomsky normal form. Let $p = 2^{k+1}$. For all integers $j \geq 1$, if $z \in L(G)$ and $|z| \geq p^j$, every derivation $S \Longrightarrow^* z$ has the same derivation tree as a derivation of the form*

$$S \Longrightarrow^* uAy$$
$$\Longrightarrow^* uv_1 A x_1 y$$
$$\Longrightarrow^* uv_1 v_2 A x_2 x_1 y$$
$$\vdots$$
$$\Longrightarrow^* uv_1 v_2 \cdots v_j A x_j \cdots x_2 x_1 y$$
$$\Longrightarrow^* uv_1 v_2 \cdots v_j w x_j \cdots x_2 x_1 y = z,$$

where $A \in V$, $v_i x_i \neq \epsilon$ for $1 \leq i \leq j$, and $|v_1 v_2 \cdots v_j x_j \cdots x_2 x_1| \leq p^j$.

Proof. Consider a derivation tree for z. As in the proof of the ordinary pumping lemma for context-free grammars, since $|z| \geq p^j = 2^{j(k+1)}$, there must be a path P of length $\geq j(k+1) + 1$ from the root S to a terminal. This path P contains $j(k+1) + 1$ variables, so some variable must occur at least $j + 1$ times. Now trace a path P' from the last node on P backup until some variable A occurs at least $j + 1$ times for the first time. The yield of the highest A in P' is of length at most $2^{j(k+1)} = p^j$. Each A gives a derivation of the form $A \implies^* v_i A x_i$; combining these with $S \implies^* u A y$ and the yield of the lowest A, $A \implies^* w$, gives a derivation of the desired form with $|v_1 v_2 \cdots v_j x_j \cdots x_2 x_1| \leq p^j$. Each $v_i x_i$ is nonempty because these correspond to a variable other than A, which must derive a nonempty string. ∎

We are now ready for the proof of Parikh's theorem.

Theorem 4.6.5. *If L is a CFL, then $\psi(L)$ is semilinear.*

Proof. We can assume without loss of generality that L does not contain ϵ, for if it does, we can first compute $\psi(L)$ for the CFL $L - \{\epsilon\}$ and then add in the vector $(0, 0, \ldots, 0)$.

So let $G = (V, \Sigma, P, S)$ be a context-free grammar in Chomsky normal form generating $L - \{\epsilon\}$, and let p be the constant in the previous lemma. Let $U \subseteq V$ be any set of variables containing S. Define L_U to be the set of all words generated by G for which there exists a derivation including precisely the variables in U—no more, no less. Now there are only finitely many L_U, and $L = \bigcup_{\{S\} \subseteq U \subseteq V} L_U$. Thus, it suffices to show that each L_U is semilinear.

Now fix an arbitrary U and assume that all derivations use only the variables from U. Let $\ell = |U|$, and define the languages

$$E = \{w \in L_U \; : \; |w| < p^\ell\}$$

and

$$F = \{vx \; : \; 1 \leq |vx| \leq p^\ell \text{ and } A \implies^* vAx \text{ for some variable } A \in U\}.$$

Note that both E and F are finite, so $\psi(EF^*)$ is semilinear. We will show that $\psi(L_U) = \psi(EF^*)$.

First, let us show that $\psi(L_U) \subseteq \psi(EF^*)$. Let $z \in L_U$; we prove that $\psi(z) \in \psi(EF^*)$ by induction on $|z|$. The base case is $|z| < p^\ell$. In this case, $z \in E \subseteq EF^*$, so $\psi(z) \in \psi(EF^*)$.

For the induction step, assume $|z| \geq p^\ell$ and $z \in L_U$. By Lemma 4.6.4, there is a derivation for z that can be written in the form

$$S \Longrightarrow^* uAy$$
$$(d_1) \Longrightarrow^* uv_1 Ax_1 y$$
$$(d_2) \Longrightarrow^* uv_1 v_2 Ax_2 x_1 y$$

$$\vdots$$

$$(d_\ell) \Longrightarrow^* uv_1 v_2 \cdots v_\ell Ax_\ell \cdots x_2 x_1 y$$
$$\Longrightarrow^* uv_1 v_2 \cdots v_\ell wx_\ell \cdots x_2 x_1 y = z,$$

where the derivations have been labeled $d_1, d_2, \ldots, d_\ell$.

Now, with each of the $\ell - 1$ variables $B \in U - \{A\}$, associate (arbitrarily) a derivation d_i if B occurs in d_i. Since there are ℓ labeled derivations and only $\ell - 1$ variables in $B \in U - \{A\}$, there must be at least one derivation d_i that is not associated with any variable. We can therefore omit d_i to get a derivation

$$S \Longrightarrow^* uv_1 \cdots v_{i-1} v_{i+1} \cdots v_\ell wx_\ell \cdots x_{i+1} x_{i-1} \cdots x_1 y = z',$$

where $z' \in L_U$. Since $|z'| < |z|$, by induction we have $\psi(z') \in \psi(EF^*)$. Now $v_i x_i \in F$, so $\psi(z) = \psi(z' v_i x_i) \in \psi(EF^*)$, as desired.

Now we prove the other direction. Let $z \in EF^*$; then $z = e_0 f_1 f_2 \cdots f_t$ for some $t \geq 0$, where $e_0 \in E$ and $f_i \in F$ for $1 \leq i \leq t$. We prove by induction on t that $\psi(z) \in \psi(L_U)$.

The base case is $t = 0$. In that case, $z = e_0 \in E$. Then by definition, $z \in L_U$, so $\psi(z) \in \psi(L_U)$.

For the induction step, assume $z = e_0 f_1 \cdots f_t$, where $e_0 \in E$ and each $f_i \in F$. Since $f_t \in F$, we can write $f_t = vx$, where $1 \leq |vx| \leq p^l$ and $A \Longrightarrow^* vAx$. By induction we know $\psi(e_0 f_1 \cdots f_{t-1}) = \psi(z')$ for some $z' \in L_U$. But since $z' \in L_U$, there exists a derivation of z' using the variable A, say $S \Longrightarrow^* v'Ax' \Longrightarrow^* v'w'x' = z'$. But then $S \Longrightarrow^* v'Ax' \Longrightarrow^* v'vAxx' \Longrightarrow^* v'vwxx' = z''$, so $z'' \in L_U$. Now $\psi(z'') = \psi(z') + \psi(vx) = \psi(e_0 f_1 \cdots f_{t-1}) + \psi(f_t) = \psi(z)$, so $\psi(z) \in \psi(L_U)$, as desired. ∎

Sometimes Parikh's theorem is useful for proving certain languages non-context-free when other methods, such as the pumping lemma, fail.

Example 4.6.6. Let us prove that $L = \{a^i b^j : j \neq i^2\}$ is not context-free. Suppose it is. Then by Parikh's theorem, the set $\psi(L) = \{(i, j) : j \neq i^2\}$ is semilinear. By Theorem 4.6.1, $T := \overline{\psi(L)} = \{(i, i^2) : i \geq 0\}$ is semilinear. But by Theorem 4.6.3, there exists a regular language $R \subseteq \{a, b\}^*$ such that $\psi(R) = T$. Now consider the morphism $h : \{a, b\}^* \to c^*$ defined by $h(a) =$

$h(b) = c$. Then $h(R) = \{c^{n^2+n} : n \geq 0\}$, which is easily seen to be nonregular using the pumping lemma, a contradiction (since regular languages are closed under application of a morphism). Thus, L is not context-free.

You might find this proof a bit unsatisfactory, as it depends on Theorem 4.6.1, which we did not prove. We can prove the result about L without Theorem 4.6.1, but it requires a bit more work. To do so, assume that $\psi(L)$ is semilinear. Then it is the union of linear sets, each of which can be written in the form $u_0 + \langle u_1, u_2, \ldots, u_j \rangle$. Let d' be the maximum of all the integers occurring in all vectors defining $\psi(L)$, and let $d = \max(d', 3)$. Now let $m = d!$ and $n = (d!)^2 - d!$. Clearly, $n \neq m^2$, so $(m, n) \in \psi(L)$, and so (m, n) belongs to some linear set $u_0 + \langle u_1, u_2, \ldots, u_j \rangle$. We first claim that some u_i, $1 \leq i \leq j$, must be of the form $(0, r)$ for some r, $1 \leq r \leq d$. For otherwise, all the first coordinates of the u_i, $1 \leq i \leq j$, are at least 1. Since $(m, n) \in u_0 + \langle u_1, u_2, \ldots, u_j \rangle$, we can write

$$(m, n) = (q_0, r_0) + \sum_{1 \leq i \leq j} a_i(q_i, r_i),$$

where $u_i = (q_i, r_i)$. Since each $q_i \geq 1$, it follows that $m \geq a_1 + a_2 + \cdots + a_j$. Now $n = r_0 + a_1 r_1 + \cdots + a_j r_j \leq (m + 1)d$. Now, since $d \geq 3$, we have $d! > d + 2$ and so $n = (d!)^2 - d! > (d + 2)d! - d! = (d + 1)d! > d(d! + 1) = d(m + 1)$, a contradiction.

Thus some u_i is of the form $(0, r)$. It follows that $(m, n) + t(0, r) \in \psi(L)$ for all $t \geq 0$. Now take $t = d!/r$; this is an integer because $1 \leq r \leq d$. Then

$$(m, n) + t(0, r) = (m, n) + \frac{d!}{r}(0, r) = (m, n + d!) = (d!, (d!)^2) \in \psi(L),$$

a contradiction.

4.7 Deterministic context-free languages

An interesting subclass of the CFLs is the deterministic context-free languages, or DCFLs.

To formally define this class, recall that a PDA is given by a 7-tuple $M = (Q, \Sigma, \Gamma, \delta, q_0, Z_0, F)$. The PDA M accepts a string x by final state if and only if $(q_0, x, Z_0) \overset{*}{\vdash} (q, \epsilon, \alpha)$ for some $q \in F$ and $\alpha \in \Gamma^*$. We say that M is *deterministic* if the following two conditions hold:

(a) $|\delta(q, a, A)| \leq 1$ for all $q \in Q$, $a \in \Sigma \cup \{\epsilon\}$, and $A \in \Gamma$;
(b) for all $q \in Q$ and $A \in \Gamma$, if $\delta(q, \epsilon, A) \neq \emptyset$, then $\delta(q, a, A) = \emptyset$ for all $a \in \Sigma$.

The intent is that condition (a) prevents a choice between two non-ϵ moves, while condition (b) prevents a choice between an ϵ move and a non-ϵ move.

If L is accepted by a DPDA by final state, then we say that L is a DCFL.

One of the most important observations about the DCFLs is that this class is closed under complement. Recall how we proved that the class of regular languages is closed under complement: we took a DFA M and created a new machine M' to accept $\overline{L(M)}$ by changing the "finality" of each state: final states became nonfinal and vice versa. We would like to do this with a DPDA, but two problems occur.

First, a DPDA M may enter a state in which it never consumes additional input symbols. This can occur because M has no defined move, or because the stack has been emptied, or because it enters an infinite loop on ϵ-transitions. If M never reads past x, then it cannot accept any string of the form xy for $y \in \Sigma^+$. If we simply changed the "finality" of each state of M to obtain M', then M' would also never read past x, and so it would also not accept any string of the form xy for $y \in \Sigma^+$. We can fix this problem by forcing M to scan its entire input.

Second, after reading a string x, M may enter a sequence of states on ϵ-transitions. Suppose that it enters at least one final state and at least one nonfinal state. Then by our definition of acceptance in PDAs, x would be accepted. However, if we simply change the finality of each state to get M', then x would still be accepted, which it should not. We can fix this problem by recording, in between states where M actually reads an input, whether or not M has seen a final state so far.

Lemma 4.7.1. *If $M = (Q, \Sigma, \Gamma, \delta, q_0, Z_0, F)$ is a DPDA, then there exists a DPDA $M' = (Q', \Sigma, \Gamma', \delta', q_0', X_0, F')$ such that $L(M) = L(M')$ and M' always scans its entire input. More formally, for all inputs $x \in \Sigma^*$, there exists a computation in M' such that $(q_0', x, X_0) \overset{*}{\vdash} (q, \epsilon, \alpha)$ for some $q \in Q'$ and $\alpha \in \Gamma'^*$.*

Proof. As earlier, the basic idea is simple: we add transitions, so there is always a next move, and we add transitions to avoid infinite loops on ϵ-moves. The actual implementation is a bit complex.

Suppose $M = (Q, \Sigma, \Gamma, \delta, q_0, Z_0, F)$. We define a machine $M' = (Q', \Sigma, \Gamma', \delta', q_0', X_0, F')$, where $Q' = Q \cup \{q_0', d, f\}$, $\Gamma' = \Gamma \cup \{X_0\}$, $F' = F \cup \{f\}$, and δ' is defined as follows:

(a) $\delta'(q_0', \epsilon, X_0) = \{(q_0, Z_0 X_0)\}$.

(b) If $\delta(q, a, X) = \emptyset$ and $\delta(q, \epsilon, X) = \emptyset$, then $\delta'(q, a, X) = \{(d, X)\}$.

(c) $\delta'(q, a, X_0) = \{(d, X_0)\}$ for all $q \in Q$ and $a \in \Sigma$.

(d) $\delta'(d, a, X) = \{(d, X)\}$ for all $a \in \Sigma$ and $X \in \Gamma'$.

(e) If M enters an infinite loop on ϵ-transitions from the configuration (q, ϵ, X), then $\delta'(q, \epsilon, X) = \{(d, X)\}$, provided no state encountered in the infinite loop is final, and $\delta'(q, \epsilon, X) = \{(f, X)\}$ otherwise.

(f) $\delta'(f, a, X) = \{(d, X)\}$ for all $a \in \Sigma$ and $X \in \Gamma'$.

(g) For all $q \in Q$, $a \in \Sigma \cup \{\epsilon\}$, $X \in \Gamma$ for which $\delta'(q, a, X)$ has not been defined earlier, $\delta'(q, a, X) = \delta(q, a, X)$.

We leave the formal proof that this construction works to the reader.   ∎

We can now prove the fact that the DCFLs are closed under complement.

Theorem 4.7.2. *If L is a DCFL then so is $\overline{L}$.*

Proof. If L is a DCFL, it is accepted by a DPDA $M = (Q, \Sigma, \Gamma, \delta, q_0, Z_0, F)$. By Lemma 4.7.1 we may assume that M scans its entire input. We now modify M by adding a code to the state that says whether or not a final state has been seen since the last "real" (i.e., non-ϵ) input. The meaning of y in the second component is that a final state has been seen; the meaning of n is that it has not; and the meaning of A is that the machine is about to read another "real" input and has not entered a final state since the last "real" input.

Formally, let $M' = (Q', \Sigma, \Gamma, \delta', q_0', Z_0, F')$, where $Q' = Q \times \{y, n, A\}$;

$$q_0' = \begin{cases} [q_0, y], & \text{if } q_0 \in F; \\ [q_0, n], & \text{if } q_0 \notin F \end{cases}$$

and $F' = Q \times \{A\}$. We also define δ' as follows: if $\delta(q, a, X) = (p, \gamma)$ for $a \in \Sigma$, then

$$\delta'([q, y], a, X) := \begin{cases} ([p, y], \gamma), & \text{if } p \in F; \\ ([p, n], \gamma), & \text{if } p \notin F; \end{cases}$$

$$\delta'([q, A], a, X) := \begin{cases} ([p, y], \gamma), & \text{if } p \in F; \\ ([p, n], \gamma), & \text{if } p \notin F; \end{cases}$$

$$\delta'([q, n], \epsilon, X) := ([q, A], X).$$

If $\delta(q, \epsilon, X) = (p, \gamma)$, then

$$\delta'([q, y], \epsilon, X) := ([p, y], \gamma)$$

$$\delta'([q, n], \epsilon, X) := \begin{cases} ([p, y], \gamma), & \text{if } p \in F; \\ ([p, n], \gamma), & \text{if } p \notin F; \end{cases}$$

We now argue that $L(M') = \overline{L(M)}$. To see this, suppose $x = a_1 a_2 \cdots a_n \in L(M)$. Then M enters a final state after reading a_n. In this case, the second component of the simulating M' will be y and cannot enter a state with second component A before the next input symbol. Hence, x is not accepted by M'. If $x \notin L(M)$, then M never enters a final state after reading a_n. In this case, the second component of the simulating M' will be n, and eventually all ϵ-moves will be exhausted, and the machine will attempt to read a "real" input. At this point the second component is changed to A and M' accepts. ∎

Theorem 4.7.2 is an important tool in proving languages not DCFLs.

Example 4.7.3. Let us prove that the language

$$L := \{w \in \{a, b\}^* \ : \ w \neq xx \text{ for all } x \in \{a, b\}^*\}$$

is not a DCFL.

Assume that L is a DCFL. Then

$$\overline{L} = \{xx \ : \ x \in \{a, b\}^*\}$$

is a DCFL, since DCFLs are closed under complement. Now every DCFL is a CFL, so $\overline{L}$ is a CFL. But $\overline{L}$ is not a CFL by the pumping lemma (see Exercise 1.16).

Sometimes Theorem 4.7.2 is of no help in proving that a particular CFL is not a DCFL. For example, consider $\text{PAL} = \{x \in \{a, b\}^* \ : \ x = x^R\}$, the palindrome language. Now $\overline{\text{PAL}}$ is also a CFL—see Exercise 1.22—so Theorem 4.7.2 alone cannot be used to show that PAL is not a DCFL. In these cases the following theorem may be useful.

Theorem 4.7.4. *Let $L \subseteq \Sigma^*$ be a language such that each Myhill–Nerode equivalence class is of finite cardinality. Then L is not a DCFL.*

Proof. Suppose L is a DCFL. Then, by Lemma 4.7.1, there exists a DPDA M accepting L that scans its entire input. It is now easy to modify this DPDA so that every move is either a pop or a push; it never replaces a symbol X on top of the stack with a string of the form γY with $X \neq Y$ (see Exercise 26).

Let $x \in \Sigma^*$. Let y_x be a string such that the height of M's stack after processing $x y_x$ is as small as possible. Our assumption about the moves of M now implies that after processing $x y_x$, M never pops or changes any of the symbols currently on the stack. Note that we could have $x y_x = z y_z$ for $x \neq z$, but there are still infinitely many strings of the form $u = x y_x$ for which after processing u, M never pops or changes any of the symbols currently on the stack.

From these infinitely many strings, by the infinite pigeonhole principle, there must be an infinite subset of the strings u such that M is in the same state after processing u (including any ϵ-moves needed to minimize the stack height). Further, there must be an infinite subset of *these* strings such that the top stack symbol after processing u is the same. Finally, there must be an infinite subset of *these* strings such that either all of them are in L or all of them are in $\overline{L}$. Thus there is an infinite set S of strings $\{u_1, u_2, \ldots\}$ such that

$$(q_0, u_i, Z_0) \overset{*}{\vdash} (q, \epsilon, A\alpha_i)$$

for some $q \in Q$, $\alpha_i \in \Gamma^*$, $A \in \Gamma$, and all $i \geq 1$, where this is a derivation of minimal stack height. Hence for all $z \in \Sigma^+$ and all $i \geq 1$, we have

$$(q_0, u_i z, Z_0) \overset{*}{\vdash} (q, z, A\alpha_i).$$

Since A is never popped from the stack in this computation, the α_i cannot contribute in any way to future configurations. It follows that, for $z \neq \epsilon$, and for all i and j, M accepts $u_i z$ if and only if it accepts $u_j z$. On the other hand, M accepts u_i if and only if it accepts u_j because we chose the set S such that either $S \subseteq L$ or $S \subseteq \overline{L}$. Hence all the (infinitely many) u_i are in the same Myhill–Nerode equivalence class for L, a contradiction. ∎

Corollary 4.7.5. *The language* PAL $= \{x \in \{a, b\}^* : x = x^R\}$ *is not a DCFL.*

Proof. We leave it to the reader as Exercise 27 to verify that in the Myhill–Nerode equivalence relation for PAL, every string is in an equivalence class by itself. ∎

4.8 Linear languages

There is an interesting subclass of the CFLs known as the *linear languages*. To define them we first define the notion of a linear grammar. A *linear grammar* is one in which no right-hand side of any production contains more than one occurrence of a variable. A language is linear if it has a linear grammar.

Example 4.8.1. The language ODDPAL $= \{x \in \{a, b\}^* : x = x^R$ and $|x|$ is odd$\}$ from Section 1.5 is linear, since it is generated by the linear grammar

$$S \to a$$
$$S \to b$$
$$S \to aSa$$
$$S \to bSb.$$

The following is a pumping lemma for linear languages.

Lemma 4.8.2. *If L is linear, then there exists a constant n such that if $z \in L$ with $|z| \geq n$, then there exists a decomposition $z = uvwxy$ with $|uvxy| \leq n$ and $|vx| \geq 1$ such that $uv^i wx^i y \in L$ for all $i \geq 0$.*

Proof. We can assume that G contains no unit productions, for otherwise we may remove them using the algorithm of Exercise 1.27, without changing the fact that the grammar is linear.

Let k be the number of variables in G, and let t be the length of the longest right-hand side of any production. We may take $n = (k + 1)t$. If $z \in L$, and $|z| \geq n$, then it is easy to see that a parse tree for z must contain some variable twice. Tracing down from the root of the parse tree, we see further that this repeated variable—call it A—must occur within the first $k + 1$ variables starting from the top. Thus we have

$$S \stackrel{*}{\Longrightarrow} uAy,$$

$$A \stackrel{*}{\Longrightarrow} vAx,$$

$$A \stackrel{*}{\Longrightarrow} w$$

for some strings u, v, w, x, y, and these last two derivations represent sentential forms derived from the closest A to the top and the second closest, respectively. Then the total distance from S to the second A from the top is a path of length at most k, so $|uvxy| \leq (k + 1)t = n$. Similarly, since G contains no unit productions, we must have $|vx| \geq 1$. Then, combining the derivations, we get

$$S \stackrel{*}{\Longrightarrow} uAy \stackrel{*}{\Longrightarrow} uv^i Ax^i y \stackrel{*}{\Longrightarrow} uv^i wx^i y$$

for all $i \geq 0$, and hence $uv^i wx^i y \in L$, as desired. ∎

We now give an example of a nonlinear CFL.

Example 4.8.3. We claim that $L = \{a^i b^i c^j d^j : i, j \geq 0\}$ is a CFL that is not linear.

To see this, use Lemma 4.8.2. Assume L is linear. Let $z = a^n b^n c^n d^n$, where n is the constant in the lemma. Consider decompositions of the form $z = uvwxy$ with $|uvxy| \leq n$ and $|vx| \geq 1$. Then we must have $v \in a^*$, $x \in d^*$. Hence, pumping with $i = 2$, we get $z' := uv^2 wx^2 y = a^{n+k} b^n c^n d^{n+l}$, where $k = |v|$, $l = |x|$, and $k + l \geq 1$, and $z' \notin L$. It follows that L is not linear.

4.9 Exercises

1. Prove that if $L = \{a^n b^n c^n : n \geq 0\}$, then $\overline{L}$ is context-free but L is not.
2. Give an example of a DCFL that is not regular.
3. Let L be a CFL. Which of the following are always CFLs?
   (a) $\frac{1}{2}L = \{x : \text{there exists } y, |y| = |x|, \text{ with } xy \in L\}$.
   (b) $L^{1/2} = \{x : xx \in L\}$.
   (c) $\{x : x^* \subseteq L\}$.
4. Let
$$L = \{w \in \{a, b\}^* : |w|_a = 2^n;\ |w|_b = 2^{n+1}\} \text{ for some } n \geq 0.$$

   Show that neither L nor $\overline{L}$ is context-free.
5. Suppose $G = (V, \Sigma, P, S)$ is a context-free grammar generating a CFL L. Show how to create a grammar G' to generate $\text{pref}(L)$, where
$$\text{pref}(L) = \{x \in \Sigma^* : \exists y \text{ such that } xy \in L\}.$$

6. (a) Prove or disprove that
$$L_3 = \{a^i b^j a^i b^j a^i b^j : i, j \geq 1\}$$

   is the intersection of two CFLs.
   (b) Generalizing (a), prove or disprove the same result (intersection of two CFLs) for
$$L_k = \{a^{i_1} b^{j_1} a^{i_2} b^{j_2} \cdots a^{i_k} b^{j_k} : i_1 = i_2 = \cdots = i_k \geq 1;$$
$$j_1 = j_2 = \cdots = j_k \geq 1\},$$

   for each $k \geq 2$.
7. Is the class of CFLs closed under the shuffle operation shuff (introduced in Section 3.3)? How about perfect shuffle?
8. If $\text{shuff}(L, \{0\})$ is a CFL, need L be a CFL?
9. Recall the definition of $\sigma(L)$ from Exercise 3.26: let $L \subseteq \Sigma^*$ be a language, and define $\sigma(L) = \{x \in \Sigma^* : xy \in L \text{ for } \underline{\text{all}}\ y \in \Sigma^*\}$. If L is context-free, must $\sigma(L)$ also be context-free?
10. Let w be the infinite word
$$w = a_1 a_2 \cdots = 1110100100001 \cdots\ ;$$

    here $a_k = 1$ if $k = F_n$ for some n, and $a_k = 0$ otherwise. Here F_n is the nth Fibonacci number, defined by $F_0 = 0$, $F_1 = 1$, and $F_n = F_{n-1} + F_{n-2}$ for $n \geq 2$. Show that the language of all finite prefixes of w
$$\{\epsilon, 1, 11, 111, 1110, 11101, \ldots\}$$

    is a co-CFL; that is, its complement is a CFL.

11. In early versions of FORTRAN, a string constant was written $d(n)Ha_1a_2 \cdots a_n$, where $d(n)$ is the decimal representation of n, and each $a_i \in \Sigma$, for some finite alphabet of legitimate characters Σ. Show that the language of all such strings is not context-free.

12. A *pure context-free grammar* (PCF grammar) is one where there is no distinction between variables and terminals; everything is a terminal. A production rewrites a single terminal as a string of terminals, possibly empty. More formally, G is a PCF grammar if $G = (\Sigma, P, S)$, where Σ is the set of terminals, P the set of productions, and S a finite set of words. Then $L(G)$, the language generated by G, is defined to be

$$L(G) = \{x \in \Sigma^* \ : \ \text{for some } s \in S, \ s \stackrel{*}{\Longrightarrow} x\}.$$

For example, the PCF grammar given by

$$(\{a, b\}, \{s \rightarrow asb\}, \{asb\})$$

generates the language

$$\{a^n sb^n \ : \ n \geq 1\}.$$

(a) Prove the following lemma. Suppose $L \subseteq \{a, b\}^*$ satisfies the following three conditions: (i) L is infinite; (ii) every word in L contains a^3 and b^3 as subwords; and (iii) there exists a real constant $c > 0$ such that each word $w \in L$ contains some subword y, $|y| \geq c|w|$, and y does not contain two consecutive occurrences of the same letter. Then L is not generated by a PCF grammar.

(b) Use (a) to prove that $a^3b^3(ab)^*$ is a regular language that is not generated by any PCF grammar.

13. The *census generating function* of a language L is defined to be $\sum_{n \geq 0} t_n X^n$, where t_n counts the number of distinct strings in L of length n. Give an example of a linear language for which the census generating function is not rational.

**14. Let L be a language over $\{0, 1, \ldots, k - 1\}$ for some integer $k \geq 1$. The language of minimal words of L, $M(L)$, is defined by taking the union of the lexicographically least word of each length (if it exists). Show that $M(L)$ is context-free if L is.

15. Let $G = (V, \Sigma, P, S)$ be a context-free grammar.
    (a) Prove that the language of all sentential forms derivable from S is context-free.
    (b) Prove that the language consisting of all sentential forms derivable by a leftmost derivation from S is context-free.

*16. Recall that a word $w \in \Sigma^*$ is said to be *unbordered* if it cannot be written in the form xyx, where $|x| \geq 1$ and $|y| \geq 0$. For example, the word 001 is unbordered, but 0010 is not (take $x = 0$ and $y = 01$). Define

$$P = \{x \in \{0, 1\}^* \; : \; x \text{ is unbordered}\}.$$

Show that P is not context-free. *Hint:* Use Ogden's lemma.

17. Suppose L is an inherently ambiguous CFL. Then we know that for every context-free grammar G with $L = L(G)$, at least one word in L has at least two different derivations in G. Show that in fact *infinitely* many words in L must have at least two different derivations in G.

18. Show that if L is a CFL and R is a regular language, then the quotient L/R is a CFL.

19. Let $u, v, w, x, y \in \Sigma^*$, and define

$$L = L(u, v, w, x, y) = \{uv^i wx^i y \; : \; i \geq 0\}.$$

Show that for all u, v, w, x, y, the language $\overline{L}$ is context-free.

20. Let # be a symbol not contained in the alphabet $\Sigma = \{a, b\}$, and consider the language

$$L = \{x\#y \; : \; x, y \in \Sigma^* \text{ and } x \text{ is not a subword of } y\}.$$

Prove or disprove that L is not a CFL.

21. Let # be a symbol not contained in the alphabet $\Sigma = \{a, b\}$, and consider the language

$$L = \{x\#y \; : \; x, y \in \Sigma^* \text{ and } x \text{ is not a subsequence of } y\}.$$

(Recall from Section 3.12 that we say x is a subsequence of y if x can be obtained by striking out 0 or more letters from y.) Prove or disprove that L is a CFL.

22. Suppose we modify our PDA model as follows: instead of requiring $\delta(q, a, A)$ to be a finite set $\{(q_1, \gamma_1), \ldots, (q_k, \gamma_k)\}$ representing the nondeterministic choices of the PDA, we allow the PDA to nondeterministically choose among a potentially *infinite* set, but this set must be context-free. More formally, we allow

$$\delta(q, a, A) = (q_1 \times L_1) \cup (q_2 \times L_2) \cup \cdots \cup (q_k \times L_k),$$

where each L_i is a CFL. We accept by empty stack. Prove or disprove that the class of languages accepted by these more powerful PDAs is precisely the class of CFLs.

*23. Recall the definition of inverse substitution from Exercise 3.15. Are the CFLs closed under inverse substitution? That is, let L be a CFL, and let s be a substitution that maps each letter a to a CFL L_a. Define

$$s^{-1}(L) = \{x \ : \ s(x) \subseteq L\}.$$

Must $s^{-1}(L)$ be context-free? How about if s maps letters to finite sets?

24. Recall the alternate definition of inverse substitution from Exercise 3.16:

$$s^{[-1]}(L) := \{x \ : \ s(x) \cap L \neq \emptyset\}.$$

Suppose s maps letters to regular languages and L is context-free. Must $s^{[-1]}(L)$ be context-free? How about if s maps letters to CFLs?

*25. Let $\alpha \geq 0$ be a real number, and define $L_\alpha = \{a^i \ b^j \ : \ i/j \leq \alpha, \ i \geq 0, \ j \geq 1\}$. Prove that L_α is context-free if and only if α is rational.

26. Show that, given a PDA M, there exists a PDA M' with the property that M' has no moves of the form $(p, \gamma Y) \in \delta(q, a, X)$ with $X \neq Y$. That is, all of the moves of M' either pop a symbol or push a string of symbols on top of the stack; none replaces the current symbol on top of the stack. Show further that if M is a DPDA, then M' can be constructed to be a DPDA, too.

27. Show that in the Myhill–Nerode equivalence relation for PAL, every string is in an equivalence class by itself.

28. Give an example of a CFL with an unambiguous grammar that is not a DCFL.

29. (T. Biedl) *Clickomania* is a game whose goal is to remove all the colored squares in an array. Squares are removed by clicking on a connected set of at least two squares of the same color and then these disappear (see http://www.clickomania.ch for more information). Consider a simplified version where the squares are arranged in a $1 \times n$ array and come in only two colors, a and b. A string of a's and b's is *solvable* if there is some choice of moves that reduces it to the empty string. For example, abbaaba can be reduced to the empty string as follows, where the underline portion denotes the part that is removed at each step:

$$\text{abb\underline{aa}ba} \rightarrow \text{a\underline{bbb}a} \rightarrow \underline{\text{aa}} \rightarrow \epsilon.$$

Show that CL, the language of all solvable strings, is a CFL.

*30. Let $M = (Q, \Sigma, \Gamma, \delta, q_0, Z_0, \emptyset)$ be a PDA that accepts by *empty stack*. Further, assume that every move of M is either a pop move or a move where a *single* symbol is pushed on top of the current stack contents.

(a) Suppose M accepts ϵ, the empty string. Prove that there must be an accepting computation for ϵ where the maximum stack height during the computation is $\leq |Q|^2|\Gamma|$.

(b) How close to the bound $|Q|^2|\Gamma|$ can you come?

31. Compute $\psi(L_7)$, where ψ is the Parikh map and $L_7 = \{x \in \{0, 1\}^* : x$ is not of the form $ww\}$.

32. If ψ is the Parikh map, find some examples of long English words w and suitable subsets of the alphabet for which:

(a) $\psi(w)$ has all entries equal to 1;

(b) $\psi(w)$ has all entries equal to 2;

(c) $\psi(w)$ has all entries equal to 3;

(d) $\psi(w)$ has all entries ≥ 2;

(e) $\psi(w)$ is a permutation of $(1, 2, 3, \ldots, n)$;

(f) $\psi(w)$ is a permutation of $(1, 2, 2, 3, 3, 3, \ldots, \overbrace{n}^{n})$.

33. In this exercise we will construct a CFL such that none of its Myhill–Nerode equivalence classes is context-free. Let

$$L = \{x \in \{a, b, c\}^* : |x|_a \neq |x|_b \text{ or } |x|_b \neq |x|_c \text{ or } |x|_a \neq |x|_c\}.$$

(a) Explain why L is context-free.

(b) Define $\gamma(x) = (|x|_a - |x|_b, |x|_b - |x|_c)$. Show that $\gamma(xy) = \gamma(x) + \gamma(y)$.

(c) Show that $x \notin L$ if and only if $\gamma(x) = (0, 0)$.

(d) Show that for all pairs of integers (i, j), there exists a string $x \in \{a, b, c\}^*$ such that $\gamma(x) = (i, j)$.

(e) Show that x is related to y under the Myhill–Nerode equivalence relation for L if and only if $\gamma(x) = \gamma(y)$.

(f) Show that each Myhill–Nerode equivalence relation for L is not context-free.

34. Show that the following morphism is *squarefree-preserving*, that is, x is squarefree if and only if $h(x)$ is squarefree.

$$0 \to \texttt{abacabcacbabcbacabacbc}$$

$$1 \to \texttt{abacabcacbcabcbabcacbc}$$

$$2 \to \texttt{abacabcbabcacbabcbacbc}$$

$$3 \to \texttt{abacabcbabcacbcabcbabc}$$

$$4 \to \texttt{abacabcbacabacbabcacbc}$$

$$5 \to \texttt{abacabcbacbcacbabcacbc}.$$

*35. Use the interchange lemma to prove that the following languages are not context-free over a sufficiently large alphabet:

(a) the language of all strings containing at least one overlap;

(b) the language of all strings containing at least one cube;

(c) the language of all strings containing at least one abelian square. (An abelian square is a string of the form xx', where x' is a permutation of x.)

*36. Is the class of CFLs closed under the cyc operation introduced in Section 3.4?

37. Recall the definition of perm(L) from Exercise 3.13.

(a) Give an example of a regular language L such that perm(L) is not context-free.

(b) Show that if L is a regular language over an alphabet of two symbols, then perm(L) is context-free.

*38. For strings x, w of equal length, define match(x, y) to be the number of indices i such that $a_i = b_i$, where $x = a_1 a_2 \cdots a_n$ and $y = b_1 b_2 \cdots b_n$. Define

$$L = \{y \in \Sigma^* \ : \ y = xw, |x| = |w|, \text{ and } \operatorname{match}(x, w) \geq 2\}.$$

Is L context-free? Your answer may depend on the cardinality of Σ.

*39. We say a word $w \in \Sigma^*$ is *balanced* if $||u|_a - |v|_a| \leq 1$ for all subwords u, v of w, with $|u| = |v|$, and all $a \in \Sigma$; otherwise w is *unbalanced*. For example, 01101 is balanced and 1100 is unbalanced.

(a) Prove that $w \in \{0, 1\}^*$ is unbalanced if and only if there exists a palindrome x such that w contains both $0x0$ and $1x1$ as subwords.

(b) Prove that the set of unbalanced words over $\{0, 1\}$ is context-free.

40. Recall the definition of $h^{-*}(L)$ from Exercise 3.71. If L is context-free, need $h^{-*}(L)$ be context-free?

41. Prove that the language of all words over $\{0, 1\}$ that are *not* prefixes of the Thue–Morse word is context-free. Generalize.

42. For a language L, define llc(L) to be the union of the lexicographically least conjugate of each member of L. Give an example of a regular language L over a two-letter alphabet such that llc(L) is not context-free.

43. For a language L, define llp(L) to be the union of the lexicographically least permutation of each member of L. Show that if L is a regular language over a two-letter alphabet, then llp(L) is context-free, while if L is over a larger alphabet, then llp(L) need not be context-free.

4.10 Projects

1. Find out about applications of the theory of formal languages to the study of natural languages, such as English. You can start with Shieber [1985] and Gazdar, Klein, Pullum, and Sag [1985].
2. Find out more about the class of languages that can be expressed as the intersection of a finite number of CFLs. What are the closure properties of this class? You can start with the paper of Liu and Weiner [1973].
3. Find out about graph grammars, a combination of formal language theory and graph theory. An immense survey is the three-volume compendium of Rozenberg [1997], Ehrig, Engels, Kreowski, and Rozenberg [1999], and Ehrig, Kreowski, Montanari, and Rozenberg [1999].

4.11 Research problems

1. Given CFLs L_1, and L_2 with $L_1 \subset L_2$ and $L_2 - L_1$ infinite, need there be a CFL L_3 with $L_1 \subset L_3 \subset L_2$ such that both $L_2 - L_3$ and $L_3 - L_1$ are infinite? This question is due to Bucher [1980].
2. Are the primitive words over $\{0, 1\}$ context-free? This classic problem has been open for at least 20 years.
3. Let $p(n)$ be a polynomial with rational coefficients such that $p(n) \in \mathbb{N}$ for all $n \in N$. Prove or disprove that the language of the base-k representations of all integers in $\{p(n) : n \geq 0\}$ is context-free if and only if the degree of p is ≤ 1.

4.12 Notes on Chapter 4

4.1 Theorem 4.1.6 is due to Ginsburg and Spanier [1963]. Our proof is new.

4.2 The theorem in this section is due to Ginsburg and Rice [1962], although our proof is different.

4.3 For Ogden's lemma, see Ogden [1968]. There are very few techniques known for proving languages not context-free. Another is the method of Bader and Moura [1982].

4.4 Theorem 4.4.1 is originally due to Maurer [1969]. Our proof is from Du and Ko [2001, pp. 149–150].
The result on the optimality of the triple construction is from Goldstine, Price, and Wotschke [1982a, b].

4.5 For the interchange lemma, see Main [1982], Ross and Winklmann [1982], Gabarro [1985], and (especially) Ogden, Ross, and Winklmann

[1985]. Boonyavatana and Slutzki [1988] compared the power of the interchange and pumping lemmas. The morphism h is from Brandenburg [1983].

4.6 Parikh's theorem was originally proved by Parikh in an obscure 1961 technical report. It later appeared as Parikh [1966]. Our proof is based on Goldstine [1977]. Also see Pilling [1973]. The second proof in Example 4.6.6 is from Du and Ko [2001, pp. 153–154].

For the closure of semilinear sets under intersection and complement, see Ginsburg [1966]. No really simple proof of this result seems to be known.

4.7 For more on DCFLs, see Fischer [1963], Schützenberger [1963], and Ginsburg and Greibach [1966].

A weaker version of Theorem 4.7.4 was observed by M. Van Biesbrouck (personal communication) after reading a similar theorem given in Martin [1997].

4.8 For the linear languages, see Ginsburg and Spanier [1966].

5

Parsing and recognition

In this chapter we investigate methods for parsing and recognition in context-free grammars (CFGs). Both problems have significant practical applications. Parsing, for example, is an essential feature of a compiler, which translates from one computer language (the "source") to another (the "target"). Typically, the source is a high-level language, while the target is machine language.

The first compilers were built in the early 1950s. Computing pioneer Grace Murray Hopper built one at Remington Rand during 1951–1952. At that time, constructing a compiler was a black art that was very time consuming. When John Backus led the project that produced a FORTRAN compiler in 1955–1957, it took 18 person-years to complete.

Today, modern parser generators, such as Yacc (which stands for "yet another compiler-compiler") and Bison, allow a single person to construct a compiler in a few hours or days. These tools are based on LALR(1) parsing, a variant of one of the parsing methods we will discuss here. Parsing is also a feature of natural language recognition systems.

In Section 5.1 we will see how to accomplish parsing in an arbitrary CFG in polynomial time. More precisely, if the grammar G is in Chomsky normal form, we can parse an arbitrary string $w \in L(G)$ of length n in $O(n^3)$ time. While a running time of $O(n^3)$ is often considered tractable in computer science, as programs get bigger and bigger, it becomes more and more essential that parsing be performed in linear time.

Can general grammars be parsed faster than cubic time? Yes, Valiant has shown that parsing can be reduced to matrix multiplication. Since it is known how to multiply two $n \times n$ matrices in $O(n^{2.376})$ steps, we can parse general grammars within this time bound. But this method is not likely to be useful for any grammars that people actually use, since it is quite complicated and the hidden constant is large.

It is currently not known if general grammars can be parsed in $O(n^2)$ time, so computer scientists instead have turned to restricting the class of grammars so that linear-time parsing can be achieved. Because of its importance to computer science, it should come as no surprise to learn that many different parsing methods have been proposed. The two main paradigms are *top-down parsing*, where we begin with the start symbol S of the grammar and attempt to determine the correct sequence of productions in a derivation starting with S, and *bottom-up parsing*, where we begin with the string w and attempt to construct a derivation by doing the productions "in reverse" until we wind up with S.

Although top-down parsing may seem more natural, it appears to be less powerful and is less often used in practice. Nevertheless, understanding its principles is instructive and we cover this topic in Section 5.3.

Most modern parser generators use a form of bottom-up parsing. We discuss bottom-up parsing in Section 5.5.

5.1 Recognition and parsing in general grammars

Suppose we are given an CFG grammar $G = (V, \Sigma, P, S)$ and we wish to determine, given a string w, whether $w \in L(G)$. This problem is less general than parsing, since we do not demand that the algorithm produce the parse tree if indeed $w \in L(G)$.

First, we convert G to Chomsky normal form (see Exercise 1.28).

Next, we use a dynamic programming algorithm due (independently) to Cocke, Younger, and Kasami, and often called the CYK algorithm. Let us write $w = a_1 a_2 \cdots a_n$ and $w[i..j] = a_i \cdots a_j$. Suppose we are trying to determine whether $A \overset{*}{\Longrightarrow} w[i..j]$. Since G is in Chomsky normal form, this is easy: if $i = j$, then we just need to check to see if $A \to a_i$ is a production in P. If $i < j$, then the first step of the derivation must look like $A \to BC$ for some variables $B, C \in V$. This implies that there exists k such that $B \overset{*}{\Longrightarrow} w[i..k]$ and $C \overset{*}{\Longrightarrow} w[k+1..j]$.

These observations suggest the following dynamic programming algorithm: determine, for all variables $A \in V$ and subwords y of w, whether $A \overset{*}{\Longrightarrow} y$. We do this in order of increasing length of y.

CYK(G, w)

Input: $G = (V, \Sigma, P, S)$ is a context-free grammar in Chomsky normal form,
    $w = a_1 a_2 \cdots a_n$ is a string

Output: $U[i, j]$ contains all variables A such that $A \overset{*}{\Longrightarrow} a_i \cdots a_j$

for $i := 1$ to n do
        $U[i, i] := \{A \in V \ : \ A \to a_i \text{ is a production}\}$
for $d := 1$ to $n - 1$ do
        for $i := 1$ to $n - d$ do
                $j := i + d$
                $U[i, j] := \emptyset$
                for $k := i$ to $j - 1$ do
                        $U[i, j] := U[i, j] \cup \{A \in V \ : \ A \to BC \text{ is a production}$
                                and $B \in U[i, k]$ and $C \in U[k + 1, j]\}$
if $(S \in U[1, n])$ then
                return(true)
else
                return(false)

Theorem 5.1.1. *Given a CFG G in Chomsky normal form and an input w of length n, we can determine in $O(n^3)$ steps whether $w \in L(G)$. Here the constant in the big-O may depend on G.*

Proof. The CYK algorithm has three nested loops. Each loop is executed at most n times.   ∎

Example 5.1.2. Let us look at an example. Consider the following grammar in Chomsky normal form:

$$S \to AB \mid \text{b}$$
$$A \to CB \mid AA \mid \text{a}$$
$$B \to AS \mid \text{b}$$
$$C \to BS \mid \text{c}.$$

For the input cabab, the CYK algorithm fills in the table, as follows:

$i \backslash j$	1	2	3	4	5
1	C	$\emptyset$	A	A	S, B
2		A	S, B	$\emptyset$	C
3			S, B	$\emptyset$	C
4				A	S, B
5					S, B

Since S is in $U[1, 5]$, it follows that cabab $\in L(G)$.

We can modify the preceding CYK algorithm to produce parse trees for strings in $L(G)$. To do so, we add a new array $CYK[A, i, j]$. The intent is that $CYK[A, i, j]$ contains the triple (B, C, k) if there exists a derivation $A \stackrel{*}{\Longrightarrow} w[i..j]$ whose first step is $A \Longrightarrow BC$ and such that $B \stackrel{*}{\Longrightarrow} w[i..k]$ and $C \stackrel{*}{\Longrightarrow} w[k + 1..j]$. We use a procedure called maketree that takes a variable A and a set of strings $\gamma_1, \gamma_2, \ldots, \gamma_l$ as arguments and returns a tree with A as the root and the γ's as children.

CYK-Make-Parse-Table(G, w)
Input: $G = (V, \Sigma, P, S)$ is a context-free grammar in Chomsky normal form
  $w = a_1 a_2 \cdots a_n$ is a string
for $i := 1$ to n do
  $U[i, i] := \{A \in V \ : \ A \to a_i$ is a production$\}$
for all variables $A \in V$, indices i, j with $1 \le i \le j \le n$
  set $CYK[A, i, j] :=$ the empty list
for $d := 1$ to $n - 1$ do
  for $i := 1$ to $n - d$ do
  $j := i + d$
  $U[i, j] := \emptyset$
  for $k := i$ to $j - 1$ do
    $U[i, j] := U[i, j] \cup \{A \in V \ : \ A \to BC$ is a production
        and $B \in U[i, k]$ and $C \in U[k + 1, j]\}$
    For each $A \to BC$ just added, append (B, C, k) to the list
        $CYK[A, i, j]$

Buildtree(A, i, j)
if $i = j$ then
  return(maketree$(A \to a_i)$) for some production $A \to a_i$
else if $CYK[A, i, j] = \emptyset$
  then error
else
  choose an element (B, C, k) from $CYK[A, i, j]$
  $l :=$ Buildtree(B, i, k)
  $r :=$ Buildtree$(C, k + 1, j)$
  return(maketree$(A \to l, r)$)

CYK-Parse(G, w)
1. Call CYK-Make-Parse-Table(G, w)
2. Return Buildtree$(S, 1, |w|)$

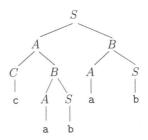

Figure 5.1: A parse tree for the string cabab

Theorem 5.1.3. *We can produce a parse tree for a string generated by a CFG in Chomsky normal form in $O(n^3)$ steps, where n is the length of the string.*

Proof. Left to the reader. ∎

Example 5.1.4. Let us continue Example 5.1.2. For the input cabab, the CYK-Make-Parse-Table algorithm creates the following entries:

$i\backslash j$	1	2	3	4	5
1	C	$\emptyset$	$A : (C, B, 1)$	$A : (A, A, 3)$	$S : (A, B, 3), (A, B, 4)$ $B : (A, S, 3), (A, S, 4)$
2		A	$S : (A, B, 2)$ $B : (A, S, 2)$	$\emptyset$	$C : (B, S, 3)$
3			S, B	$\emptyset$	$C : (B, S, 3)$
4				A	$S : (A, B, 4)$ $B : (A, S, 4)$
5					S, B

One resulting parse tree is shown in Figure 5.1.

5.2 Earley's method

Earley's method is a general parsing method that runs in $O(n^3)$ time on general grammars, $O(n^2)$ time on unambiguous grammars, and can be modified to run in linear time on LR(1) grammars.

Like the CYK parsing algorithm, it works in two stages. First, it builds a parsing table for the input string. Once this is complete, we can recognize whether the input is in $L(G)$ or not. Next, we can use the information in the parsing table to construct a parse tree for w.

We start with the construction of the parsing table. The table is an array $M = (M_{i,j})_{0 \le i \le j \le n}$, where $w = a_1 a_2 \cdots a_n$ is the input and $G = (V, \Sigma, P, S)$

is the grammar. Each entry holds a number of *items*, which are objects of the form $A \to \alpha \bullet \beta$, where $A \to \alpha\beta$ is a production of P. The $\bullet$ serves as a placeholder. An item is said to be *complete* if it is of the form $A \to \alpha\bullet$.

The goal is to generate the entries of the table M such that the item $A \to \alpha \bullet \beta$ is in $M_{i,j}$ if and only if the production $A \to \alpha\beta$ is in P and there exists $\delta \in (V \cup \Sigma)^*$ such that

$$S \overset{*}{\Longrightarrow} a_1 a_2 \cdots a_i A\delta \quad \text{and} \quad \alpha \overset{*}{\Longrightarrow} a_{i+1} \cdots a_j \tag{5.1}$$

both hold.

Once this is done, we can recognize whether $w \in L(G)$ quickly, as follows.

Lemma 5.2.1. *We have $w \in L(G)$ if and only if there exists an item of the form $S \to \alpha\bullet \in M_{0,n}$.*

Proof. If $w \in L(G)$, then there is a derivation of the form $S \Longrightarrow \alpha \overset{*}{\Longrightarrow} w$. Now (5.1) is satisfied for $i = 0$, $A = S$, $\delta = \epsilon$, and $j = n$, so $S \to \alpha\bullet \in M_{0,n}$.

On the other hand, if $S \to \alpha\bullet \in M_{0,n}$, then $\alpha \overset{*}{\Longrightarrow} a_1 a_2 \cdots a_n$ and $S \to \alpha$ is a production of P, so putting these together we get $S \overset{*}{\Longrightarrow} w$. ∎

The following algorithm constructs the parsing table:

`Make-Earley-Table`

A. Add $S \to \bullet\gamma$ to $M_{0,0}$ for all productions $S \to \gamma$ in P.

Do the following steps until no more items can be added to M:

    B. If $M_{i,j}$ contains $A \to \alpha \bullet a_{j+1}\beta$, then add $A \to \alpha a_{j+1} \bullet \beta$ to $M_{i,j+1}$;

    C. If $M_{i,j}$ contains $A \to \alpha \bullet B\beta$ and $M_{j,k}$ contains $B \to \gamma\bullet$, then add $A \to \alpha B \bullet \beta$ to $M_{i,k}$;

    D. If $M_{i,j}$ contains $A \to \alpha \bullet B\beta$, then add $B \to \bullet\gamma$ to $M_{j,j}$ for all $B \to \gamma$ in P.

Example 5.2.2. Consider the following grammar, where S is the start symbol:

$$S \to T{+}S$$
$$S \to T$$
$$T \to F{*}T$$
$$T \to F$$
$$F \to (S)$$
$$F \to \mathsf{a}.$$

This grammar generates some simple algebraic expressions over the alphabet $\Sigma = \{\mathsf{a}, +, *, (,)\}$.

Consider applying Earley's algorithm to $w = (\text{a} + \text{a}) * \text{a}$. We can, if we choose, do the algorithm in order of increasing j. Initially, by step A, we put

$$S \to \bullet T + S \quad \text{and} \quad S \to \bullet T \text{ in } M_{0,0}.$$

Then, by step D, we put

$$T \to \bullet F * T \quad \text{and} \quad T \to \bullet F \text{ in } M_{0,0}.$$

Finally, by step D again, we put

$$F \to \bullet(S) \quad \text{and} \quad F \to \bullet \text{a in } M_{0,0}.$$

Next, by step B we put

$$F \to (\bullet S) \text{ in } M_{0,1}.$$

By step D we put

$$S \to \bullet T + S \quad \text{and} \quad S \to \bullet T \text{ in } M_{1,1}.$$

Then by step D we add, successively,

$$T \to \bullet F * T, \quad T \to \bullet F, \quad F \to \bullet(S), \quad \text{and} \quad F \to \bullet \text{a to } M_{1,1}.$$

Next, by step B we add

$$F \to \text{a} \bullet \text{ to } M_{1,2}.$$

And so, by step C ($i = 1, j = 1, k = 2$), since $M_{1,1}$ contains $T \to \bullet F * T$ and $M_{1,2}$ contains $F \to \text{a} \bullet$, we add $T \to F \bullet * T$ to $M_{1,2}$.

Eventually, we find the following contents of the parsing table:

$M_{0,0}$	$S \to \bullet T + S$	$S \to \bullet T$	$T \to \bullet F * T$
	$T \to \bullet F$	$F \to \bullet(S)$	$F \to \bullet \text{a}$
$M_{0,1}$	$F \to (\bullet S)$		
$M_{0,2}$	$F \to (S \bullet)$		
$M_{0,4}$	$F \to (S \bullet)$		
$M_{0,5}$	$F \to (S) \bullet$	$S \to T \bullet$	$T \to F \bullet * T$
	$S \to T \bullet + S$	$T \to F \bullet$	
$M_{0,6}$	$T \to F * \bullet T$	$\cdot$	
$M_{0,7}$	$T \to F * T \bullet$	$S \to T \bullet + S$	$S \to T \bullet$
$M_{1,1}$	$S \to \bullet T + S$	$S \to \bullet T$	$T \to \bullet F * T$
	$T \to \bullet F$	$F \to \bullet(S)$	$F \to \bullet \text{a}$
$M_{1,2}$	$F \to \text{a} \bullet$	$T \to F \bullet * T$	$T \to F \bullet$
	$S \to T \bullet + S$	$S \to T \bullet$	
$M_{1,3}$	$S \to T + \bullet S$		
$M_{1,4}$	$S \to T + S \bullet$		
$M_{3,3}$	$S \to \bullet T + S$	$S \to \bullet T$	$T \to \bullet F * T$
	$T \to \bullet F$	$F \to \bullet(S)$	$F \to \bullet \text{a}$
$M_{3,4}$	$F \to \text{a} \bullet$	$T \to F \bullet * T$	$T \to F \bullet$
	$S \to T \bullet + S$	$S \to T \bullet$	
$M_{6,6}$	$T \to \bullet F * T$	$T \to \bullet F$	$F \to \bullet(S)$
	$F \to \bullet \text{a}$		
$M_{6,7}$	$F \to \text{a} \bullet$	$T \to F \bullet * T$	$T \to F \bullet$

The next theorem proves that Earley's method works.

Theorem 5.2.3. *The item $C \to \eta \bullet \gamma$ gets added to $M_{u,v}$ iff the production $C \to \eta\gamma$ is in P, $\eta \overset{*}{\Longrightarrow} w[u+1..v]$, and there exists $\delta \in (V \cup \Sigma)^*$ such that $S \overset{*}{\Longrightarrow} w[1..u]C\delta$.*

Proof. Suppose $C \to \eta \bullet \gamma$ gets added to $M_{u,v}$. We prove the desired result by induction on the number of items currently added in all entries of M.

For the base case, after step A has been performed, we have that $S \to \bullet\gamma$ is in $M_{0,0}$, so $\eta = \epsilon$, $C = S$, and we can take $\delta = \epsilon$.

Now let us prove the induction step. Suppose $C \to \eta \bullet \gamma$ is added to $M_{u,v}$. This can occur in either step B, C, or D of the algorithm.

If it occurs in step B, then $u = i$, $v = j+1$, $\eta = \alpha a_{j+1}$, $\gamma = \beta$, and $A = C$. Then $M_{i,j}$ contains $A \to \alpha \bullet a_{j+1}\beta$, which must have been added at an earlier step. By induction $\alpha \overset{*}{\Longrightarrow} w[i+1..j]$ and $S \overset{*}{\Longrightarrow} w[1..i]A\delta$. Hence, $\eta = \alpha a_{j+1} \overset{*}{\Longrightarrow} w[i+1..j+1]$.

If it occurs in step C, then $\eta = \alpha B$, $\gamma = \beta$, $u = i$, $v = k$, and $C = A$. Then $M_{i,j}$ contains the item $A \to \alpha \bullet B\beta$, which must have been added at an earlier step. By induction, $\alpha \overset{*}{\Longrightarrow} w[i+1..j]$ and $S \overset{*}{\Longrightarrow} w[1..i]A\delta$. Also, $M_{j,k}$ contains $B \to \gamma\bullet$, so by induction $\gamma \overset{*}{\Longrightarrow} w[j+1..k]$. Hence,

$$\eta = \alpha B \overset{*}{\Longrightarrow} w[i+1..j]B$$
$$\Longrightarrow w[i+1..j]\gamma, \quad \text{since } B \to \gamma \text{ is in } P$$
$$\overset{*}{\Longrightarrow} w[i+1..j]w[j+1..k] = w[i+1..k].$$

And we already have $S \overset{*}{\Longrightarrow} w[1..i]A\delta$.

If it occurs in step D, then $\eta = \epsilon$, $C = B$, and $u = v = j$. By induction, $\alpha \overset{*}{\Longrightarrow} w[i+1..j]$ and there exists δ such that $S \overset{*}{\Longrightarrow} w[1..i]A\delta$. Hence,

$$S \overset{*}{\Longrightarrow} w[1..i]A\delta$$
$$\Longrightarrow w[1..i]\alpha B\beta\delta$$
$$\overset{*}{\Longrightarrow} w[1..i]w[i+1..j]B\beta\delta = w[1..j]B\beta\delta.$$

This completes one direction of the proof.

For the other direction, we will prove that $C \to \bullet\eta\gamma \in M_{u,u}$ and $C \to \eta \bullet \gamma \in M_{u,v}$. In order to do this, we prove two lemmas. Let $\mu \in (V \cup \Sigma)^*$.

Lemma 5.2.4. *If $A \to \alpha \bullet \mu\beta$ is in $M_{i,j}$ and $\mu \overset{*}{\Longrightarrow} w[j+1..k]$, then $A \to \alpha\mu \bullet \beta$ is in $M_{i,k}$.*

Proof. By induction on r, the length of the derivation $\mu \overset{*}{\Longrightarrow} w[j+1..k]$.

The base case is $r = 0$. In this case we have $\mu = w[j + 1..k]$ and then $A \to \alpha \bullet w[j + 1..k]\beta \in M_{i,j}$. Hence,

$$A \to \alpha a_{j+1} \bullet w[j + 2..k]\beta \qquad \text{gets added to } M_{i,j+1} \text{ by step B}$$
$$A \to \alpha a_{j+1}a_{j+2} \bullet w[j + 3..k]\beta \qquad \text{gets added to } M_{i,j+2} \text{ by step B}$$
$$\vdots$$
$$A \to \alpha w[j + 1..k] \bullet \beta \qquad \text{gets added to } M_{i,k} \text{ by step B.}$$

For the induction step, assume $r > 0$. Then μ must contain a variable, say, $\mu = \mu_1 B \mu_2$ for $B \in V$. Since $\mu \overset{*}{\Longrightarrow} w[j + 1..k]$, we have

$$\mu_1 \overset{*}{\Longrightarrow} w[j + 1..l]$$
$$B \Longrightarrow \gamma \overset{*}{\Longrightarrow} w[l + 1..m], \quad \text{where } B \to \gamma \text{ is a production}$$
$$\mu_2 \overset{*}{\Longrightarrow} w[m + 1..k]$$

for some integers l, m and the preceding derivations from μ_1, γ, μ_2 each take $<r$ steps. Now $A \to \alpha \bullet \mu\beta \in M_{i,j}$; that is,

$$A \to \alpha \bullet \mu_1 B \mu_2 \beta \in M_{i,j}, \tag{5.2}$$

so

$$A \to \alpha \mu_1 \bullet B \mu_2 \beta \in M_{i,l} \tag{5.3}$$

by induction and (5.2). Now

$$B \to \bullet \gamma \in M_{l,l} \tag{5.4}$$

by step D applied to Eq. (5.3). Hence,

$$B \to \gamma \bullet \in M_{l,m} \tag{5.5}$$

by (5.4) and induction. Now

$$A \to \alpha \mu_1 B \bullet \mu_2 \beta \in M_{i,m} \tag{5.6}$$

by step C and Eqs. (5.3) and (5.5). Finally, $A \to \alpha \mu_1 B \mu_2 \bullet \beta \in M_{i,k}$ by Eq. (5.6) and induction. Thus, Lemma 5.2.4 is proved. ∎

Lemma 5.2.5. *If $S \overset{*}{\Longrightarrow} w[1..i]B\delta$, then $B \to \bullet \gamma \in M_{i,i}$ for all productions $B \to \gamma \in P$.*

Proof. By induction on r, the length of the derivation $S \overset{*}{\Longrightarrow} w[1..i]B\delta$.

The base case is $r = 0$. Then $i = 0$, $S = B$, $\delta = \epsilon$, and by step A we have $S \to \bullet \gamma \in M_{0,0}$ for all productions $S \to \gamma \in P$.

For the induction step, assume $r \geq 1$. Then look at the step of the derivation where the displayed occurrence of B is introduced:

$$S \overset{*}{\Longrightarrow} \mu A \delta_1 \Longrightarrow \mu \alpha B \beta \delta_1 \overset{*}{\Longrightarrow} w[1..i]B\delta,$$

where $A \to \alpha B \beta$ is a production in P and $\mu \alpha \overset{*}{\Longrightarrow} w_1 w_2 \cdots w_i$. Define j so that

$$\mu \overset{*}{\Longrightarrow} w[1..j];$$
$$\alpha \overset{*}{\Longrightarrow} w[j+1..i].$$

Hence, $A \to {\bullet}\alpha B \beta \in M_{j,j}$ by induction applied to the derivation $S \overset{*}{\Longrightarrow} \mu A \delta_1 \overset{*}{\Longrightarrow} w[1..j]A\delta_1$. Hence, $A \to \alpha \bullet B\beta \in M_{j,i}$ by Lemma 5.2.4. Thus, $B \to {\bullet}\gamma \in M_{i,i}$ by step D. ∎

We can now complete the proof of Theorem 5.2.3.

If $\eta \overset{*}{\Longrightarrow} w[u+1..v]$ and there exists a δ such that $S \overset{*}{\Longrightarrow} w[1..u]C\delta$, then $C \to {\bullet}\eta\gamma \in M_{u,u}$ by Lemma 5.2.5. Then $C \to \eta \bullet \gamma \in M_{u,v}$ by Lemma 5.2.4 with $A = C$, $\alpha = \epsilon$, $\mu = \eta$, $\gamma = \beta$, $i = u$, $j = u$, and $k = v$. ∎

Next we prove a theorem about how efficiently Earley's method can be implemented.

Theorem 5.2.6. *The parse table $M = (M_{i,j})$ can be constructed in $O(n^3)$ steps, where $n = |w|$.*

Proof. We compute the table in order of increasing j. It suffices to see that all the entries in $M_{i,j}$ for all i can be computed in $O(n^2)$ steps. There are $O(n)$ possible entries, and for each one we have to do at most $O(n)$ work in step C. ∎

Theorem 5.2.7. *If G is an unambiguous grammar with no useless symbols, no unit productions, and no ϵ-productions, then $M = (M_{i,j})$ can be constructed in $O(n^2)$ steps, where $n = |w|$.*

Proof. We use three data structures:

- I_j, $0 \leq j \leq n$, a list of pairs $(A \to \alpha \bullet \beta, i)$ such that $(A \to \alpha \bullet \beta, i) \in I_j$ if and only if $A \to \alpha \bullet \beta \in M_{i,j}$;
- $L_j(X)$, $0 \leq j \leq n$, $X \in V \cup \Sigma$, a list of pairs $(A \to \alpha \bullet X\beta, i)$ such that $A \to \alpha \bullet X\beta \in M_{i,j}$;
- BV_j, $0 \leq j \leq n$, a bit vector, initially all 0, that for each item $A \to \alpha \bullet \beta$ tells whether the pair $(A \to \alpha \bullet \beta, j)$ has already been added to I_j.

A subroutine ADD maintains these lists. Here is the code for ADD:

ADD$((A \rightarrow \alpha \bullet X\beta, i), j)$
1. append $(A \rightarrow \alpha \bullet X\beta, i)$ to I_j
2. append $(A \rightarrow \alpha \bullet X\beta, i)$ to $L_j(X)$
3. If $i = j$, set $BV_j[A \rightarrow \alpha \bullet X\beta]$ to 1.
4. If $X \in V$, for all productions $X \rightarrow \gamma$ do
       if $BV_j[X \rightarrow \gamma \bullet] = 1$
           then call ADD $((A \rightarrow \alpha X \bullet \beta, i), j)$

Our implementation of Earley's algorithm now implements steps A–D as follows:

A. For all productions $S \rightarrow \alpha$, call ADD$((S \rightarrow \bullet\alpha, 0), 0)$.
For $j = 0, 1, \ldots, n$ do:
  B. If $j > 0$ then do
       for each pair $(A \rightarrow \alpha \bullet w_j\beta, i)$ on the list $L_{j-1}(w_j)$,
       call ADD $((A \rightarrow \alpha w_j \bullet \beta, i), j)$
1. For each pair on the list I_j do:
     If the pair is of the form $(B \rightarrow \gamma\bullet, i)$
       C. For each pair $(A \rightarrow \alpha \bullet B\beta, k)$ on the list $L_i(B)$, call
         ADD$((A \rightarrow \alpha B \bullet \beta, k), j)$
     If the pair is of the form $(A \rightarrow \alpha \bullet B\beta, i)$
       D. If $BV_j[B \rightarrow \bullet\gamma] = 0$, then call ADD$((B \rightarrow \bullet\gamma, j), j)$.

Note that I_j lengthens as the algorithm proceeds.

We claim that the algorithm presented is correct and uses $O(n^2)$ steps. The correctness proof is left to the reader; the only trick is that step 4 of ADD is needed if $(A \rightarrow \alpha \bullet B\beta, i)$ is added to I_j *after* the pair $(B \rightarrow \gamma\bullet, j)$ is considered in line 1.

For the time bound, note that there exists a constant c such that at most $c(j + 1)$ pairs appear on the list I_j. For if the pair is of the form $(A \rightarrow \alpha \bullet \beta, i)$ with $\alpha \neq \epsilon$, then by Exercise 9 we try to add this item to I_j at most once, since G is unambiguous. If the pair is of the form $(A \rightarrow \bullet\beta, i)$, then it is added only in steps A and D, and in step D the bit vector is checked before the item is added. Thus the total number of pairs is $\leq \sum_{0 \leq j \leq n} c(j + 1) = O(n^2)$.

The running time now follows if we can show that the total time associated with a list entry is $O(1)$. We do so by an amortized analysis argument. We allocate \$2 to each list entry. \$1 is used to pay for the cost of examining the entry in line 1, and \$1 is used to pay for the cost of adding the entry to a list. But our algorithm examines and adds each entry at most once. Thus the total cost is $O(n^2)$. ∎

Up until now we have used Earley's algorithm as a recognizer, not a parser. We now discuss how the parsing table constructed by the algorithm may be used to parse.

PARSE $(A \rightarrow \beta\bullet, i, j)$
  { Finds a rightmost derivation of $w[i + 1..j]$ starting with production
    $A \rightarrow \beta$. }

If $\beta = X_1 X_2 \cdots X_m$, set $k := m$ and $l := j$
Repeat until $k = 0$:
  If $X_k \in \Sigma$
    set $k := k - 1$ and $l := l - 1$
  Else $\{X_k \in V\}$
    (*) find a complete item of the form $X_k \rightarrow \gamma\bullet$ in $M_{r,l}$ for some r
        such that $A \rightarrow X_1 X_2 \cdots X_{k-1} \bullet X_k \cdots X_m \in M_{i,r}$
    Call PARSE$(X_k \rightarrow \gamma\bullet, r, l)$
    Set $k := k - 1$ and $l := r$

This algorithm can be used to obtain a rightmost derivation of the input string. We call PARSE with the arguments $(S \rightarrow \alpha\bullet, 0, n)$, where $S \rightarrow \alpha\bullet$ is an item in $M_{0,n}$.

Theorem 5.2.8. *Assume that G contains neither ϵ-productions nor unit productions and that the table $[M_{i,j}]$ has already been computed. If $A \Longrightarrow \beta \overset{*}{\Longrightarrow} w_{i+1} \cdots w_j$, then a call to PARSE$(A \rightarrow \beta\bullet, i, j)$ produces a parse of $w_{i+1} \cdots w_j$ starting with $A \rightarrow \beta$ in $O((j - i)^2)$ steps.*

Proof. For correctness, observe that if you have shown $X_{k+1} \cdots X_m \overset{*}{\Longrightarrow} w_{l+1} \cdots w_j$, then

$$A \Longrightarrow \beta = X_1 X_2 \cdots X_{k-1} X_k X_{k+1} \cdots X_m \overset{*}{\Longrightarrow} X_1 X_2 \cdots X_k w_{l+1} \cdots w_j.$$

But $A \rightarrow X_1 \cdots X_{k-1} \bullet X_k \cdots X_m \in M_{i,r}$, so $X_1 \cdots X_{k-1} \overset{*}{\Longrightarrow} w_{i+1} \cdots w_r$. Hence, $A \overset{*}{\Longrightarrow} w_{i+1} \cdots w_r X_k w_{l+1} \cdots w_j$. But $X_k \rightarrow \gamma\bullet \in M_{r,l}$, so $\gamma \overset{*}{\Longrightarrow} w_{r+1} \cdots w_l$. Hence,

$$A \overset{*}{\Longrightarrow} w_{i+1} \cdots w_r \gamma w_{l+1} \cdots w_j \overset{*}{\Longrightarrow} w_{i+1} \cdots w_r w_{r+1} \cdots w_l w_{l+1} \cdots w_j,$$

as desired.

For the running time analysis, let us prove by induction on $j - i$ that the running time of the call PARSE($A \to \beta \bullet, i, j$) is bounded by $c(j - i)^2$ for some constant c. This is clearly true if $j - i = 1$. Now suppose $\beta = X_1 X_2 \cdots X_m$ and that $X_j \stackrel{*}{\Longrightarrow} w_{i_j+1} \cdots w_{i_{j+1}}$ for $1 \le j \le m$. Note $i = i_1$ and $j = i_{m+1}$. In step (*) we need to examine all lists $M_{r,l}$ for $r = l, l - 1, \ldots, i$ until the desired item is found. This can be done in $d(j - i)$ steps for some constant d. The total cost is therefore

$$\le c((i_2 - i_1)^2 + \cdots + (i_{m+1} - i_m)^2) + d((i_2 - i_1) + \cdots + (i_{m+1} - i_m)).$$

By telescoping cancelation, the second sum is just $d(j - i)$. Since G does not contain ϵ-productions or unit productions, $1 < m \le j - i$. Now by Exercise 13, $((i_2 - i_1)^2 + \cdots + (i_{m+1} - i_m)^2)$ is bounded by $(j - i - 1)^2 + 1 = (j - i)^2 - 2(j - i) + 2$. Hence, taking $c = d$, the desired inequality follows. ∎

5.3 Top-down parsing

As mentioned previously, a top-down parser attempts to construct the derivation tree for a word $w \in L(G)$ from the "top down," that is, by starting with the start symbol S of the grammar and choosing the correct productions in order.

The most popular top-down methods are called LL(k). The first L stands for left-to-right scan of the input, the second L stands for producing a leftmost derivation, and the k refers to the number of symbols of "lookahead" that are allowed. Lookahead is a feature of many parsing algorithms, and refers to how many symbols of the input past the current position the algorithm is allowed to refer to.

In this section we focus on LL(1) parsing. It is known that LL(1) parsers are not as powerful as LL(k) parsers for arbitrary k; in fact, there are examples known of grammars that can be parsed with LL(k) parsers but not LL($k - 1$).

It is conceptually easy to think of a top-down parser as a one-state nondeterministic pushdown automaton (PDA) with a write-only output tape, as shown in Figure 5.2.

The *configuration* of such a parser is

$$[a_i a_{i+1} \cdots a_n \$, \gamma_j \gamma_{j-1} \cdots \gamma_2 \gamma_1 \#, n_1 n_2 \cdots n_k].$$

Here the input is $a_1 \cdots a_n$, the current stack contents is $\gamma_j \cdots \gamma_1$, with the top symbol on the stack being γ_j, and $n_1 \cdots n_k$ is the output.

Input tape

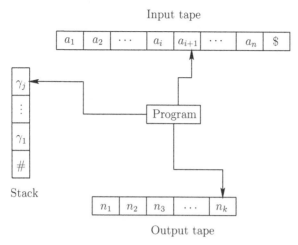

Figure 5.2: Top-down parser illustrated

The *initial configuration* of the parser is

$$[a_1 a_2 \cdots a_n \$, S\#, \epsilon].$$

Note: the special symbol $ should be thought of as the "end-of-input" marker, and the special symbol # is the "bottom-of-stack" marker.

At any stage in the computation, the parser can do exactly one of three things:

1. If the symbol on the top of the stack is a variable X, the parser pops X and pushes the string $\alpha_1 \cdots \alpha_t$, where $X \to \alpha_1 \cdots \alpha_t$ is a production in G. The parser then writes the appropriate production, or a code for it, on the output tape. (In general, there may be several such productions with X on the left-hand side; the parser must choose the right one, based on X and the current symbol being scanned.)

2. If the symbol on the top of the stack is a terminal x, it is compared with the current input symbol a. If $x = a$, the stack is popped and the input pointer is advanced one cell. If $x \neq a$, the parser writes "reject" on the output tape and halts.

3. If the symbol on the top of the stack is # and the input is $, the parser writes "accept" on the output tape and halts.

The decision about what to do is based on a transition function $M(\gamma, x)$.

$\gamma \backslash x$	a	b	c	$
S	$S \to AB$	$S \to AB$	$S \to c$	Reject
A	$A \to aS$	$A \to b$	Reject	Reject
B	$B \to AS$	$B \to AS$	$B \to c$	Reject
a	Pop	Reject	Reject	Reject
b	Reject	Pop	Reject	Reject
c	Reject	Reject	Pop	Reject
#	Reject	Reject	Reject	Accept

Figure 5.3: LL(1) parsing table

Example 5.3.1. Consider a grammar G with the following numbered productions:

1. $S \to AB$;
2. $S \to c$;
3. $A \to aS$;
4. $A \to b$;
5. $B \to AS$;
6. $B \to c$.

Then the transition function $M(\gamma, x)$ is as given in Figure 5.3.

For example, here are the configurations of the parser on input acbbc:

$(acbbc\$, S\#, \epsilon) \vdash (acbbc\$, AB\#, 1) \vdash (acbbc\$, aSB\#, 13)$
$\qquad \vdash (cbbc\$, SB\#, 13) \vdash (cbbc\$, cB\#, 132) \vdash (bbc\$, B\#, 132)$
$\qquad \vdash (bbc\$, AS\#, 1325) \vdash (bbc\$, bS\#, 13254) \vdash (bc\$, S\#, 13254)$
$\qquad \vdash (bc\$, AB\#, 132541) \vdash (bc\$, bB\#, 1325414) \vdash (c\$, B\#, 1325414)$
$\qquad \vdash (c\$, c\#, 13254146) \vdash (\$, \#, 13254146). \qquad\qquad (5.7)$

This corresponds to using the productions 1, 3, 2, 5, 4, 1, 4, 6 in a leftmost derivation of acbbc.

The whole game of LL(1) parsing is to construct the transition function M. The parser must know which production to use, based only on the current symbol on top of the stack and the current input symbol being scanned.

To compute M, we introduce two functions:

- FIRST(α), defined for all $\alpha \in (\Sigma \cup V)^*$;
- FOLLOW(A), defined for all $A \in V$.

The range of each of these functions is a set of symbols.

Intuitively, we put a terminal a in FIRST(α) if it is possible to derive a sentential form from α that begins with a.

Formally, we define

$$\text{FIRST}(\alpha) = \{a \in \Sigma \; : \; \text{there exists a derivation } \alpha \overset{*}{\Longrightarrow} a\beta \text{ for some}$$

$$\beta \in (\Sigma \cup V)^*\} \cup \{\epsilon \; : \; \text{there exists a derivation } \alpha \overset{*}{\Longrightarrow} \epsilon\}. \quad (5.8)$$

The heuristic description of FOLLOW(A) is as follows: we put a terminal a in FOLLOW(A) if it could appear immediately following A in some sentential form derivable from S.

Formally, we define

$$\text{FOLLOW}(A) = \{a \in \Sigma \; : \; \text{there exists a derivation } S \overset{*}{\Longrightarrow} \alpha A a\beta \text{ for some}$$

$$\alpha, \beta \in (V \cup \Sigma)^*\} \cup \{\$ \; : \; \text{there exists a derivation } S \overset{*}{\Longrightarrow} \alpha A$$

$$\text{for some } \alpha \in (V \cup \Sigma)^*\}. \quad (5.9)$$

Example 5.3.2. Consider the following grammar G:

$$S \rightarrow AB \mid \text{a}$$
$$A \rightarrow CD$$
$$B \rightarrow \text{b}AB \mid \epsilon$$
$$C \rightarrow \text{d}S\text{d} \mid \text{c}$$
$$D \rightarrow \text{c}CD \mid \epsilon.$$

Then FIRST(AB) = $\{\text{c}, \text{d}\}$, because we have the two derivations:

$$AB \Longrightarrow CDB \Longrightarrow \text{d}S\text{d}DB;$$
$$AB \Longrightarrow CDB \Longrightarrow \text{c}DB.$$

Similarly, we have

$$\text{FIRST}(\text{a}) = \{\text{a}\};$$
$$\text{FIRST}(CD) = \{\text{c}, \text{d}\};$$
$$\text{FIRST}(\text{b}AB) = \{\text{b}\};$$
$$\text{FIRST}(\epsilon) = \{\epsilon\};$$
$$\text{FIRST}(\text{d}S\text{d}) = \{\text{d}\};$$
$$\text{FIRST}(\text{c}) = \{\text{c}\};$$
$$\text{FIRST}(\text{c}CD) = \{\text{c}\}.$$

We also have FOLLOW(C) = {$, b, c, d}, because we have the derivations

$$S \Longrightarrow AB \Longrightarrow A \Longrightarrow CD \Longrightarrow C;$$
$$S \Longrightarrow AB \Longrightarrow CDB \Longrightarrow CB \Longrightarrow CbAB;$$
$$S \Longrightarrow AB \Longrightarrow CDB \Longrightarrow CcCD;$$
$$S \Longrightarrow AB \Longrightarrow CDB \Longrightarrow dSdDB \Longrightarrow dABdDB \Longrightarrow dCDBdDB \Longrightarrow$$
$$dCBdDB \Longrightarrow dCdDB.$$

Similarly, we have

$$\text{FOLLOW}(S) = \{\$, d\};$$
$$\text{FOLLOW}(A) = \{\$, b, d\};$$
$$\text{FOLLOW}(B) = \{\$, d\};$$
$$\text{FOLLOW}(D) = \{\$, b, d\}.$$

Now we give an algorithm to compute $M(\gamma, x)$, assuming we have algorithms for FIRST and FOLLOW (which we discuss next).

Compute-LL-Table

1. $M(a, a) = $ "pop" for all $a \in \Sigma$;
2. $M(\#, \$) = $ "accept";
3. For each production $X \to \alpha$ do
   (a) For each terminal $b \in \text{FIRST}(\alpha)$, set $M(X, b) = $ "apply production $X \to \alpha$";
   (b) If $\epsilon \in \text{FIRST}(\alpha)$, set $M(X, b) = $ "apply production $X \to \alpha$" for all $b \in \text{FOLLOW}(X)$;
4. $M(X, b) = $ "reject" for all other cases.

Example 5.3.3. Let us compute the LL(1) parsing table for the grammar G of Example 5.3.2 (see Figure 5.4). (Blank spaces mean "reject.")

Note: It is possible that the function $M(\gamma, x)$ is multiply defined. In that case, we say the parsing table has a *conflict*, and the corresponding grammar is not LL(1).

There are several approaches to handle conflicts in LL(1) grammars. We can try to provide disambiguating rules that tell which of several productions we should choose if there is a conflict. We can try all the possibilities, which forces backtracking. We can attempt to rewrite the grammar to obtain an equivalent LL(1) grammar. Finally, we can use more symbols of lookahead, which leads to LL(2), LL(3), and so on.

$\gamma \backslash x$	a	b	c	d	$
S	$S \to$ a		$S \to AB$	$S \to AB$	
A			$A \to CD$	$A \to CD$	
B		$B \to$ bAB		$B \to \epsilon$	$B \to \epsilon$
C			$C \to$ c	$C \to$ dSd	
D		$D \to \epsilon$	$D \to$ cCD	$D \to \epsilon$	$D \to \epsilon$
a	Pop				
b		Pop			
c			Pop		
d				Pop	
#					Accept

Figure 5.4: Parsing table $M(\gamma, x)$ for G of Example 5.3.2

Definition. We say grammar G is LL(1) if $M(\gamma, x)$ is single-valued. We say a language L is LL(1) if there exists some LL(1) grammar G such that $L = L(G)$.

The term LL(1) arises as follows: the first L stands for a left-to-right scan of the input, the second L stands for the fact that the method produces a leftmost derivation, and the 1 refers to 1 symbol of lookahead.

Theorem 5.3.4. *If G is an LL(1) grammar, then G has a deterministic top-down parser given by the algorithm to compute $M(\gamma, x)$ given in* Compute-LL-Table.

Proof. We show that if $z \in L(G)$, then the parser correctly constructs the leftmost derivation of z and if $z \notin L(G)$, then the parser rejects z.

Let $z = a_1 a_2 \cdots a_n$. The initial configuration of the parser is

$$[a_1 a_2 \cdots a_n \$, S\#, \epsilon].$$

The program first examines $M(S, a_1)$. If the entry is "reject," that means $a_1 \notin$ FIRST(α) for all α with $S \to \alpha$ a production. Hence, no string in $L(G)$ derivable from S can begin with a_1. Hence, $z \notin L(G)$.

Suppose $M(S, a_1)$ does contain a production. Then the production is $S \to \alpha$ and can come from 3(a) or 3(b). If it comes from 3(a), then $a_1 \in$ FIRST(α). Since $M(\gamma, x)$ is single-valued, if $S \to \beta$ is any other S-production, $a_1 \notin$ FIRST(β). If 3(b), then $\epsilon \in$ FIRST(α), $a_1 \in$ FOLLOW(S), and $a_1 \notin$ FIRST(β) for any other S-production $S \to \beta$. Hence, $a_1 = \$$, $z = \epsilon$, and $S \to \alpha$ is the first production used to derive z.

We have shown that if z is derivable from S, then the parser correctly determines the first production used.

Similarly, suppose that after several moves the parser has reached the configuration

$$[a_k a_{k+1} \cdots a_n \$, A x_1 x_2 \cdots x_p \#, y].$$

We want to show that it correctly determines the next production.

If $M(A, a_k) =$ "reject", then I claim we cannot derive a string beginning with a_k from $A x_1 x_2 \cdots x_p$. For we know $a_k \notin \text{FIRST}(\alpha)$ for all A-productions $A \to \alpha$. It is possible however, that $A \overset{*}{\Longrightarrow} \epsilon$. In that case, $a_k \in \text{FOLLOW}(A)$, so by 3(b), $M(A, a_k) \neq$ "reject."

Now suppose $M(A, a_k)$ is a production. Then it must contain only one of the form $A \to \alpha$. If this production came from step 3(a), then $a_k \in \text{FIRST}(\alpha)$ and the production must be applied to derive $a_k a_{k+1} \cdots a_n$, since $a_k \notin \text{FIRST}(\beta)$ for all other β.

If it came from step 3(b), then $\epsilon \in \text{FIRST}(\alpha), a_k \notin \text{FIRST}(\alpha)$. Thus we must transform A to ϵ first to derive $a_k a_{k+1} \cdots a_n$ from $A x_1 x_2 \cdots x_p$. Then we derive $a_k \cdots a_n$ from $x_1 \cdots x_p$. Hence the parser chooses the correct production here, too.

To complete the proof we observe that eventually a_k appears on the top of the stack and is popped. Thus we eventually either accept or reject z, and we accept if and only if a sequence of derivations actually produced z.   ∎

It remains to see how to compute the sets FIRST and FOLLOW.

To compute $\text{FIRST}(\alpha)$ we first show how to compute $\text{FIRST}(X)$ when $X \in V$; then we show how to use this to compute $\text{FIRST}(\alpha)$ for $\alpha \in (V \cup \Sigma)^*$. Here is the algorithm for $\text{FIRST}(X)$:

COMPUTE-FIRST(G)

Input: $G = (V, \Sigma, P, S)$ is a context-free grammar
1. Initialize $F(B) = \emptyset$ for all $B \in V$, and $F(a) = \{a\}$ for all $a \in \Sigma$.
2. For each production of G do
3.   (i) If the production is $A \to a\alpha$ for $a \in \Sigma$, set $F(A) := F(A) \cup \{a\}$.
        (ii) If the production is $A \to \epsilon$, set $F(A) := F(A) \cup \{\epsilon\}$.
        (iii) If the production is $A \to Y_1 Y_2 \cdots Y_k$
              (a) If there is a smallest index j such that $\epsilon \notin F(Y_j)$,
              set $F(A) := F(A) \cup (F(Y_1) \cup F(Y_2) \cup \cdots \cup F(Y_j) - \{\epsilon\})$
              (b) If there is no such index, set $F(A) := F(A) \cup F(Y_1)$
                 $\cup F(Y_2) \cup \cdots \cup F(Y_k)$.
4. If any of the sets $F(B)$ were changed in size, return to step 2.
5. Otherwise set $\text{FIRST}(A) := F(A)$ for all $A \in V$.

Theorem 5.3.5. *The preceding algorithm correctly computes* FIRST(X) *for* $X \in V$.

Proof. First, let us show that at all times during the algorithm's execution we have $F(X) \subseteq$ FIRST(X) for $X \in V \cup \Sigma$. This is clearly true after step 1. Now assume it is true for all iterations up to iteration k; we prove it for iteration k. At this step, a symbol gets added to $F(X)$ only as a result of steps 3(i), (ii), or (iii).

In step (i), we add a to $F(A)$ if and only if there exists a production $A \to a\alpha$, and indeed $a \in$ FIRST(A). In step (ii), we add ϵ to $F(A)$ if and only if there exists a production $A \to \epsilon$, but then $\epsilon \in$ FIRST(A). Finally, in step (iii), there are two possibilities. In possibility (a), there is a smallest index j such that $\epsilon \notin F(Y_j)$. In this case, $\epsilon \in$ FIRST(Y_i) for $1 \le i < j$, so by induction $Y_i \overset{*}{\Longrightarrow} \epsilon$ for $1 \le i < j$. Hence all the terminals in $F(Y_i)$ for $1 \le i < j$ are in FIRST(Y_i). A similar argument applies to possibility (b).

Next, let us show that if $x \in$ FIRST(A), then x eventually gets added to $F(A)$ by some step of the algorithm. Let $x \in$ FIRST(A). There are two cases to consider:

Case 1: $x = a \in \Sigma$. Then there exists a derivation

$$A \Longrightarrow \gamma_1 \Longrightarrow \gamma_2 \Longrightarrow \cdots \Longrightarrow \gamma_{n-1} \Longrightarrow \gamma_n = a\beta; \qquad (5.10)$$

without loss of generality, let this be the shortest such that it results in a beginning a right-hand side derivable from A. We claim that a is added to $F(A)$ before or during the nth iteration.

If $n = 1$, then $A \Longrightarrow a\beta$ is a production of G, so a is added to FIRST(A) during step 3(i). Suppose our claim is true for all variables A and terminals a for all $n < n'$. We prove the claim holds for $n = n'$. Suppose (5.10) holds. Then let $\gamma_1 = Y_1 Y_2 \cdots Y_s$, where $Y_i \in V \cup \Sigma$. Thus,

$$A \Longrightarrow Y_1 Y_2 \cdots Y_s \overset{*}{\Longrightarrow} a\beta.$$

Now there exists j such that $Y_i \overset{*}{\Longrightarrow} \epsilon$ with $1 \le i < j$, $Y_j \overset{*}{\Longrightarrow} a\alpha$, and $Y_{j+1} \cdots Y_s \overset{*}{\Longrightarrow} \delta$, where $\alpha\delta = \beta$. All these derivations are of length $< n'$, so by induction $a \in F(Y_j)$. Hence, a is added to $F(A)$ at the latest at step n'.

Case 2: $x = \epsilon$. Similar to Case 1, and left to the reader. ■

Now that we know how to compute FIRST(X) for $X \in V \cup \Sigma \cup \{\epsilon\}$, we show how to compute FIRST(α) for an arbitrary sentential form α.

Lemma 5.3.6. *If* $\alpha = Z_1 Z_1 \cdots Z_m$, *where* $Z_i \in V \cup \Sigma$ *for* $1 \leq i \leq m, m \geq 2$, *then*

$$
\text{FIRST}(\alpha) = \begin{cases}
\text{FIRST}(Z_1) \cup \cdots \cup \text{FIRST}(Z_j) - \{\epsilon\}, & \begin{array}{l}\text{if there exists a small-}\\ \text{est index } j, 1 \leq j \leq m\end{array} \\
\text{FIRST}(Z_1) \cup \cdots \cup \text{FIRST}(Z_m), & \begin{array}{l}\text{such that } \epsilon \notin \text{FIRST}\\ (Z_j); \text{ otherwise}\end{array}
\end{cases}
$$

Proof. Left to the reader. ∎

Now we turn to the computation of FOLLOW(X).

COMPUTE-FOLLOW(G)

Input: $G = (V, \Sigma, P, S)$ is a context-free grammar with no useless symbols
1. Initialize $H(B) = \emptyset$ for all $B \in V$, $B \neq S$ and $H(S) = \{\$\}$.
2. For each production of G do
3.   For each variable X on the right-hand side of the production, write the production as $A \to \alpha X \beta$ and
        (i) add all the terminals in FIRST(β) to $H(X)$; do not add ϵ;
        (ii) if $\epsilon \in \text{FIRST}(\beta)$, add all symbols of $H(A)$ to $H(X)$.
4. If any of the sets $H(B)$ were changed in size, return to step 2.
5. Otherwise set FOLLOW(A) := $H(A)$ for all $A \in V$.

Theorem 5.3.7. *The algorithm* COMPUTE-FOLLOW *correctly computes* FOLLOW(X) *for all* $X \in V$.

Proof. First, let us prove that the invariant $H(A) \subseteq \text{FOLLOW}(A)$ holds at every step of the algorithm. We do this by induction on the number of iterations of step 2.

Initially, we have $H(A) = \emptyset \subseteq \text{FOLLOW}(A)$ for all $A \neq S$. Also, $H(S) = \{\$\}$, and $\$ \in \text{FOLLOW}(S)$ because of the derivation $S \overset{*}{\Longrightarrow} S$.

Now assume that the invariant holds at step i; we prove it for step $i + 1$. A symbol can be added to $H(X)$ in step (i) or (ii). Suppose $a \in \Sigma$ is added in step (i). Then $a \in \text{FIRST}(\beta)$, so there is a derivation $\beta \overset{*}{\Longrightarrow} a\gamma$ for some $\gamma \in (V \cup \Sigma)^*$. Combining this with the derivation $A \overset{*}{\Longrightarrow} \alpha X \beta$, we get $A \overset{*}{\Longrightarrow} \alpha X \beta \overset{*}{\Longrightarrow} \alpha X a\gamma$, so indeed $a \in \text{FOLLOW}(X)$.

If step (ii) is taken, then we have $\epsilon \in \text{FIRST}(\beta)$, and hence there is a derivation $\beta \overset{*}{\Longrightarrow} \epsilon$. Let $a \in H(A)$. Then by induction $a \in \text{FOLLOW}(A)$. If

$a \in \Sigma$, then there is a derivation $S \overset{*}{\Longrightarrow} \delta Aa\gamma$. Combining this with the production $A \to \alpha X\beta$, we get the derivation

$$S \overset{*}{\Longrightarrow} \delta Aa\gamma \Longrightarrow \delta\alpha X\beta a\gamma \overset{*}{\Longrightarrow} \delta\alpha Xa\gamma,$$

so indeed $a \in \text{FOLLOW}(X)$. If $a = \$$, then there is a derivation $S \overset{*}{\Longrightarrow} \delta A$. Combining this with $A \to \alpha X\beta$, we get

$$S \overset{*}{\Longrightarrow} \delta A \Longrightarrow \delta\alpha X\beta \overset{*}{\Longrightarrow} \delta\alpha X,$$

so indeed $\$ \in \text{FOLLOW}(X)$.

The converse is left to the reader. ∎

5.4 Removing LL(1) conflicts

In this section we look at two basic techniques for converting a grammar to LL(1) form. They are not always guaranteed to work, but they are useful in many situations.

The first technique is removing left recursion. We say a grammar has *immediate left recursion* if there exists a variable E with a production of the form $E \to E\alpha$. Immediate left recursion can be removed from a grammar without ϵ-productions as follows. Suppose the E-productions are

$$E \to E\alpha_1 \mid E\alpha_2 \mid \cdots \mid E\alpha_k \mid \beta_1 \mid \beta_2 \mid \cdots \mid \beta_j,$$

where no β_i starts with E. Then we remove these productions from the grammar and replace them with the productions

$$E \to \beta_1 E' \mid \beta_2 E' \mid \cdots \mid \beta_j E';$$
$$E' \to \alpha_1 E' \mid \alpha_2 E' \mid \cdots \mid \alpha_k E' \mid \epsilon.$$

It is easy to see that this change does not affect the language generated by the grammar.

Example 5.4.1. The production rules

$$E \to EA \mid EB \mid \text{c} \mid \text{d}$$

would be replaced by

$$E \to \text{c}E' \mid \text{d}E';$$
$$E' \to AE' \mid BE' \mid \epsilon.$$

However, it is also possible to have left recursion consisting of several steps, as in the grammar given next.

$$S \to Aa \mid b;$$
$$A \to Sd \mid \epsilon.$$

This type of left recursion can be removed as follows:

REMOVE-LEFT-RECURSION(G)

Input: $G = (V, \Sigma, P, S)$ is a context-free grammar
1. Arrange the variables in V in some order $A_1, A_2, \ldots, A_n$.
2. For $i := 1$ to n do
3.   For $j := 1$ to $i - 1$ do
4.   Suppose the A_j-productions are $A_j \to \delta_1 \mid \delta_2 \mid \cdots \mid \delta_k$.
        Replace each production $A_i \to A_j \gamma$ with $A_i \to \delta_1 \gamma \mid \delta_2 \gamma \mid \cdots \mid \delta_k \gamma$.
5.   Eliminate immediate left recursion among the A_i as mentioned earlier.

Example 5.4.2. Suppose we start with the grammar

$$A_1 \to A_2 a \mid b;$$
$$A_2 \to A_2 c \mid A_1 d \mid \epsilon.$$

Then step 4 of the preceding algorithm results in the new grammar

$$A_1 \to A_2 a \mid b;$$
$$A_2 \to A_2 c \mid A_2 ad \mid bd \mid \epsilon.$$

Finally, step 5 gives

$$A_1 \to A_2 a \mid b;$$
$$A_2 \to bd A_2' \mid A_2';$$
$$A_2' \to c A_2' \mid ad A_2' \mid \epsilon.$$

The second method to attempt to resolve LL(1) conflicts is called "factoring." The idea here is that if two or more productions have right-hand sides that begin in the same way, this common prefix may be "factored" out by introducing a new variable.

Example 5.4.3. Consider the "if-then-else" grammar

$$S \to iEtSeS \mid iEtS \mid x;$$
$$E \to y.$$

We observe that the right-hand sides of the two productions $S \to iEtSeS$ and $S \to iEtS$ share a common prefix of $iEtS$. This suggests introducing a new variable S' and creating the grammar

$$S \to iEtSS' \mid \text{x};$$
$$S' \to eS \mid \epsilon;$$
$$E \to \text{y}.$$

This idea can be turned into an algorithm as follows:

FACTOR(G)

Input: $G = (V, \Sigma, P, S)$ is a context-free grammar

1. For each variable $A \in V$ do
2.   Find the longest prefix α common to two or more right-hand sides of A-productions.
3.   If $\alpha \neq \epsilon$, replace productions $A \to \alpha\beta_1 \mid \cdots \mid \alpha\beta_n \mid \gamma_1 \mid \gamma_2 \mid \ldots \mid \gamma_m$
     with productions $A \to \alpha A' \mid \gamma_1 \mid \gamma_2 \mid \ldots \mid \gamma_m$
     $$A' \to \beta_1 \mid \beta_2 \mid \cdots \mid \beta_n$$
     where A' is a new variable.
4.   Repeat until no two right-hand sides of A-productions share a nontrivial common prefix.

5.5 Bottom-up parsing

In the previous two sections we covered some aspects of top-down parsing. In this section we continue our study of parsing methods by turning to bottom-up parsing.

A bottom-up parsing method constructs a derivation by starting with a string x and attempting to find the immediately previous sentential forms. The best-known bottom-up methods are the LR(k) methods. Here the L stands for left-to-right scan of the input and the R stands for a rightmost derivation, produced in reverse by the algorithm. Once again the number k refers to the number of symbols of lookahead performed by the algorithm.

We focus here on LR(0) parsing. While LR(0) parsing is generally considered too weak for practical parsers, it shares aspects with more complicated methods that make it worthy of study.

The LR(0) algorithm depends on some specialized terminology. Suppose we have a grammar $G = (V, \Sigma, P, S)$ with no useless symbols. Recall from Section 5.2 that an *item* is a production of G with a dot in the middle. A *right sentential form* is a sentential form that can appear somewhere in a rightmost derivation in G. A *handle* of a right sentential form is a substring that could be introduced in the immediately preceding step of a rightmost derivation. More formally, if $S \overset{*}{\Longrightarrow}_{\text{rm}} \delta A w \Longrightarrow_{\text{rm}} \delta \alpha w$, for some $\delta, \alpha \in (V \cup \Sigma)^*$, $A \in V$, and $w \in \Sigma^*$, then α is said to be a *handle* of $\delta \alpha w$. A *viable prefix* of a right sentential form $\gamma \in (V \cup \Sigma)^*$ is any prefix of γ ending at or to the left of the right end of a handle of γ. Finally, we say that an item $A \to \alpha \bullet \beta$ is *valid for a viable prefix* γ if there is a rightmost derivation

$$S \overset{*}{\Longrightarrow}_{\text{rm}} \delta A w \Longrightarrow_{\text{rm}} \delta \alpha \beta w$$

and $\gamma = \delta \alpha$.

Example 5.5.1. Consider the following grammar G:

$$S \to T$$
$$T \to aTa$$
$$T \to bTb$$
$$T \to c.$$

Then $S \Longrightarrow T \Longrightarrow aTa \Longrightarrow abTba \Longrightarrow abcba$ is a rightmost derivation of abcba. Also, $\gamma = abTba$ is a right sentential form and bTb is a handle of γ. The viable prefixes of $abTba$ are ϵ, a, ab, abT, and $abTb$. The item $T \to bT \bullet b$ is valid for viable prefix abT, as is shown by the rightmost derivation $S \overset{*}{\Longrightarrow} aTa \Longrightarrow_{\text{rm}} abTba$. (Take $\delta = $ a, $A = T$, $w = $ a, $\alpha = bT$, $\beta = $ b.)

The interesting thing about viable prefixes is that for *any* grammar G without useless symbols—whether LR(0) or not—there is a deterministic finite automaton (DFA) that accepts the viable prefixes of G, and furthermore, the name of the corresponding state is the set of valid items for that viable prefix.

We now show how to compute this DFA, which we call the Knuth DFA. Given $G = (V, \Sigma, P, S)$, we first show how to compute a certain NFA-ϵ $M(G) = (Q, \Delta, \delta, q_0, F)$, where

- $Q = \text{items}(G) \cup \{q_0\}$;
- $\Delta = \Sigma \cup V$;
- $F = Q$;

and δ is defined as follows:

1. $\delta(q_0, \epsilon) = \{S \to \bullet \alpha \ : \ S \to \alpha$ is a production of $G\}$;
2. $\delta(A \to \alpha \bullet B\beta, \epsilon) = \{B \to \bullet \rho \ : \ B \to \rho$ is a production of $G\}$;
3. $\delta(A \to \alpha \bullet X\beta, X) = \{A \to \alpha X \bullet \beta\}$, $X \in V \cup \Sigma$.

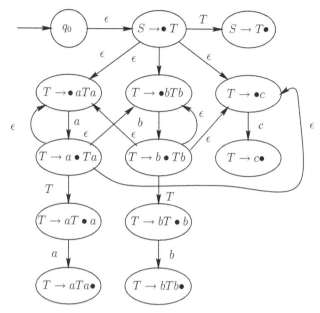

Figure 5.5: Knuth NFA-ϵ for the grammar of Example 5.5.1

We call this NFA-ϵ the Knuth NFA-ϵ. The Knuth DFA is computed from the Knuth NFA-ϵ by the usual subset construction.

Example 5.5.2. The NFA-ϵ in Figure 5.5 is the Knuth NFA-ϵ corresponding to the grammar of Example 5.5.1. The DFA in Figure 5.6 is obtained by the subset construction. (Useless transitions have been deleted.)

Theorem 5.5.3. *Assume G is a grammar with no useless symbols. Then the corresponding Knuth NFA-ϵ has the following property: $A \to \alpha \bullet \beta \in \delta(q_0, \gamma)$ iff $A \to \alpha \bullet \beta$ is valid for γ.*

Proof. Suppose $A \to \alpha \bullet \beta \in \delta(q_0, \gamma)$. We must show

$$A \to \alpha \bullet \beta \text{ is valid for } \gamma. \tag{5.11}$$

A natural way to prove (5.11) would be by induction on $|\gamma|$, but the Knuth NFA-ϵ we constructed has some edges labeled ϵ. So instead we prove assertion (5.11) by induction on the length l of the shortest path labeled γ from q_0 to $A \to \alpha \bullet \beta$.

The base case is $l = 1$. Then $\gamma = \epsilon$. Then we have the situation represented in Figure 5.7.

Then $S \to \bullet\beta$ is in $\delta(q_0, \gamma)$. Now $S \overset{*}{\Longrightarrow} \delta A w \Longrightarrow \delta\alpha\beta w$ with $A = S, w = \epsilon, \alpha = \epsilon$, and $\delta = \epsilon$. Hence, $S \to \bullet\beta$ is valid for γ.

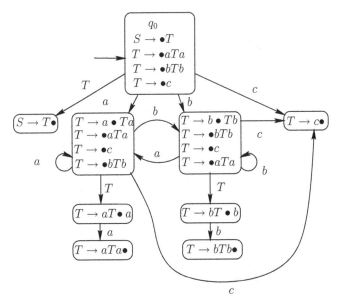

Figure 5.6: Knuth DFA for the grammar of Example 5.5.1

Now assume (5.11) holds for all paths of length $<l$; we prove it for a path of length l. Let there be a path labeled γ from q_0 to $A \rightarrow \alpha \bullet \beta$. There are two cases to consider:

Case 1: The last edge in the path is labeled with a nonempty symbol $X \in V \cup \Sigma$ (see Figure 5.8).

Write $\gamma = \gamma'X$ and $\alpha = \alpha'X$. Then, by induction, $A \rightarrow \alpha' \bullet X\beta$ is valid for γ'. Hence there exists a derivation

$$S \stackrel{*}{\Longrightarrow} \delta Aw \Longrightarrow \delta\alpha'X\beta w$$

with $\delta\alpha' = \gamma'$. Thus, $\gamma'X = \delta\alpha'X = \delta\alpha$. It follows that $A \rightarrow \alpha'X \bullet \beta$ is valid for γ.

Case 2: The last edge in the path is labeled ϵ. In this case we have the situation represented in Figure 5.9.

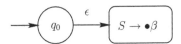

Figure 5.7: Base case of the proof

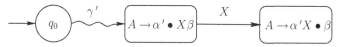

Figure 5.8: Case 1 of the induction step

Hence, by induction, $B \to \alpha' \bullet A\beta'$ is valid for γ. This means there exists a rightmost derivation

$$S \xRightarrow{*} \delta Bw \Longrightarrow \delta\alpha' A\beta' w,$$

where $\gamma = \delta\alpha'$. Now, since there are no useless symbols, β' must eventually derive some terminal string, so suppose $\beta' \xRightarrow{*} x$. Then

$$S \xRightarrow{*} \delta Bw \Longrightarrow \delta\alpha' A\beta' w \xRightarrow{*} \delta\alpha' A x w \Longrightarrow \delta\alpha'\beta x w.$$

Thus, $A \to \bullet\beta$ is indeed valid for $\delta\alpha' = \gamma$. This completes the proof of one direction.

For the other direction, suppose $A \to \alpha \bullet \beta$ is valid for γ. This means there is a rightmost derivation

$$S \xRightarrow{*} \delta' Aw \Longrightarrow \delta'\alpha\beta w, \tag{5.12}$$

where $\gamma = \delta'\alpha$. If we could show that $\delta(q_0, \delta')$ contains $A \to \bullet\alpha\beta$, then by successively applying rule (3) of the definition of the Knuth NFA-ϵ, it would follow that $\delta(q_0, \delta'\alpha)$ contains $A \to \alpha \bullet \beta$, as desired.

So let us prove by induction on the length of the rightmost derivation (5.12) that $\delta(q_0, \delta')$ contains $A \to \bullet\alpha\beta$.

The base case is when this derivation is of length 1. Then $\delta' = \epsilon$, $A = S$, and $w = \epsilon$. Then $\delta(q_0, \epsilon)$ contains $A \to \bullet\alpha\beta$ by rule (1).

For the induction step, suppose

$$S \xRightarrow{*} \delta_2 Bx \Longrightarrow \delta_2\delta_3 A\delta_4 x \xRightarrow{*} \delta_2\delta_3 Ayx,$$

where $B \to \delta_3 A\delta_4$ is a production. Thus, $\delta' = \delta_2\delta_3$ and $yx = w$. By induction we know $B \leftarrow \bullet\delta_3 A\delta_4$ is in $\delta(q_0, \delta_2)$. Then by rule (3) we have that $B \to \delta_3 \bullet A\delta_4$ is in $\delta(q_0, \delta_2\delta_3)$. Finally, by rule (2) we conclude $A \to \bullet\alpha\beta$ is in $\delta(q_0, \delta_2\delta_3) = \delta(q_0, \delta')$. The proof is complete. ∎

We now formally define the concept of LR(0) grammar.

Figure 5.9: Case 2 of the induction step

Definition. A grammar $G = (V, \Sigma, P, S)$ is LR(0) if each of the following conditions holds:

(a) G has no useless symbols.

(b) The start symbol S does not appear on the right-hand side of any production.

(c) For all viable prefixes γ, if $A \to \alpha \bullet$ is a complete item valid for γ, then no other complete item nor any item with a terminal immediately to the right of the $\bullet$ is valid for γ.

How do we parse using the Knuth DFA? An LR(0) parser is a deterministic PDA that generates a rightmost derivation. The stack of the DPDA holds a viable prefix of a right sentential form α, including all variables of α. Actually, the stack holds this viable prefix together with states of the Knuth DFA interspersed between symbols of the viable prefix. The remainder of α appears as the unexpended input.

Initially, the LR(0) parser is in a configuration (q, w, q_0), where q_0 now means the initial state of the corresponding Knuth DFA for the grammar. (Our description uses only a single state q, but allows the PDA to pop multiple symbols in a single step. Any implementation by a normal PDA would require extra states to handle these pops.)

At each step, the parser has two choices: (i) to shift a symbol from the input to the stack, updating the state of the Knuth DFA, or (ii) to "reduce" or pop $2|\alpha|$ symbols from the stack, where $A \to \alpha \bullet$ is a complete item on top of the stack, and then push A and the appropriate state of the Knuth DFA back on top of the stack. For this reason, LR parsers are sometimes called *shift-reduce* parsers.

More formally, an LR(0) parser behaves as follows: a typical configuration before a move looks like

$$(q, a_t a_{t+1} \cdots a_n, q_k X_k q_{k-1} X_{k-1} \cdots q_1 X_1 q_0),$$

where $x = a_1 \cdots a_n$ is the input, $X_1 \cdots X_k a_t a_{t+1} \cdots a_n$ is the current right sentential form, and $q_j = \delta(q_{j-1}, X_j)$, $1 \leq j \leq k$, where δ is the transition function of the Knuth DFA. If q_k contains a complete item of the form $A \to \alpha \bullet$, then $\alpha = X_{i+1} \cdots X_k$ for some $i \geq 0$, and the new configuration is

$$(q, a_t a_{t+1} \cdots a_n, q' A q_i X_i q_{i-1} \cdots q_1 X_1 q_0),$$

where $q' = \delta(q_i, A)$. Otherwise, the new configuration is

$$(q, a_{t+1} \cdots a_n, q' a_t q_k X_k q_{k-1} X_{k-1} \cdots q_1 X_1 q_0),$$

where $q' = \delta(q_k, a_t)$. We accept, by emptying the stack, if there is a complete item $S \to \alpha \bullet$ on top of the stack.

Let us prove that the LR(0) parsing method works. First we prove the following theorem.

Theorem 5.5.4. *Let G be an* LR(0) *grammar, let $x \in L(G)$, and let $\alpha \neq S$ be a right sentential form appearing in a derivation of x, that is, suppose $S \overset{*}{\Longrightarrow} \alpha \overset{*}{\Longrightarrow} x$ by a rightmost derivation. Then there is a unique right sentential form β such that $S \overset{*}{\Longrightarrow} \beta \Longrightarrow \alpha \overset{*}{\Longrightarrow} x$.*

Proof. Suppose the right sentential form is $\alpha = X_1 X_2 \cdots X_k y$, $y \in \Sigma^*$, and one rightmost derivation is $S \overset{*}{\Longrightarrow} X_1 X_2 \cdots X_j A y \Longrightarrow \alpha = X_1 X_2 \cdots X_k y \overset{*}{\Longrightarrow} x$, using the production $A \to X_{j+1} \cdots X_k$. Suppose there is another possible right sentential form previous to α, and consider the corresponding right end of the handle in α. There are three possibilities:

(i) the handle ends to the right of X_k (and hence the end is inside y);
(ii) the handle ends at X_k;
(iii) the handle ends at X_t for some $t < k$.

Consider $s = \delta(q_0, X_1 X_2 \cdots X_k)$ in the Knuth DFA for G. Then s contains a complete item, namely $A \to X_{j+1} \cdots X_k \bullet$. But by the LR(0) rules, this means that s contains no other complete items (ruling out case (ii)) and contains no items with a terminal immediately to the right of the dot (ruling out case (i)).

Finally, we have to rule out case (iii). To do so, suppose there is a rightmost derivation

$$X_1 X_2 \cdots X_r B X_{t+1} \cdots X_k y \Longrightarrow X_1 X_2 \cdots X_k y$$

using a production $B \to X_{r+1} \cdots X_t$. Since the derivation is rightmost,

$$\text{each of } X_{t+1}, \ldots, X_k \text{ is a terminal.} \tag{5.13}$$

Now complete item $B \to X_{r+1} \cdots X_t \bullet$ is valid for viable prefix $X_1 \cdots X_t$, but then, since $X_1 X_2 \cdots X_k$ is also a viable prefix, there must be some other item valid for $X_1 \cdots X_t$. And by (5.13), this item must have a terminal to the right of the dot or be complete. But this would violate the LR(0) rules, a contradiction. ∎

Corollary 5.5.5. *If G is* LR(0)*, then it is unambiguous.*

Proof. For every right sentential form in the derivation of $w \in L(G)$, there is only one previous right sentential form. ∎

Now we prove that the LR(0) algorithm works.

Theorem 5.5.6. *Let M be the DPDA specified earlier, based on the LR(0) grammar G. Then $L(G) = L_e(M)$, where by L_e we mean acceptance by empty stack.*

Proof. First we prove that $L_e(M) \subseteq L(G)$.

Suppose that $x \in L_e(M)$. We will prove that $x \in L(G)$ by producing a rightmost derivation of x.

We define α_i, the right sentential form represented by the configuration of the DPDA M at step i, to be the string $X_1 X_2 \cdots X_k y$ if the DPDA at step i has configuration

$$(q, y, s_k X_k s_{k-1} \cdots s_1 X_1 s_0).$$

We will prove the following two assertions by induction on i. Let $\alpha_{-1} = \alpha_0$.

1. $\delta(q_0, X_1 X_2 \cdots X_j) = s_j$ for all j, $0 \le j \le k$, where δ is the transition function of the associated Knuth DFA.
2. Either $\alpha_i \Longrightarrow_{rm} \alpha_{i-1}$ or $\alpha_i = \alpha_{i-1}$.

For $i = 0$, both (1) and (2) are true. (1) is true since the initial configuration of the DPDA is (q, x, q_0), and $\delta(q_0, \epsilon) = q_0$. (2) is true since $\alpha_0 = \alpha_{-1} = x$.

Now assume the assertions are true for steps $<i$; we prove them for i.

Suppose the configuration of the DPDA before step i is $(q, y, s_k X_k s_{k-1} \cdots s_1 X_1 s_0)$. At step i the DPDA either reduces or shifts.

(A) Reduce move: If the DPDA makes a reduce move, we know that s_k contains a complete item $A \to \gamma \bullet$. By induction $s_k = \delta(q_0, X_1 X_2 \cdots X_k)$. Since δ is the transition function for the Knuth automaton, we know that $A \to \gamma \bullet$ is valid for viable prefix $X_1 X_2 \cdots X_k$. In other words, there exists a rightmost derivation

$$S \overset{*}{\Longrightarrow} \beta A z \Longrightarrow \beta \gamma z,$$

where $\beta \gamma = X_1 X_2 \cdots X_k$. It follows that γ is a suffix of $X_1 X_2 \cdots X_k$ and hence when we pop $2|\gamma|$ symbols from the stack we are left with

$$s_j X_j s_{j-1} \cdots s_1 X_1 s_0$$

for some j, with $X_1 \cdots X_j = \beta$, $X_{j+1} \cdots X_k = \gamma$. Then we push A and $\delta(s_j, A)$ maintaining the invariant (1).

On the other hand, the invariant (2) is preserved because we have

$$\alpha_i = X_1 X_2 \cdots X_j A y \Longrightarrow X_1 X_2 \cdots X_j \gamma y = X_1 X_2 \cdots X_k y = \alpha_{i-1}.$$

(B) Shift move: If the DPDA makes a shift move, the invariant (1) is trivially preserved and (2) is preserved because $\alpha_i = \alpha_{i-1}$.

Finally, since $x \in L_e(M)$, we know the DPDA eventually empties its stack and accepts its input. This can occur only if at some step, say step n, the configuration is $(q, \epsilon, s_k X_k s_{k-1} \cdots s_1 X_1 s_0)$ and s_k contains a complete item of the form $S \to \gamma \bullet$. If this is the case, by the reasoning given earlier, there is a rightmost derivation

$$S \overset{*}{\Longrightarrow} \beta S z \Longrightarrow \beta \gamma z,$$

with $X_1 X_2 \cdots X_k = \beta \gamma$. However, since S does not appear on the right-hand side of any production, we must have $S = \beta S z$, so it follows that $\beta = \epsilon$ and $z = \epsilon$. Hence, $X_1 X_2 \cdots X_k = \gamma$. Now define $\alpha_{n+1} = S$. Then we have $\alpha_i \overset{*}{\Longrightarrow} \alpha_{i-1}$ for $1 \le i \le n + 1$. Since $\alpha_0 = x$, this gives a derivation of x in G.

Now let us show that $L(G) \subseteq L_e(M)$. Let $x \in L(G)$. As we have seen in Theorem 5.5.4, there is only one rightmost derivation $S \overset{*}{\Longrightarrow} x$. Suppose this derivation is of length n and

$$S = \alpha_n \Longrightarrow \alpha_{n-1} \Longrightarrow \cdots \Longrightarrow \alpha_0 = x.$$

We want to argue that M, when given x, eventually pops its stack and halts. To do so, we need to create a measure of "progress" toward an accepting computation. Suppose $C = (q, y, s_k X_k s_{k-1} \cdots s_1 X_1 s_0)$ is a configuration of M on input x. If $X_1 X_2 \cdots X_k y = \alpha_i$, then we define the *weight* of C to be $n - i + |y|$. We then argue that each move of the DPDA is correct and reduces the weight of its configuration.

Initially, the configuration is (q, x, q_0), with weight $n + |x|$. At each step, M either reduces or shifts. Consider what happens at step i.

If M reduces, then there must be a complete item on top of the stack. By Theorem 5.5.4, there is only one handle in $X_1 \cdots X_k y$ and it must be $X_{j+1} \cdots X_k$ with corresponding production $A \to X_{j+1} \cdots X_k$. The machine now performs a reduce move, and the corresponding weight decreases by 1.

If M shifts, then there is no complete item on top of the stack. We now argue that shifting is the right thing to do. Suppose there were a complete item $A \to \gamma$ buried in the stack. Then this complete item would have been added at some point. Consider the very next step. Since a complete item is on top, we would do a reduce move, popping $2|\gamma|$ symbols from the stack, so if $\gamma \ne \epsilon$, this complete item gets popped from the stack and cannot be buried. If $\gamma = \epsilon$, then A and $\delta(s_k, A)$ are put on top of $A \to \bullet$ in the stack. If, in any future step, $X_1 X_2 \cdots X_k$ has not risen to the top of the stack, then there will be a variable on top of $X_1 X_2 \cdots X_k$. But then ϵ (via $A \to \epsilon$) cannot be the handle of any right sentential form $X_1 X_2 \cdots X_k \epsilon \beta$, where β contains a variable, because then $X_1 X_2 \cdots X_k A \beta \Longrightarrow X_1 X_2 \cdots X_k \beta$ would not be a rightmost derivation. Thus the handle must include some symbols of the input, and shifting is the right thing to do. This reduces the weight of the configuration by 1.

Eventually, the weight of the configuration becomes 0. At this point, we have $i = n$ and $y = \epsilon$, and the DPDA pops its stack, accepting. Thus, $x \in L_e(M)$. ∎

5.6 Exercises

1. Consider the grammar G given by the following productions:

$$S \rightarrow AB \mid \text{b}$$
$$A \rightarrow BC \mid \text{a}$$
$$B \rightarrow AS \mid CB \mid \text{b}$$
$$C \rightarrow SS \mid \text{a}.$$

   Using the CYK algorithm, show that babbbab $\in$ L(G) and find a parse tree for this string. Show the tables in the algorithms.

2. Suppose G is a CFG and $w \in L(G)$. Show how to compute the number of distinct parse trees for w in G in polynomial time.

3. Give an example of a grammar for which constructing the parse table by Earley's method uses $\Omega(n^3)$ steps. *Hint:* Consider the grammar $S \rightarrow SS \mid$ a.

4. Compute the table $M(\gamma, x)$ for the grammar

$$S \rightarrow \text{a}A \mid \text{a}B$$
$$A \rightarrow \text{a}$$
$$B \rightarrow \text{b}.$$

   Is this grammar LL(1)?

5. Find an LL(1) grammar for the following set: the set of strings over $\{\text{a}, \text{b}\}^*$ containing an equal number of a's and b's. Be sure to prove that your grammar is correct and that it is LL(1).

6. Let G be a CFG with no useless symbols. Prove that G is an LL(1) grammar if and only if, for any two distinct productions of the form $X \rightarrow \alpha$, and $X \rightarrow \beta$, the following holds: if x and y are in FOLLOW(X), then FIRST(αx) $\cap$ FIRST(βy) = $\emptyset$. The symbols x and y need not be distinct.

7. Show that every regular language has an $LL(1)$ grammar.

8. Give an example of an LR(0) grammar such that there exists a viable prefix γ and items $A \rightarrow \bullet$, $B \rightarrow \alpha \bullet \beta$, which are both valid for γ.

9. Let $G = (V, \Sigma, P, S)$ be an unambiguous grammar with no useless symbols and $w_1 w_2 \cdots w_n$ be a string in Σ^*. Show that if $\alpha \neq \epsilon$, the algorithm to construct the Earley table attempts to add an item $A \rightarrow \alpha \bullet \beta$ to M_{ij} at most once.

10. Give an example of a grammar that is LL($k + 1$) but not LL(k).
*11. Give an example of a context-free language that is LL($k + 1$) but not LL(k).
**12. Give an example of a context-free language that is not LL(k) for any k.
13. Show that if $i, j, m, i_1, \ldots, i_{m+1}$ are all integers with $i_1 = i$, $i_{m+1} = j$, $m \geq 2$, and $i_1 < i_2 < \cdots < i_m < i_{m+1}$, then $((i_2 - i_1)^2 + \cdots + (i_{m+1} - i_m)^2)$ is bounded by $(j - i - 1)^2 + 1$.
14. Let G be an $LR(0)$ grammar with $A \rightarrow \alpha\bullet, \alpha \neq \epsilon$, valid for some viable prefix γ. Prove that no other item can be valid for γ.

5.7 Projects

1. Study software packages for LR parsing, such as Yacc and Bison. How do they compare in terms of features and efficiency?
2. Read about Valiant's method for recognition in $o(n^3)$ time. You can start with Valiant [1975].

5.8 Notes on Chapter 5

For Valiant's result on parsing general CFGs, see Valiant [1975].

5.1 For the CYK algorithm, see, for example, Younger [1967].

5.2 Earley's original paper is Earley [1970], but this is somewhat difficult to read. I have followed Urbanek [1990] for one direction of the proof of Theorem 5.2.3. While very clever, this paper unfortunately contains several typographical errors. I have followed Aho and Ullman [1972] for other parts of the presentation.

5.3 For two early papers on top-down parsing, see Rosenkrantz and Stearns [1970] and Lewis and Stearns [1968]. Our presentation is based on the book of Drobot [1989], but we have corrected many errors.

5.4 The material in this section is based on Aho, Sethi, and Ullman [1986].

5.5 For LR(k) grammars, see Knuth [1965].

The material in this section is based on Hopcroft and Ullman [1979], but the proof of correctness (Theorem 5.5.6) is new and improved.

6

Turing machines

In this chapter we explore some advanced topics relating to Turing machines (TMs): Kolmogorov complexity and unsolvability aspects of context-free grammars and languages. We begin by discussing unrestricted grammars and their languages.

6.1 Unrestricted grammars

In previous chapters we have studied context-free grammars (CFGs) and variants as LL(1) and LR(0) grammars. None of these grammars is powerful enough to generate the class of recursively enumerable languages. We introduce a new model, the unrestricted grammar, which has more power.

In an unrestricted grammar, both the left and right side of productions can be any string of variables and terminals, subject to the left side being nonempty. In other words, a production is of the form $\alpha \to \beta$, with $\alpha \in (V \cup \Sigma)^+$ and $\beta \in (V \cup \Sigma)^*$. We apply a production in the same manner as for other kinds of grammars; that is, if a sentential form is $\gamma\alpha\delta$, then we can apply the production $\alpha \to \beta$ to get the new sentential form $\gamma\beta\delta$. As usual we write $\gamma\alpha\delta \Longrightarrow \gamma\beta\delta$ and let $\overset{*}{\Longrightarrow}$ be the reflexive, transitive closure of $\Longrightarrow$. Finally, as usual we define $L(G)$ for an unrestricted grammar G to be $\{w \in \Sigma^* : S \overset{*}{\Longrightarrow} w\}$.

Example 6.1.1. The following is an unrestricted grammar for the language $\{a^{i^2} : i \geq 1\}$:

$$S \to BRAE$$
$$B \to BRAA$$
$$RA \to aAR$$
$$Ra \to aR$$
$$RE \to E$$
$$B \to X$$

$$XA \to X$$
$$Xa \to aX$$
$$XE \to \epsilon.$$

Here is the idea behind this example. It is based on the identity $1 + 3 + 5 + \cdots + (2n - 1) = n^2$. The B and E symbols are endmarkers. The first two productions create strings of the form $B(RAA)^i RAE$ for all $i \geq 0$. Thus, each R has an odd number of As to its right. Each R then moves to the right, creating a new a for each A encountered. When R hits E at the right, it disappears. Finally, the symbol B changes to X and causes the As, X, and E to disappear. Here are two examples of derivations using this grammar:

$S \Longrightarrow BRAE \Longrightarrow BaARE \Longrightarrow BaAE \Longrightarrow XaAE \Longrightarrow aXAE \Longrightarrow aXE \Longrightarrow$ a.

$S \stackrel{*}{\Longrightarrow} BRAARAE \Longrightarrow BRAARAARAE \Longrightarrow BaARARAARAE$
$\Longrightarrow BaARARAAaARE \Longrightarrow BaAaARRAAaARE$
$\Longrightarrow BaAaARaARAaARE \Longrightarrow BaAaARaARAaAE$
$\Longrightarrow BaAaARaAaARaAE \Longrightarrow BaAaAaRAaARaAE$
$\Longrightarrow BaAaAaaARaARaAE \Longrightarrow BaAaAaaAaRARaAE$
$\Longrightarrow BaAaAaaAaaARRaAE \Longrightarrow BaAaAaaAaaARaRAE$
$\Longrightarrow BaAaAaaAaaAaRRAE \Longrightarrow BaAaAaaAaaAaRaARE$
$\Longrightarrow BaAaAaaAaaAaRaAE \Longrightarrow BaAaAaaAaaAaaARAE$
$\Longrightarrow BaAaAaaAaaAaaaARE \Longrightarrow BaAaAaaAaaAaaaAE$
$\Longrightarrow XaAaAaaAaaAaaaAE \Longrightarrow aXAaAaaAaaAaaaAE$
$\Longrightarrow aXaAaaAaaAaaaAE \Longrightarrow aaXAaaAaaAaaaAE$
$\Longrightarrow aaXaaAaaAaaaAE \stackrel{*}{\Longrightarrow} aaaaaaaaaXAE$
$\Longrightarrow aaaaaaaaaXE \Longrightarrow aaaaaaaaa.$

The following two theorems characterize the power of unrestricted grammars.

Theorem 6.1.2. *Let $G = (V, \Sigma, P, S)$ be an unrestricted grammar. Then $L(G)$ is recursively enumerable.*

Proof. We show how to construct a TM accepting $L(G)$. Our TM is a nondeterministic four-tape model. Tape 1 holds the input w, and will never change. Tape 2 holds a sentential form. Tape 3 holds the left side of a production, and tape 4 holds the corresponding right side.

Initially, we write S on tape 2. Now, we perform the following loop forever, until a halting state is reached. First, we nondeterministically choose a cell on tape 2. Then, we nondeterministically choose a production rule $\alpha \to \beta$ and write α on tape 3 and β on tape 4. Then we see if the symbols on tape 3 match the symbols beginning in the cell being scanned on tape 2. If they do, we replace the symbols with the contents of tape 4; this will require shifting the rest of the symbols on tape 2 to the left if $|\alpha| > |\beta|$ and to the right if $|\alpha| < |\beta|$. Next, we compare the contents of tape 1 with tape 2; if they agree, we accept. Otherwise, we return to the beginning of the loop.

We know from Exercise 1.29 that a nondeterministic four-tape machine is equivalent to a deterministic one-tape machine, and hence $L(G)$ is recursively enumerable.   ■

Theorem 6.1.3. *Let L be a recursively enumerable language. Then there exists an unrestricted grammar G such that $L(G) = L$.*

Proof. If L is recursively enumerable, then there exists a deterministic one-tape TM M accepting L. We now modify M to get a nondeterministic "language generator" M' as follows: M' has two tracks. Starting with an initially blank tape, M' writes a nondeterministically-chosen string $w \in \Sigma^*$ on track 1. Then it copies w to track 2. Then it simulates M on track 1, and if M accepts, M' erases track 1, copies track 2 back to the tape (so the second track disappears and there is now just one track), and enters the halting state h. If M does not accept, M' crashes (by not having a next move).

In order to erase the tape, we need a small technical trick. Using Exercise 1.30, we can assume that M' never writes a blank symbol B; instead, it writes a new symbol $\overline{\mathrm{B}}$. Furthermore, we may assume that M' stops with the tape head immediately to the right of w, scanning a B or $\overline{\mathrm{B}}$. Thus, M' has the following behavior: it starts with a blank tape, and after some computation, it eventually halts with a nondeterministically chosen member of $L(M)$ (if one exists) written on its tape, followed by some number of $\overline{\mathrm{B}}$ symbols, with the rest of the tape consisting of B symbols. We assume the tape head is scanning the first B or $\overline{\mathrm{B}}$ symbol when the machine halts.

Once we have such an $M' = (Q, \Sigma, \Gamma, \delta, q_0, h)$, we create an unrestricted grammar mimicking its computations, with productions as follows:

$S \to q_0 S_1$

$S_1 \to \mathrm{B} S_1 \mid T$

$pX \to qY$ for all $X, Y \in \Gamma$, $p, q \in Q$ such that $(q, Y, S) \in \delta(p, X)$

$pX \to Yq$ for all $X, Y \in \Gamma$, $p, q \in Q$ such that $(q, Y, R) \in \delta(p, X)$

$ZpX \rightarrow qZY$ for all $X, Y, Z \in \Gamma$, $p, q \in Q$ such that $(q, Y, L) \in \delta(p, X)$

$h\overline{B} \rightarrow h$

$h\mathrm{B} \rightarrow h$

$hT \rightarrow \epsilon$.

To see that this construction works, note that the productions have been designed in such a way that intermediate sentential forms represent configurations of M'. Starting with S, we derive a string of the form $q_0\mathrm{B}^n$ for some n. We then perform moves of M' until h is reached, after which point the remaining $\overline{B}$ and B symbols are removed, and the h symbol is removed. The resulting string is the contents of the tape of M', which contains a nondeterministically chosen element of $L(M)$, if one exists.   ∎

6.2 Kolmogorov complexity

In this section we discuss the basic notions of Kolmogorov complexity.

When is a string of symbols complex? Intuitively, a string such as

$$010101010101010101010101010$$

is not complex, because there is an easy way to describe it, whereas a string such as

$$0110101011001110010001010$$

is complex because it appears to have no simple description.

Here is another way to think about it. Suppose I flip a fair coin, recording 0 for heads and 1 for tails. If I produce 0110101011001110010001010 and claim that it is a record of 25 tosses, no one would be surprised. But a few eyebrows would be raised if I produced 010101010101010101010101010 as my record of tosses. Thus complexity and randomness are linked.

Laplace noticed this connection two centuries ago. In 1819, he wrote

> In the game of heads and tails, if heads comes up a hundred times in a row then this appears to us extraordinary, because the almost infinite number of combinations that can arise in a hundred throws are divided in regular sequences, or those in which we observe a rule that is easy to grasp, and in irregular sequences, that are incomparably more numerous.

Kolmogorov complexity is a way to measure the complexity, or randomness, of a finite string. *Roughly speaking*, the Kolmogorov complexity $C(x)$ of a string x is the size (number of bits) in the shortest Pascal program P + input i that will print x and then halt. (If you do not like Pascal, feel free to substitute C, APL, or your favorite programming language.)

If the Kolmogorov complexity of a string x is small, then there is a simple way to describe x. If the Kolmogorov complexity of x is large, then x is hard to describe; we say it is "complex", "random", or possesses "high information content."

We can also view the combination of program and input (P, i) as an optimal way to compress x. In this interpretation, instead of storing x, we could store (P, i), since we could always recover x by running P on input i. (Note that this approach disregards the running time of P on input i.)

For a more formal definition of Kolmogorov complexity, we need a universal TM U. The input to U is a self-delimiting binary encoding of a TM T, followed by $y \in \{0, 1\}^*$, the input for T. By *self-delimiting* we mean that given $e(T)y$ we can tell where the encoding of T ends and y begins. We assume that T's input alphabet, as well as U's, is $\{0, 1\}$. U then simulates T on input y. It is assumed that T has an output tape, and the output of U is what T outputs if and when it halts.

Then $C(x)$ is formally defined to be the length of a shortest input $e(T)y$ that causes U to output x.

Theorem 6.2.1. *We have $C(x) \leq |x| + O(1)$.*

Note that the constant in the big-O is independent of x.

Proof. Informally, we can use the following Pascal program:

```
program print(input);
begin
     write(input);
end.
```

Clearly, the length of this program is $|x| + c$, where c is the number of characters in the preceding template.

Formally, there exists some TM T that simply copies the input to the output. Then the input to U is $e(T)x$, which is of length $|x| + |e(T)| = |x| + O(1)$. ∎

Example 6.2.2. Let us show $C(xx) \leq C(x) + O(1)$. Informally, given a Pascal program P to print x, we simply call it twice to print xx. The extra cost to build the "wrapper" program and call P twice corresponds to the $O(1)$ term.

The next theorem, called the invariance theorem, shows that the particular choice of programming language or universal TM is irrelevant, at least up to an additive constant.

Theorem 6.2.3. *Suppose we define* C_{APL}, C_{JAVA}, *and so on, analogously. Then we have, for example,*

$$C_{APL}(x) \leq C(x) + O(1);$$
$$C(x) \leq C_{APL}(x) + O(1).$$

Thus all these measures are the same up to an additive constant.

Proof. We prove $C(x) \leq C_{APL}(x) + O(1)$, leaving the other direction to the reader. Suppose $C_{APL}(x) = d$. Then there exists an APL program p to print out x, of size d. Now write an APL interpreter as a TM T; such a machine can be fed with p to output x. Thus, $C(x) \leq d + O(1)$ as desired, since $C(x) \leq |e(T)p| = |e(T)| + |p|$. ∎

We can think of the representation of a string x as $e(T)y$ as a sort of optimal "compression" method (like the Unix `compress` command). The $e(T)$ captures the "regular" aspects of x, while the y captures the "irregular" aspects of x.

We call a string x *incompressible* or *random* if $C(x) \geq |x|$. We cannot explicitly exhibit long incompressible strings x, but we can prove they exist:

Theorem 6.2.4. *For all $n \geq 0$, there exists at least one string x of length n such that $C(x) \geq |x|$.*

Proof. There are 2^n strings of length n, but at most $1 + 2 + \cdots + 2^{n-1} = 2^n - 1$ shorter descriptions. ∎

Unfortunately, Kolmogorov complexity is uncomputable, so perfect compression is unattainable.

Theorem 6.2.5. *The quantity $C(x)$ is uncomputable.*

Proof. Assume $C(x)$ is computable by a TM T that takes x as input. Create a new TM T' that, on input l, examines all strings of size l in lexicographic order until it finds a string y with $C(y) \geq |y| = l$, using T as a subroutine. Such a string exists by Theorem 6.2.4. Then T' outputs y.

Now let us compute the Kolmogorov complexity of y. On the one hand, we have $C(y) \geq l$. On the other hand, the string y is completely determined by T' and l, so $C(y) \leq |e(T')| + (\log_2 l) + 1$.

$$l \leq C(y) \leq |e(T)| + (\log_2 l) + c \qquad (6.1)$$

for a constant c. Now choose l sufficiently large so that $l > |e(T)| + (\log_2 l) + c$. This inequality contradicts Eq. (6.1). ∎

6.3 The incompressibility method

The basic idea in this method is that "most" strings cannot be compressed very much. Generally speaking, a proof works by selecting a typical instance and arguing about its properties. In the incompressibility method, we pick a random "incompressible" string and argue about it.

Example 6.3.1. Let $\pi(x)$ denote the number of primes $\leq x$. A celebrated theorem known as the prime number theorem states that $\pi(x) \sim \frac{x}{\log x}$. Using the incompressibility method, however, we can prove the weaker inequality $\pi(n) > cn/(\log n)^2$ for infinitely many n. In fact, we show that this inequality is true for infinitely many n of the form $n = 1 + \lfloor 2^d m (\log_2 m)^2 \rfloor$ for a constant d.

Consider the ordinary binary representation of the nonnegative integers, so that, for example, 43 is represented by 101011. If $n \geq 1$ is represented by a string x, then it is easy to see that $|x| = \lfloor \log_2 n \rfloor + 1$. Unfortunately, there are also other possible representations for 43, such as 0101011. To avoid the "leading zeroes" problem, we can define a 1–1 mapping between the natural numbers and elements of $\{0, 1\}^*$ as follows: $e(n)$ is defined to be the string obtained by taking the ordinary base-2 expansion of $n + 1$ and then dropping the leading bit 1. For example, the representations of the first eight natural numbers are given in the following table:

n	$e(n)$
0	ϵ
1	0
2	1
3	00
4	01
5	10
6	11
7	000

Note that $|e(n)| = \lfloor \log_2(n + 1) \rfloor + 1 - 1 = \lfloor \log_2(n + 1) \rfloor$. Now $t + 1 \leq 2t$ for $t \geq 1$, so

$$\log_2(t + 1) \leq \log_2(2t) \leq (\log_2 t) + 1. \tag{6.2}$$

It follows that

$$(\log_2 n) - 1 \leq |e(n)| \leq (\log_2 n) + 1. \tag{6.3}$$

Previously we defined a binary string x to be random if $C(x) \geq |x|$. Since we now have a bijection between binary strings and natural numbers, we can define a natural number N to be *random* if $C(e(N)) \geq |e(N)|$. By Theorem 6.2.4, there exist infinitely many random integers.

We will also need a *prefix-free* encoding of the natural numbers. By *prefix-free*, we mean that no prefix of an encoding of a number m is the encoding of some other number. Prefix-free encodings are useful because they enable us to encode k-tuples of integers by simply concatenating the encodings. The prefix-free property then ensures unique decoding.

There are many different ways to create prefix-free encodings, but the following one will suffice for us. Given a natural number m, we define

$$E(m) = 1^{|e(|e(m)|)|} 0 e(|e(m)|) e(m).$$

Here are some examples of this encoding.

m	$E(m)$
0	0
1	1000
2	1001
3	10100
4	10101
5	10110
6	10111
7	11000000

From (6.3) we get

$$|E(m)| \leq 2(\log_2((\log_2 m) + 1) + 1) + 1 + (\log_2 m) + 1$$
$$\leq 2(\log_2 \log_2 m + 2) + \log_2 m + 2$$
$$= 2 \log_2 \log_2 m + \log_2 m + 6.$$

Before we get started on the main result, let us use the ideas given earlier to give a proof that there are infinitely many prime numbers. Suppose there are only finitely many primes, say $p_1, p_2, \ldots, p_k$, and let N be random. Then

$$C(e(N)) \geq |e(N)| \geq (\log_2 N) - 1. \tag{6.4}$$

On the other hand, from the well-known result that every integer can be factored as a product of primes, we can write $N = p_1^{a_1} \cdots p_k^{a_k}$ for nonnegative integers $a_1, a_2, \ldots, a_k$. Clearly, $a_i \leq \log_2 N$ for $1 \leq i \leq k$. It follows that we can encode N by $e(T)E(a_1)E(a_2) \cdots E(a_k)$, where T is a TM that reconstructs N from the exponents in its prime factorization. The length of this representation is $O(k \log_2 \log_2 N)$, which contradicts (6.4).

Now let us prove $\pi(n) > cn/(\log n)^2$ for infinitely many n. We note that an integer N can be encoded by the string $x := e(T)E(m)e(N/p_m)$, where p_m is the largest prime dividing N and T is a TM that deduces m, computes p_m, and multiplies it by N/p_m to get N. If N is random, then the length of x must be at least as long as $e(N)$. Hence we have

$$|e(T)E(m)e(N/p_m)| \geq (\log_2 N) - 1$$

for infinitely many N. In fact, among these infinitely many N, there must be infinitely many distinct m, for otherwise all random N could be factorized into some finite set of primes, which is impossible as we have seen earlier.

Using the preceding inequalities for E and e, we get

$$\log_2 p_m \leq \log_2 m + 2 \log_2 \log_2 m + d$$

for some constant $d \geq 1$. Now, raising 2 to both sides, we get $p_m \leq 2^d m (\log_2 m)^2$. Now set $n = \lfloor 2^d m (\log_2 m)^2 \rfloor + 1$. We then have $\pi(n) \geq m$.

It now remains to see that $m \geq \frac{n}{2^d (\log_2 n)^2}$. Assume, contrary to what we want to prove, that

$$m < \frac{n}{2^d (\log_2 n)^2}. \qquad (6.5)$$

From our definition of n, we have

$$2^d m (\log_2 m)^2 < n \leq 2^d m (\log_2 m)^2 + 1. \qquad (6.6)$$

Thus,

$$\log_2 n > d + \log_2 m + 2 \log_2 \log_2 m. \qquad (6.7)$$

Now, using (6.5) first and then (6.7), we get, for $m \geq 2$,

$$\begin{aligned}
n &> 2^d m (\log_2 n)^2 \\
&> 2^d m (d + \log_2 m + 2 \log_2 \log_2 m)^2 \\
&\geq 2^d m (\log_2 m + 1)^2 \\
&> 2^d m (\log_2 m)^2 + 1,
\end{aligned}$$

which contradicts (6.6). Thus our assumption in (6.5) is false and hence $m \geq \frac{n}{2^d (\log_2 n)^2}$. Since $\pi(n) \geq m$, we get $\pi(n) \geq \frac{n}{2^d (\log_2 n)^2}$, our desired result.

We now turn to applications of the incompressibility method to formal languages, specifically, to proving that certain languages are not regular.

Example 6.3.2. Let $L = \{0^k 1^k : k \geq 1\}$. We prove that L is not regular. Suppose it were. Then it would be accepted by a deterministic finite automaton (DFA) $M = (Q, \Sigma, \delta, q_0, F)$. We could then encode each integer n by providing a description of M (in $O(1)$ bits) and $q = \delta(q_0, 0^n)$ (in $O(1)$ bits), because then n is uniquely specified as the least i with $\delta(q, 1^i) \in F$. Hence, $C(e(n))) = O(1)$. But there exist infinitely many n with $C(e(n)) \geq \log_2 n + O(1)$, a contradiction.

We can generalize the previous example, as follows:

Lemma 6.3.3. *Let $L \subseteq \Sigma^*$ be regular, and define $L_x = \{y : xy \in L\}$. Then there exists a constant c such that for each x, if z is the nth string in L_x in lexicographic order, then $C(z) \leq C(e(n)) + c$.*

Proof. The string z can be encoded by the DFA for L (in $O(1)$ bits), plus the state of the DFA after processing x (in $O(1)$ bits), and the encoding $e(n)$. ∎

We now consider some applications of this lemma.

Example 6.3.4. Let us prove that $L = \{1^p : p \text{ prime}\}$ is not regular. Let $x = 1^{p_k}$, where p_k is the kth prime. Then the second element of L_x is $y = 1^{p_{k+1} - p_k}$. But as $k \to \infty$, the difference $p_{k+1} - p_k$ is unbounded (because, for example, the $n - 1$ consecutive numbers $n! + 2, n! + 3, n! + 4, \ldots, n! + n$ are all composite for $n \geq 2$). Hence, $C(1^{p_{k+1} - p_k})$ is unbounded. However, by Lemma 6.3.3, we have $C(y) \leq C(e(2)) + c = O(1)$, a contradiction.

Example 6.3.5. Let us prove that $L = \{xx^R w : x, w \in \{0, 1\}^+\}$ is not regular. Let $x = (01)^m$, where m is random (i.e., $C(e(m)) \geq |e(m)| \geq \log_2 m - 1$). Then the lexicographically first element of L_x is $y = (10)^m 0$. Hence, $C(y) = O(1)$. But $C(y) \geq \log_2 m + O(1)$, a contradiction.

Example 6.3.6. Let us prove that $L = \{0^i 1^j : \gcd(i, j) = 1\}$ is not regular. Let $x = 0^{(p-1)!} 1$, where p is a prime, and $|e(p)| = n$. Then the second word in L_x is $y = 1^{p-1}$, which gives $C(y) = O(1)$. But $C(e(p)) \leq C(y) + O(1)$, and there are infinitely many primes, so $C(e(p)) = O(1)$ for infinitely many primes p, a contradiction.

6.4 The busy beaver problem

In this section we describe a problem of Rado on TMs now known as the *busy beaver problem*. We assume that our TMs are deterministic and have a tape alphabet consisting of a single symbol 1 and the usual blank symbol B. (In Rado's original description, the symbol 0 was used as a blank.) We also assume

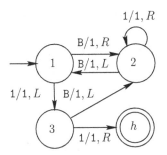

Figure 6.1: A three-state busy beaver

that our TM has a single "doubly infinite" tape, initially completely blank, and that the machine must move either right or left at each step—it cannot remain stationary. There is a single halting state from which no transitions emerge, and this halting state is not counted in the total number of states.

Rado's function $\Sigma(n)$ is defined to be the maximum number of (not necessarily consecutive) 1s left on the tape after such an n-state TM halts. He also defined a function $S(n)$ that counts the maximum number of moves that can be made by an n-state halting TM of this form.

For example, consider the three-state TM as shown in Figure 6.1.

If this machine is started with a tape of all blanks, it halts after 13 moves with six consecutive 1s on the tape—check this. This shows that $\Sigma(3) \geq 6$ and $S(3) \geq 13$. In fact, it can be shown that $\Sigma(3) = 6$ and $S(3) = 21$.

If a TM writes the maximum possible number of 1s for its number of states—that is, $\Sigma(n)$ 1s—then it is called a "busy beaver." Busy beavers are hard to find, even for relatively small n, for two reasons. First, the search space is extremely large: there are $(4(n + 1))^{2n}$ different TMs with n states. (For each nonhalting state, there are two transitions out, so there are $2n$ total transitions, and each transition has two possibilities for the symbol being written, two possibilities for the direction to move—left or right, and $(n + 1)$ possibilities for what state to go to—including the halting state.) Second, it is in general not possible to determine whether a particular TM will halt, so it may not be easy to distinguish between a machine that goes into an infinite loop from one that goes for thousands, millions, or billions of steps before halting. For example, it is known (by explicitly producing an example) that $S(6) \geq 10^{2879}$. It is also known that $\Sigma(6) \geq 10^{1439}$.

In fact, we will show in a moment that neither $\Sigma(n)$ nor $S(n)$ is computable function. This means that there is no halting TM that, on arbitrary input n, will always halt and successfully compute these functions. Nevertheless, it is possible to compute $\Sigma(n)$ and $S(n)$ for some small values of n by a brute-force approach, and this has been done by many investigators.

n	$\Sigma(n)$	$S(n)$	Source
1	1	1	Lin and Rado
2	4	6	Lin and Rado
3	6	21	Lin and Rado
4	13	107	Brady
5	$\geq 4{,}098$	$\geq 47{,}176{,}870$	Marxen and Buntrock
6	$\geq 10^{1439}$	$\geq 10^{2879}$	Ligocki and Ligocki

Figure 6.2: $\Sigma(n)$ and $S(n)$ for $1 \leq n \leq 6$

Figure 6.2 shows what is known about $\Sigma(n)$ and $S(n)$ for $1 \leq n \leq 6$.
Figure 6.3 illustrates the six-state TM that makes about $> 10^{2879}$ moves before halting with about 10^{1439} 1s on its tape.
Now let us prove that neither $\Sigma(n)$ nor $S(n)$ is computable.

Theorem 6.4.1. *The function $\Sigma(n)$ is not computable by a TM.*

Proof. The idea is to show that if $f(n)$ is any computable function, then there exists n_0 such that $\Sigma(n) > f(n)$ for $n \geq n_0$.
Our model of computable function is that a TM calculating $f(n)$ starts with a tape with a block of n 1s immediately to the right of the starting blank and halts after a finite number of moves with a block of $f(n)$ consecutive 1s on the tape.
Let f be an arbitrary computable function and define

$$F(x) = \sum_{0 \leq i \leq x} (f(i) + i^2).$$

Since f is computable, so is F. In fact, there is a TM M_F that, for all strings y, when started in the configuration $yB1^x q_0 B$ halts in the configuration $yB1^x B1^{F(x)} hB$. Assume M_F has n states.

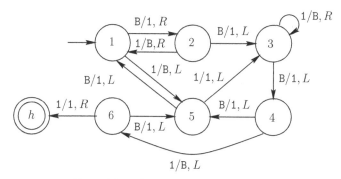

Figure 6.3: A six-state busy beaver candidate

Consider a TM M that, on input ϵ, first writes x 1s on an initially blank tape and then halts with its head on the blank immediately following the rightmost 1. This can be done with $x + 1$ states. Next, M simulates M_F on this tape, resulting in the configuration $B1^x B1^{F(x)} h B$. Finally, M simulates M_F again on this tape, resulting in the configuration $B1^x B1^{F(x)} B1^{F(F(x))} h B$. This machine has $x + 1 + 2n$ states.

Now any busy beaver machine of $x + 1 + 2n$ states will leave at least as many 1s as M does when started on input ϵ. Hence we have

$$\Sigma(x + 1 + 2n) \geq x + F(x) + F(F(x)).$$

But from its definition, $F(x) \geq x^2$, and there exists a constant c_1 such that $x^2 > x + 1 + 2n$ for all $x \geq c_1$. It follows that $F(x) > x + 1 + 2n$ for $x \geq c_1$. Now from its definition we have $F(x) > F(y)$ if $x > y$, so we have $F(F(x)) > F(x + 1 + 2n)$ for $x \geq c_1$. It follows that

$$\Sigma(x + 1 + 2n) \geq x + F(x) + F(F(x)) > F(F(x)) > F(x + 1 + 2n)$$
$$\geq f(x + 1 + 2n)$$

for $x \geq c_1$. It follows that Σ is eventually greater than f. Since f was arbitrary, Σ is noncomputable. ∎

Corollary 6.4.2. *The function $S(n)$ is also noncomputable.*

Proof. There exists a TM M with n states that writes $\Sigma(n)$ 1s on its tape before halting. Such a TM must make at least $\Sigma(n)$ moves. Hence, $S(n) \geq \Sigma(n)$. Since $\Sigma(n)$ is eventually greater than any computable function, so is $S(n)$. Hence, S is also noncomputable. ∎

6.5 The Post correspondence problem

In this section we discuss a famous unsolvable problem, the *Post correspondence problem*, often abbreviated as PCP. The problem is very simple to describe: we are given as input two morphisms $g, h : \Sigma^* \to \Delta^*$, and the question we would like to solve is, does there exist a nonempty word $x \in \Sigma^*$ such that $g(x) = h(x)$?

Example 6.5.1. Consider the morphisms g and h defined by

$$\begin{aligned}
g(1) &= 001 & h(1) &= 00 \\
g(2) &= 11 & h(2) &= 011 \\
g(3) &= 01 & h(3) &= 000 \\
g(4) &= 010 & h(4) &= 10.
\end{aligned}$$

This instance of PCP has no solution, for if $g(x) = h(x)$, then x must start with 1; however, this choice results in one more 1 in the image of g than in the image of h, and subsequence choices of letters do not allow this difference to be made up.

On the other hand, the PCP instance defined by

$$g(1) = 0 \qquad h(1) = 1$$
$$g(2) = 1 \qquad h(2) = 011$$
$$g(3) = 011 \qquad h(2) = 0.$$

has a solution, but the shortest nonempty x with $g(x) = h(x)$ has length 75. (One such solution is $x = 3113323111233312311231233123131123123311331$ $231223323212222112211323321221222.$)

We now prove

Theorem 6.5.2. *PCP is unsolvable.*

Proof Idea. The basic idea is simple; we reduce from the halting problem. Given a TM M and an input w, we structure our morphisms so that there is a solution x to $f(x) = g(x)$ iff there is an accepting computation for M on w. To do this, we force $f(u)$ to "lag behind" $g(u)$, and it can "catch up" only if the computation halts.

The details, however, are somewhat messy. First, we define a variant of PCP called MPCP (the modified Post correspondence problem). In this variant, we look for a solution to $f(x) = g(x)$, but demand that x start with a given fixed letter. Then we show that the halting problem reduces to MPCP, and MPCP reduces to PCP.

Proof. More precisely, MPCP is defined as follows: we are given morphisms $g, h : \Sigma^* \to \Delta^*$, where $\Sigma = \{0, 1, \dots, k\}$, and we want to know if there is a word w such that $g(0w) = h(0w)$.

Let us show that MPCP reduces to PCP. To make the notation a little less cumbersome, we introduce the following notation for morphisms: if the domain alphabet Σ has an obvious ordering, such as $\Sigma = \{1, 2, \dots, k\}$, we write $g = (w_1, w_2, \dots, w_k)$ to denote that $f(i) = w_i$ for $1 \leq i \leq k$.

Suppose $g = (w_1, w_2, \dots, w_k)$ and $h = (x_1, x_2, \dots, x_k)$ be an instance of MPCP. We convert this to an instance of PCP as follows: we introduce two new symbols $\sharp$ and $\flat$ not in the alphabet of the w_i and x_i, and we let $g' = (y_0, y_1, \dots, y_{k+1})$ and $h' = (z_0, z_1, \dots, z_{k+1})$, where $y_0 := \sharp y_1, z_0 := z_1,$

$y_{k+1} := \flat$, $z_{k+1} := \sharp\flat$, and

$$y_i := w_i \, \mathrm{III} \overbrace{\sharp\cdots\sharp}^{|w_i|}, \qquad z_i := \overbrace{\sharp\cdots\sharp}^{|x_i|} \mathrm{III}\, x_i$$

for $1 \le i \le k$. For example, if $g = (10111, 1, 10)$ and $h = (10, 111, 0)$, then $g' = (\sharp1\sharp0\sharp1\sharp1\sharp1\sharp, 1\sharp0\sharp1\sharp1\sharp1\sharp, \sharp1\sharp, 1\sharp0\sharp, \flat)$ and $h' = (\sharp1\sharp0, \sharp1\sharp0, \sharp1\sharp1\sharp1, \sharp0, \sharp\flat)$.

We now argue that MPCP is solvable for g and h if and only if PCP is solvable for g' and h'. Suppose $1i_2i_3\cdots i_r$ is a solution to MPCP for g and h. Then it is easy to see that $0i_2\cdots i_r(k+1)$ is a solution to PCP for g' and h'. On the other hand, if $i_1, i_2, \ldots, i_r$ is a solution to PCP for g' and h', then we must have $i_1 = 0$, for otherwise the images of the solution under g' and h' would begin with two different letters. Similarly, we must have $i_r = k + 1$, for otherwise the images of the solution under g' and h' would end with two different letters. Now let j be the smallest integer such that $i_j = k + 1$. Then $i_1i_2\cdots i_j$ is a solution to PCP for g' and h', and $1i_2\cdots i_{j-1}$ is then a solution to MPCP for g and h. We have now shown that MPCP reduces to PCP.

It remains to show that the halting problem reduces to MPCP. Suppose we are given a TM $M = (Q, \Sigma, \Gamma, \delta, q_0, h)$ and an input $w \in \Sigma^*$. We construct an instance of MPCP as follows. To simplify the construction, we give the corresponding values of the morphisms g and h in the following table, without specifying the input alphabet:

Group	Image of g	Image of h	Condition
Group 1	$\sharp$	$\sharp q_0 B w \sharp$	
Group 2	$\sharp$	$\sharp$	
	X	X	
			for $X \in \Gamma$
Group 3a	qX	Yp	if $\delta(q, X) = (p, Y, R)$
	ZqX	pZy	if $\delta(q, X) = (p, Y, L)$
	qX	pY	if $\delta(q, X) = (p, Y, S)$
Group 3b	$q\sharp$	$Yp\sharp$	if $\delta(q, B) = (p, Y, R)$
	$Zq\sharp$	$pZY\sharp$	if $\delta(q, B) = (p, Y, L)$
	$q\sharp$	$pY\sharp$	if $\delta(q, B) = (p, Y, S)$
			for $q \in Q - \{h\}$, $p \in Q$, $X, Y, Z \in \Gamma$
Group 4	XhY	h	
	Xh	h	
	hY	h	
			for $X, Y \in \Gamma$
Group 5	$h\sharp\sharp$	$\sharp$	

We now claim that M halts on w if and only if MPCP has a solution for the two morphisms defined this table. (Note that the image of 0 is given by the first line of the table.)

To see this, suppose M halts on w. Then there is a sequence of configurations $C_1 = q_0 B w, C_2, \ldots, C_t = \alpha h \beta$ representing an accepting computation. We leave it to the reader to see that we can then choose a sequence of pairs matching this computation, resulting in $g(x) = h(x) = \sharp C_1 \sharp C_2 \sharp \cdots \sharp C_t \sharp z$ for some string z.

Now suppose MPCP has a solution x. It is not hard to see that such a solution corresponds to a computation of M. Consider forming $g(x)$ and $h(x)$ symbol by symbol. Then since $g(x)$ must begin $\sharp$ and $h(x)$ begin $\sharp q_0 B w \sharp$, and because the pairs in Groups 2 and 3 do not increase the length of the image of h, there is no way the length of the image of g can "catch up" unless pairs in Groups 4 and 5 are used. But we cannot use these symbols unless the halting state h is reached, so M must halt. ∎

Now let us see an application of the PCP.

Theorem 6.5.3. *The following problem is unsolvable: given an arbitrary CFG G, decide if it is ambiguous.*

Proof. We show that if we could decide ambiguity for CFGs, we could solve the PCP.

Let $\Sigma = \{1, 2, \ldots, k\}$, and let $g, h : \Sigma^* \to \Delta^*$ be the morphisms from an instance of PCP. Without loss of generality, we may assume that Σ and Δ are disjoint. We now construct a grammar G with the productions

$$
\begin{aligned}
S &\to S_1 \mid S_2 \\
S_1 &\to g(i)\, i, & 1 \le i \le k \\
S_1 &\to g(i)\, S_1\, i, & 1 \le i \le k \\
S_2 &\to h(i)\, i, & 1 \le i \le k \\
S_2 &\to h(i)\, S_2\, i, & 1 \le i \le k.
\end{aligned}
$$

We claim that G is ambiguous iff the PCP instance has a solution.

Suppose G is ambiguous. Now it is easy to see that the subgrammars defined by taking either S_1 or S_2 to be the start symbol are each unambiguous, so any ambiguity results from a word generated by S_1 and S_2. If a word w is derived from both, then we have

$$
w = g(i_1)g(i_2) \cdots g(i_r) i_r \cdots i_2 i_1 = h(j_1)h(j_2) \cdots g(j_s) j_s \cdots j_2 j_1
$$

for some nonempty words $i_1 i_2 \cdots i_r, j_1 j_2 \cdots j_s \in \Sigma^*$. But then, since Σ and Δ are disjoint, we must have $r = s$ and $i_1 = j_1, i_2 = j_2, \ldots, i_r = j_r$. Then $g(i_1 \cdots i_r) = h(i_1 \cdots i_r)$ and so we have a solution to PCP.

Similarly, if we have a solution $i_1 i_2 \cdots i_r$ to PCP, then the word $g(i_1)g(i_2) \cdots g(i_r)i_r i_{r-1} \cdots i_2 i_1$ has two distinct leftmost derivations in G, one starting $S \Longrightarrow S_1$ and the other starting $S \Longrightarrow S_2$. ∎

6.6 Unsolvability and context-free languages

In this section we discuss some unsolvability results dealing with context-free languages and grammars. First we discuss two languages: valid(M), the language of valid computations of a TM, and invalid(M), the language of invalid computations of a TM.

A *valid computation* of a TM $M = (Q, \Sigma, \Gamma, \delta, q_0, h)$ is defined to be a string of the form $w_1 \# w_2^R \# w_3 \# w_4^R \# \cdots \# w_{2k}^R \#$ or $w_1 \# w_2^R \# w_3 \# w_4^R \# \cdots \# w_{2k-1} \#$ for some integer $k \geq 1$, $n = 2k$, or $2k - 1$ as appropriate, where $\#$ is a symbol not in Γ or Q such that

1. Each w_i is a valid configuration of M.
2. w_1 is a valid initial configuration of M; that is, it is of the form $q_0 B x$ for $x \in \Sigma^*$.
3. w_n is a valid accepting or final configuration of M, that is, of the form $y h z$, where h is the halting state.
4. $w_i \vdash w_{i+1}$ for $1 \leq i < n$.

The language of all valid computations of M is denoted valid(M). The language of invalid computations of M, denoted invalid(M), is defined to be $(\Gamma \cup Q \cup \{\#\})^*$—valid($M$).

Theorem 6.6.1. *There exists an algorithm that, given a TM M as input, produces two CFGs G_1 and G_2 such that* valid(M) $= L(G_1) \cap L(G_2)$.

Proof. It is actually somewhat easier to sketch the construction of two pushdown automatons (PDAs) M_1 and M_2 that accept $L_1 := L(G_1)$ and $L_2 := L(G_2)$, respectively. By Theorem 1.5.7 we know that we can effectively produce CFGs from these PDAs.

Both L_1 and L_2 consist of strings of the form $x_1 \# x_2 \# x_3 \cdots \# x_m \#$. We use M_1 to enforce the condition $x_i \vdash x_{i+1}^R$ for i odd and M_2 to enforce the condition $x_i^R \vdash x_{i+1}$ for i even. The machine M_2 also checks to see that x_1 is a valid initial configuration of M. The condition that x_m (respectively x_m^R) is a valid final configuration is checked by M_1 or M_2, respectively, according to whether m is odd or even.

Define $L_3 = \{y\#z^R : y \vdash z\}$. We sketch how L_3 may be accepted by a PDA M_3. The PDA reads the input up to # and ensures that y is really a valid configuration (i.e., of the form $\Gamma^* Q \Gamma^*$). As it does so, it computes z^R on the fly and pushes it onto its stack.

In more detail, M_3 reads each symbol of y and pushes it onto its stack until it reads a state p. Then M_3 stores p in its finite control and reads the next symbol X. It now looks up the corresponding transition in its finite control. If $\delta(p, X) = (q, Y, R)$, then M_3 pushes qY onto its stack. If $\delta(p, X) = (q, Y, S)$, then M_3 pushes Yq onto its stack. Finally, if $\delta(p, X) = (q, Y, L)$, then M_3 reads the symbol on top of the stack (call it Z). Then M_3 pops the Z and pushes YZq in its place. (We have described the usual case, but some special cases are needed if # appears in this process.) Finally, M_3 reads the rest of the input symbols up to the # and pushes them onto its stack. Now M_3 pops its stack and compares it to the rest of the input, symbol by symbol. It accepts if they agree; otherwise it rejects.

In a similar way we can construct a PDA for $L_4 := \{y^R\#z : y \vdash z\}$. Now define

$$L_1 = (L_3\#)^*(\{\epsilon\} \cup \Gamma^* h \Gamma^* \#);$$
$$L_2 = q_0 B \Sigma^* \#(L_4\#)^*(\{\epsilon\} \cup \Gamma^* h \Gamma^* \#).$$

Given PDAs M_3 accepting L_3 and M_4 accepting L_4 we can easily construct PDAs M_5 accepting L_1 and M_6 accepting L_2. Finally, we claim that valid$(M) = L_1 \cap L_2$. ∎

Now we can use Theorem 6.6.1 to prove an unsolvability result about grammars.

Theorem 6.6.2. *The following problem is unsolvable: given two CFGs G_1 and G_2, decide if $L(G_1) \cap L(G_2) = \emptyset$.*

Proof. Suppose there were an algorithm to solve the given problem. Then we could solve the following problem (the emptiness problem for TMs): given a TM M, decide if $L(M) = \emptyset$. To see this, we reduce the emptiness problem for TMs to our grammar problem. Given a TM M, we use Theorem 6.6.1 to create G_1 and G_2 such that valid$(M) = L(G_1) \cap L(G_2)$. Now we use our hypothesized algorithm to decide if $L(G_1) \cap L(G_2) = \emptyset$. Note that this occurs iff valid$(M) = \emptyset$, which occurs if and only if $L(M) = \emptyset$. Hence we could decide if $L(M) = \emptyset$, which is known to be unsolvable. ∎

Even more results can be obtained using invalid(M).

Theorem 6.6.3. *There exists an algorithm that, given a TM M, produces a CFG G such that* invalid$(M) = L(G)$.

Proof. The proof is generally along the lines of the proof of Theorem 6.6.1, but is somewhat simpler because we do not need to ensure that $w_i \vdash w_{i+1}$ for all i; instead it suffices to find a single i for which $w_i \not\vdash w_{i+1}$.

We claim that if w represents an invalid computation, then at least one of the following conditions holds:

1. w is not of the form $x_1 \# x_2 \# \cdots x_m \#$, where each x_i is a configuration;
2. $x_1 \notin q_0 B \Sigma^*$;
3. $x_m \notin \Gamma^* h \Gamma^*$;
4. $x_i \not\vdash x_{i+1}^R$ for some odd i;
5. $x_i^R \not\vdash x_{i+1}$ for some even i.

It is easy to check conditions (1)–(3) with a finite automaton, while conditions (4) and (5) can be checked with a single PDA using the same kind of argument we used in proving Theorem 6.6.1. Hence we can constructively create a CFG G such that invalid$(M) = L(G)$. ■

Using Theorem 6.6.3 we can prove a large number of unsolvability results about context-free grammars. Here are several; others are given in the exercises.

Corollary 6.6.4. *The following problem is unsolvable: given a CFG $G = (V, \Sigma, P, S)$, decide if $L(G) = \Sigma^*$.*

Proof. We reduce from the emptiness problem for TMs. Given a TM M, we can effectively construct a CFG G such that invalid$(M) = L(G)$. Now note that invalid$(M) = \Sigma^*$ if and only if $L(M) = \emptyset$, where $\Sigma = \Gamma \cup Q \cup \{\#\}$. ■

Corollary 6.6.5. *The following problem is unsolvable: given two CFGs G_1 and G_2, decide if $L(G_1) = L(G_2)$.*

Proof. We reduce from the problem, given a CFG G_1, is $L(G_1) = \Sigma^*$. We can easily construct a grammar G_2 such that $L(G_2) = \Sigma^*$. Hence, $L(G_1) = L(G_2)$ if and only if $L(G_1) = \Sigma^*$, and this reduction gives the desired result. ■

Theorem 6.6.6. *The following problem is unsolvable: given a CFG G, decide if $L(G)$ is regular.*

Proof. Let $G = (V, \Sigma, P, S)$ and let $L = L(G)$. Suppose $|\Sigma|$ is large enough that the problem of deciding if $L(G) = \Sigma^*$ is unsolvable. Let $L_0 \subseteq \Sigma^*$ be a nonregular, context-free language generated by a CFG G_0. Consider the language $L_1 - L_0 \# \Sigma^* \cup \Sigma^* \# L$. Since the class of context-free languages is effectively closed under concatenation and union, L_1 is a context-free language, and a CFG G_1 such that $L_1 = L(G_1)$ can be effectively computed from G and G_0. We claim L_1 is regular if and only if $L = \Sigma^*$.

Suppose $L = \Sigma^*$. Then $L_1 = \Sigma^*\#\Sigma^*$ is a regular language. Now suppose $L \neq \Sigma^*$. Then there exists $w \notin L$, and we have $L_1/\#w = L_0$. Since the class of regular languages is closed under quotient, if L_1 is regular, then L_0 is regular. By assumption, L_0 is not regular, so L_1 must not be regular as well. Thus, L_1 is regular if and only if $L = \Sigma^*$. Since the problem of deciding if $L = \Sigma^*$ is unsolvable, the result follows. ∎

The next result shows that even if a "birdie" tells you that a given CFG generates a regular language, there is no algorithm to compute an equivalent DFA.

Theorem 6.6.7. *There exists no algorithm that, given a CFG G such that $L(G)$ is regular, produces a DFA A such that $L(A) = L(G)$.*

Proof. Suppose to the contrary that such an algorithm exists. Let $M = (Q, \Sigma, \Gamma, \delta, q_0, h)$ be a TM such that $L(M)$ is not recursive. By Theorem 6.6.3, there exists an algorithm to compute a CFG G' such that $L(G') = \text{invalid}(M)$. Let $\Delta = \Gamma \cup Q \cup Q \cup \{\#\}$. For $x \in \Sigma^*$, define

$$F_x = \{q_0 y \# z \ : \ y \neq x \text{ and } z \in \Delta^*\}.$$

The language F_x is regular, and a DFA B accepting F_x can easily be computed. Given the DFA B and the grammar G', a CFG G_x such that $L(G_x) = \text{invalid}(M) \cup F_x$ can be effectively computed.

If $x \in L(M)$, then $L(G_x) = \Delta^* - \{w\}$, where w is the accepting computation of M on x. If $x \notin L(M)$, then $L(G_x) = \Delta^*$. In either case, $L(G_x)$ is regular. By our initial assumption, we can compute a DFA A such that $L(A) = L(G_x)$. Given such a DFA A, we can decide whether or not $L(G_x) = \Delta^*$, and hence decide whether or not $x \in L(M)$. This is a contradiction, since $L(M)$ is not recursive.

6.7 Complexity and regular languages

In this section we prove several fundamental results about the computational complexity of problems dealing with regular languages.

We start with the *universality problem* for regular expressions and non-deterministic finite automaton (NFAs). Given a regular expression r over a base alphabet Δ (respectively, an NFA M with input alphabet Δ), we would like to know if $L(r) \neq \Delta^*$ (respectively, if $L(M) \neq \Delta^*$). Perhaps surprisingly, both of these problems are PSPACE-complete.

We start with regular expressions. The fundamental result is the following lemma.

Lemma 6.7.1. *Let* $T = (Q, \Sigma, \Gamma, \delta, q_0, h)$ *be a one-tape deterministic TM and* $p(n)$ *be a polynomial such that* T *never uses more than* $p(|x|)$ *cells on input* x. *Let* # *be a new symbol not in* Γ, *and let* $\Delta = \Gamma \cup Q$. *Then there is a polynomial* $q(n)$ *such that we can construct a regular expression* r_x *in* $\leq q(n)$ *steps, such that* $L(r_x) \neq (\Delta \cup \{\#\})^*$ *if and only if* T *accepts* x.

Proof Idea. Although the details are somewhat messy, the basic idea is simple. We encode a computation of the TM T as a string of successive configurations, separated by the delimiter #. Then we construct the regular expression r_x so that it specifies all strings that do *not* represent accepting configurations. A string might fail to represent an accepting configuration because it is in the wrong format, or because the initial configuration is wrong, or because T never enters the halting state h, or because in two consecutive configurations, the second does not follow from the first by a valid move of T. All these possibilities can be specified by r_x.

Proof. We represent a computation of T as a string

$$\#x_1\#x_2\# \cdots \#x_k\#,$$

where each x_i is a configuration, that is, a string in $\Gamma^* Q \Gamma^*$. We will assume that T always has a next move, which can be accomplished by creating a new "dead state" to enter if there is no move, and we will also assume that T simply stays in the halting state without moving its tape head once the halting state is reached.

We will further assume that the length of each configuration between # signs is $p(n) + 1$, which we can achieve by padding on the right with the blank symbol B, if necessary. The "+1" term comes from the fact that each configuration contains a state symbol.

Now we construct r_x to specify strings that are not valid accepting computations. A string y fails to represent an accepting computation if and only if at least one of the following conditions is met:

A: y is not of the form $\#x_1\#x_2\# \cdots \#x_k\#$ for some $k \geq 1$, where each x_i is of length $p(n) + 1$ and all but one symbol of x_i is in Γ, with the exception being in Q.

B: y begins with something other than $\#q_0 B a_1 a_2 \cdots a_n B \cdots B\#$, where $x = a_1 a_2 \cdots a_n$ and the number of blanks is $p(n) - n$.

C: The halting state h never appears in a configuration.

D: y has a subword of the form $\#x_i\#x_{i+1}\#$, where x_{i+1} does not follow from x_i in one step of T.

Now we can construct regular expressions A, B, C, and D for each of the conditions.

For A, we need to specify subexpressions

A_1: strings containing less than two instances of $\#$: $\Delta^* + \Delta^*\#\Delta^*$;

A_2: strings not beginning or ending with $\#$: $\Delta(\Delta + \#)^* + (\Delta + \#)^*\Delta$;

A_3: strings with no $q \in Q$ appearing between two consecutive occurrences of $\#$: $(\Delta + \#)^*\#\Delta^*\#(\Delta + \#)^*$;

A_4: strings with two or more occurrences of $q \in Q$ appearing between two consecutive occurrences of $\#$: $(\Delta + \#)^*\#\Delta^*Q\Delta^*Q\Delta^*\#(\Delta + \#)^*$;

A_5: strings with more than $p(n) + 1$ symbols of Δ appearing between two consecutive occurrences of $\#$: $(\Delta + \#)^*\#\Delta^{p(n)+2}\Delta^*\#(\Delta + \#)^*$;

A_6: strings with fewer than $p(n) + 1$ symbols of Δ appearing between two consecutive occurrences of $\#$: $(\Delta + \#)^*\#(\epsilon + \Delta + \Delta^2 + \cdots + \Delta^{p(n)})\#(\Delta + \#)^*$.

Now $A = A_1 + A_2 + A_3 + A_4 + A_5 + A_6$.

We construct B as the union $B = B_0 + B_1 + B_2 + \cdots + B_{p(n)+1}$, where each B_i represents a configuration that differs from the correct initial configuration in the ith location. So, letting $a_0 = \text{B}$, we define

$$B_0 = \#(\Delta - \{q_0\})\Delta^{p(n)}\#(\Delta + \#)^*;$$
$$B_i = \#\Delta^i(\Gamma - \{a_{i-1}\})\Delta^{p(n)-i}\#(\Delta + \#)^*, \quad 1 \le i \le n + 1;$$
$$B_j = \#\Delta^j(\Gamma - \{\text{B}\})\Delta^{p(n)-j}\#(\Delta + \#)^*, \quad n + 2 \le j \le p(n).$$

We construct C as $(\Delta - \{h\} + \#)^*$.

Finally, to construct D, we observe that given any four consecutive symbols $c_1c_2c_3c_4$ of a configuration, we can determine what symbol will replace c_2 in the next configuration, that is, the symbol $p(n) + 2$ symbols to the right of c_2. Thus, assuming the possible moves are

$$\delta(p, X) = \begin{cases} (q, Y, L) \\ (q, Y, R) \\ (q, Y, S) \end{cases}$$

we can define a function $f(c_1 c_2 c_3 c_4)$ as follows (where U, V, W, X, Y, Z are in Γ, and $p, q \in Q$):

$c_1 c_2 c_3 c_4$	$f(c_1 c_2 c_3 c_4)$
$UVWZ$	V
$pXVW$	Y if left move q if right move Y if stationary move
$VpXW$	V if left move Y if right move q if stationary move
$VWpX$	q if left move W if right move W if stationary move
$UVWp$	V

There are also some additional cases involving the delimiter #, which we leave to the reader.

Now, given f, we can define a regular expression for D as follows:

$$D = \bigcup_{c_1, c_2, c_3, c_4} (\Delta + \#)^* c_1 c_2 c_3 c_4 (\Delta + \#)^{p(n)-1} (\Delta \cup \{\#\} - \{f(c_1 c_2 c_3 c_4)\}) (\Delta + \#)^*.$$

Now it is easy to see that the length of r_x is a polynomial that depends only on x and T. Furthermore, r_x denotes $(\Delta \cup \{\#\})^*$ if and only if T does not accept x.

Now we want to create a language L_{regex} that encodes the problem "Is $L(r_x) \neq \Sigma^*$," but there is a slight technical problem to overcome. The problem is that the regular expressions are over an arbitrary alphabet, while L_{regex} must be over a fixed alphabet. To solve this problem, we simply encode regular expressions so that the first alphabetic symbol is represented by [1], the second by [10], the third by [11], and so on. Thus, we define L_{regex} to be the set of all encodings of regular expressions r, over the alphabet

$$[,], (,), \emptyset, \epsilon, +, *, 0, 1,$$

such that $L(r) \neq (\Delta \cup \{\#\})^*$.

Theorem 6.7.2. L_{regex} *is* PSPACE-*complete.*

Proof. First, let us prove that L_{regex} is in PSPACE. By Theorem 1.8.4 (Savitch's theorem), it suffices to give a nondeterministic polynomial-space-bounded TM that accepts L_{regex}.

Given an encoded regular expression r_e as input, we decode it to determine r. Now we convert r to an NFA-ϵ M with $n = O(|r_e|)$ states using the usual technique. We now guess the string x that is not in $L(M)$ symbol by symbol, and simulate M on x. If we find that M fails to accept x, we accept the input r_e. If our guess fails, and we have guessed at least 2^n symbols, we reject. (We can count up to 2^n using $O(n)$ space.)

Now we prove that if $L \in$ PSPACE, then $L \leq L_{\text{regex}}$. Let M be a deterministic TM accepting L. Then by Lemma 6.7.1 we can construct a regular expression r_x of polynomial size in x such that $L(r_x) \neq (\Delta \cup \{\#\})^*$ if and only if $x \in L$. Now convert r_x to its encoding. ∎

Corollary 6.7.3. *The following problem is* PSPACE-*complete: given an NFA* $M = (Q, \Sigma, \delta, q_0, F)$, *decide if* $L(M) \neq \Sigma^*$.

Our proof that the universality problem for regular expressions and NFAs is PSPACE-complete no longer works for a unary alphabet. Over a unary alphabet, we have the following.

Theorem 6.7.4. *Let* $\Sigma = \{a\}$. *Consider the following problem: given a unary regular expression* r, *decide if* $L(r) \neq \Sigma^*$. *Then this problem is* NP-*complete.*

Proof. First, let us see that the problem is in NP. Given a regular expression of size k, we can easily convert it to an equivalent NFA M with $n = O(k)$ states using the standard algorithm. Now we guess a length m such that $a^m \notin L(M)$ and then verify our guess using the Boolean matrix technique of Theorem 3.8.4. If there is indeed such a word not in $L(M)$, then one exists of length $m < 2^n$. (To see this, convert M to a DFA with at most 2^n states. If a string labels a path to a nonfinal state, there must be such a path of length $<2^n$.)

To show the problem is NP-hard, we reduce from 3-SAT. Suppose we have an instance of 3-SAT, say a formula $\varphi = C_1 \wedge C_2 \wedge \cdots \wedge C_n$, where each C_i is a clause, using variables $x_1, x_2, \ldots, x_k$ and their negations. Let p_i denote the ith prime. We now construct an integer y_i based on each clause C_i, which is most easily defined in terms of an example. If the clause C_1 is $(x_3 \vee \overline{x_5} \vee x_6)$, then we let y_1 be the unique integer, $0 \leq y_1 < p_3 p_5 p_6 = 5 \cdot 11 \cdot 13 = 715$ such that

$$y_1 \equiv 0 \ (\mathrm{mod} \ p_3)$$
$$y_1 \equiv 1 \ (\mathrm{mod} \ p_5)$$
$$y_1 \equiv 0 \ (\mathrm{mod} \ p_6).$$

So in this case, $y_1 = 650$. Note that the right side of a congruence is 1 if the corresponding variable is negated in the clause; 0 otherwise. Now we make the regular expression $E = E_0 + \cdots + E_n$, where

$$E_0 = \bigcup_{1 \le i \le k} \bigcup_{2 \le j < p_i} \mathsf{a}^j (\mathsf{a}^{p_i})^*$$

and, in the example we chose earlier,

$$E_1 = \mathsf{a}^{y_1} (\mathsf{a}^{p_3 p_5 p_6})^*$$

and the other E_i are defined similarly, based on the variables that occur in their clauses.

I now claim $L(E) \ne \mathsf{a}^*$ if and only if φ is satisfiable. For the way E is constructed, it omits a string if and only if it corresponds to a satisfying assignment. E_0, for example, specifies all strings that correspond to invalid assignments, where we assign a value of 2 or more to a variable.   ■

6.8 Exercises

1. Use a more efficient encoding than E in Example 6.3.1 to obtain the result $\pi(x) \ge c \frac{x}{(\log x)(\log \log x)^2}$ infinitely often.

2. Use Kolmogorov complexity and the incompressibility method to prove that the language

$$L = \{xx \ : \ x \in \{0, 1\}^*\}$$

   is not regular.

3. A common creationist claim is that gene duplication cannot generate information. Prove the creationists wrong by showing that there exist infinitely many strings x such that $C(xx) > C(x)$.

4. Let H be the entropy function defined by $H(\alpha, \beta) = -\alpha \log_2 \alpha - \beta \log_2 \beta$. Suppose a binary string x of length n is chosen by flipping a coin with a bias of α, $0 \le \alpha \le \frac{1}{2}$, where $\beta = 1 - \alpha$ is the probability of tails. Show that with very high probability, such a string satisfies $C(x) \asymp H(\alpha, \beta)n$.

5. Show that the following problems are recursively unsolvable:
   (a) Given a CFG G and a regular expression r, is $L(G) = L(r)$?
   (b) Given a CFG G and a regular expression r, is $L(r) \subseteq L(G)$?
   (c) Given CFGs G_1 and G_2, is $L(G_1) \subseteq L(G_2)$?

6. Prove that the following decision problem is unsolvable. Given a grammar G over an alphabet Σ, is $\Sigma^* - L(G)$ finite?

7. Show that the following decision problem is solvable: given an arbitrary CFG G and an arbitrary regular expression r as input, decide whether or not $L(G) \subseteq L(r)$.

8. Show the following problem is recursively unsolvable: given a CFG G, is $L(G)$ a linear language?

9. Suppose the definition of unrestricted grammar is relaxed to allow productions of the form $\epsilon \to \alpha$. In other words, at any time during a derivation the string α can be inserted between any two symbols. Show that this new model of unrestricted grammar also generates the class of recursively enumerable languages.

10. Give an unrestricted grammar for $\{ww \ : \ w \in \{0, 1\}^*\}$.

11. Give an unrestricted grammar for the language

$$\{a^i \ : \ i \geq 4 \text{ is not a prime}\}.$$

Give a sketch of the proof that your grammar is correct.

12. Show that the language of Kolmogorov-incompressible strings is not recursive.

13. From Theorem 6.2.4 we know that, for all $n \geq 0$, there is at least one string x of length n with $C(x) \geq n$. Prove that in fact there are 2^{n-c} such strings, for some constant c.

14. Let L_1, L_2 be context-free languages. Show that the following problem is unsolvable: decide whether or not L_1/L_2 is context-free.

15. Prove that there exists a constant c such that there are infinitely many strings x and y, where x is a subword of y, and $C(x) > 2^{C(y)-c}$.

16. Prove that the following problem is PSPACE-complete: given an NFA $M = (Q, \Sigma, \delta, q_0, F)$, decide if $\Sigma^* - L(M)$ is finite.

17. Prove that the following problem is unsolvable: given a string x, determine if $C(x) < |x|$.

**18. Recall the definition of pattern matching a text given in Exercise 3.70: $p \in \Sigma^*$ matches $t \in \Delta^*$ if there is a nonerasing morphism $h : \Sigma^* \to \Delta^*$ such that $h(p) = t$.

(a) Show that if the alphabets Σ and Δ are of fixed size, then we can decide if p matches t in time polynomial in $|p|$ and $|t|$.

(b) Show that the problem of deciding if p matches t for arbitrary alphabets is NP-complete.

(c) Suppose we are given a pattern p and an NFA M, and we want to decide if p matches t for some $t \in L(M)$. Show that this problem is PSPACE-complete.

(d) Suppose we are given a pattern p and a CFG G, and we want to decide if p matches t for some $t \in L(G)$. Show that this problem is unsolvable even if p is just the pattern xx.

19. Which of the following PCP instances have solutions?

(a) $(11, 01, 011), (1, 110, 0)$;

(b) $(11, 01, 101), (0, 011, 1)$;

(c) $(0, 01, 1), (1, 0, 101)$.

20. Show that the PCP is solvable if the images of the two morphisms are over a unary alphabet.

21. Show that the following problem is PSPACE-complete: given n DFAs $M_1, M_2, \ldots, M_n$, decide if there exists a string accepted by all of them. *Hint:* Use the automata to check that a string represents a valid computation of a polynomial-space-bounded TM.

22. Show that the following problem is PSPACE-complete: given an NFA M, decide if it accepts some string unambiguously, that is, if there exists some accepted string for which there is only one acceptance path in the NFA.

6.9 Projects

1. Read papers about constructing "bad" examples of the PCP. Start with Lorentz [2001] and Zhao [2003].

6.10 Research problems

1. Try finding busy beaver TMs for some variations on the TM model given here: for larger alphabets, for one-directional tapes, and so on.

6.11 Notes on Chapter 6

6.1 Unrestricted grammars are sometimes called Type 0 grammars. The grammar in Example 6.1.1 is due to J. Rideout.

Our proof of Theorem 6.1.3 is based on a suggestion of A. F. Nevraumont.

6.2 An excellent introduction to Kolmogorov complexity can be found in Li and Vitányi [1997]. Although the concept is attributed to Kolmogorov, similar ideas were proposed about the same time by R. Solomonoff and G. J. Chaitin.

6.3 The proof in Example 6.3.1 that $\pi(x) \geq cx/(\log x)^2$ infinitely often is sketched in Li and Vitányi [1997, pp. 4–5], where it is attributed to J. Tromp, improving a result of P. Berman, which in turn was based on a proof of G. Chaitin [1979].

The material on proofs of nonregularity is based on Li and Vitányi [1995].

6.4 The busy beaver problem was introduced by Rado [1962]. Lin and Rado [1965] gave the busy beavers with one, two, and three states, and Brady [1983] solved the case of four states. Marxen and Buntrock [1990] gave a candidate for the busy beaver with five states. The best example known on six states is due to Ligocki and Ligocki in December 2007 and can be found at `http://www.drb.insel.de/~heiner/BB/simLig62_b.html`. Heniner Marxen's Web page, `http://www.drb.insel.de/~heiner/BB/`, is the best online resource for the problem.

6.5 The PCP is due to Post [1946].

For a Web page giving record examples of the PCP, see `http://www.theory.informatik.uni-kassel.de/~stamer/pcp/pcpcontest_en.html`.

Theorem 6.5.3 is due to Cantor [1962], Floyd [1962], and Chomsky and Schützenberger [1963].

6.6 The results in this section are from Bar-Hillel, Perles, and Shamir [1961] and Ginsburg and Rose [1963].

6.7 Our presentation of Theorem 6.7.2 is based strongly on that in Aho, Hopcroft, and Ullman [1974, §10.6].

7

Other language classes

In this chapter we discuss some less familiar language classes, such as the context-sensitive languages (CLs) and the 2DPDA languages.

7.1 Context-sensitive languages

In this section we introduce a variant on the context-free grammar, known as the *context-sensitive grammar* or CSG.

A grammar $G = (V, \Sigma, P, S)$ is said to be *context-sensitive* if every production in P is of the form $\alpha B \gamma \to \alpha \beta \gamma$ for some $\alpha, \gamma \in (V \cup \Sigma)^*$, $\beta \in (V \cup \Sigma)^+$, and $B \in V$. A language L is said to be context-sensitive (or a *CSL*) if $L - \{\epsilon\}$ is generated by some CSG. (The funny condition involving ϵ arises because a CSG cannot have ϵ-productions, and hence, cannot generate ϵ.)

The name *context-sensitive* comes from the fact that we can consider the allowed productions to be of the form $B \to \beta$, but they can be applied only in the "context" α—γ.

Example 7.1.1. Consider the following CFG G_1:

$$S \to ABSc$$
$$S \to Abc$$
$$BA \to CA$$
$$CA \to CB$$
$$CB \to AB$$
$$Bb \to bb$$
$$A \to a.$$

We claim that $L(G_1) = \{a^n b^n c^n : n \geq 1\}$. Here is an informal argument that this is the case. Note that $BA \overset{*}{\Longrightarrow} AB$ by the series of context-sensitive productions $BA \Longrightarrow CA \Longrightarrow CB \Longrightarrow AB$. We argue that $a^n b^n c^n \in L(G_1)$ for all $n \geq 1$. We can use the following derivation:

$$\begin{aligned}
S &\Longrightarrow ABSc \Longrightarrow ABABScc \overset{*}{\Longrightarrow} (AB)^{n-1} Sc^{n-1} \\
&\Longrightarrow (AB)^{n-1} Abc^n = A(BA)^{n-1} bc^n \\
&\overset{*}{\Longrightarrow} A(AB)^{n-2} ABbc^n \\
&\Longrightarrow A(AB)^{n-2} Abbc^n = AA(BA)^{n-2} bbc^n \\
&\overset{*}{\Longrightarrow} AA(AB)^{n-2} bbc^n = AA(AB)^{n-3} ABbbc^n \\
&\Longrightarrow AA(AB)^{n-3} Abbbc^n = AAA(BA)^{n-3} bbbc^n \\
&\overset{*}{\Longrightarrow} A^n b^n c^n \overset{*}{\Longrightarrow} a^n b^n c^n.
\end{aligned}$$

It remains to see that $L(G_1) \subseteq \{a^n b^n c^n : n \geq 1\}$. The basic idea is that any derivation of a terminal string must proceed roughly along the lines given earlier. We leave the argument as an exercise.

There is an alternative characterization of CSLs in terms of grammars. We say a grammar $G = (V, \Sigma, P, S)$ is *length-increasing* if every production in P is of the form $\alpha \to \beta$, with $\alpha, \beta \in (V \cup \Sigma)^+$ and $|\alpha| \leq |\beta|$. (As before, a length-increasing grammar cannot generate the empty string.)

Example 7.1.2. Consider the following length-increasing grammar G_2:

$$\begin{aligned}
S &\to aBSc \\
S &\to abc \\
Ba &\to aB \\
Bb &\to bb.
\end{aligned}$$

We claim that $L(G_2) = \{a^n b^n c^n : n \geq 1\}$.

Theorem 7.1.3. *A language L is generated by a length-increasing grammar if and only if L is context-sensitive.*

Proof. Clearly, if L is generated by a CSG, then it is generated by a length-increasing grammar, because every CSG is actually length increasing.

To prove the other direction, we show how to take a length-increasing grammar and transform it by a series of steps into a CSG, without changing the language generated.

First, we do a transformation that changes all the occurrences of a terminal in a production to a variable. Namely, we replace every occurrence of a in a production (on both sides) with the new variable C_a, for each $a \in \Sigma$. Then we add productions (*) $C_a \to a$ for each $a \in \Sigma$. Clearly, this does not change the language generated. Furthermore, these new productions are already context-sensitive.

Now the right-hand sides of all productions (except those labeled (*)) consist of strings of variables only. The rest of the transformation will be by example. Take a production of the form $CDE \to JKLMN$. Delete it and add the following productions:

$$CDE \to A_1 DE$$
$$A_1 DE \to A_1 A_2 E$$
$$A_1 A_2 E \to A_1 A_2 A_3$$
$$A_1 A_2 A_3 \to J A_2 A_3$$
$$J A_2 A_3 \to J K A_3$$
$$J K A_3 \to J K L M N.$$

The effect of these productions is to replace CDE with $JKLMN$, via a series of productions that are of the desired form. Note that all but the first production have a distinguished variable A_i that does not appear in any other productions, so the productions must be used in the order given, and cannot be used in any other situation. (Different distinguished variables are used in other productions, of course).

Here is a formal proof that the preceding construction works.

Deleting the terminals a that appear in productions and replacing them by C_a and then adding the productions $C_a \to a$ clearly does not change the language, so we will concentrate on the second part of the construction, for which an example was already given, namely, how to replace the production $CDE \to JKLMN$ with a "chain" of productions of the desired form. In what follows, we will use that example and refer to the variables such as A_1, A_2, A_3 as *auxiliary variables.*

Let G be the original CSG and let G' denote the grammar modified as described earlier.

Claim: $\alpha \overset{*}{\Longrightarrow} \beta$ in G if and only if $\alpha \overset{*}{\Longrightarrow} \beta$ in G' and α, β contain no auxiliary variables.

Proof: Suppose $\alpha \overset{*}{\Longrightarrow} \beta$ in G. We prove by induction on the length of the derivation that $\alpha \overset{*}{\Longrightarrow} \beta$ in G'. Clearly, this is true for derivations of length 0. Now suppose $\alpha \overset{*}{\Longrightarrow} \beta$ in G, and consider the last production used. Without loss of generality, assume it was $CDE \to JKLMN$. Then

$$\alpha = \alpha_1 CDE\alpha_2 \Longrightarrow^{i-1} \alpha_1 JKLMN\alpha_2 = \beta.$$

By induction, $\alpha \implies^* \alpha_1 CDE\alpha_2$ in G', and from the series of productions given before, we easily see $CDE \implies^* JKLMN$ in G', so $\alpha \implies^* \alpha_1 JKLMN\alpha_2 = \beta$ in G'.

The other direction is a little harder. Suppose $\alpha \overset{*}{\implies} \beta$ in G' and α, β contain no auxiliary variables. Then if this derivation is of length 0, it clearly also occurs in G. For the induction step, assume that $\alpha \implies^i \beta$ in G'. Without loss of generality, assume that $CDE \to A_1 DE$ is the first production used in the derivation in G'. Then all the other productions listed in the chain (introducing the other auxiliary variables A_2, A_3, ...) must eventually be used, and in the order listed; otherwise the auxiliary variables do not disappear. For example, once A_1 is introduced the production $A_1 DE \to A_1 A_2 E$ must eventually be used, as there is no other production involving A_1 that does not have an A_2 to its right, and so on. This is *not* to say that other productions could not be used in between productions of the chain for CDE; in fact, this may well happen. Then I claim that we can assume that all the productions listed in the chain for CDE are actually used one after the other in the order listed, with no intervening productions. For assume some other productions "intrude," namely

$$\alpha_1 CDE\beta_1 \implies \alpha_1 A_1 DE\beta_1 \overset{*}{\implies} \alpha_2 A_1 DE\beta_2 \implies \alpha_2 A_1 A_2 E\beta_2.$$

Then it is clear that in fact $\alpha_1 \overset{*}{\implies} \alpha_2$ (since the productions involving A_1 are very specific) and $DE\beta_1 \implies^* DE\beta_2$ (for the same reason). Hence we could just as well have used the following derivation in G':

$$\alpha_1 CDE\beta_1 \overset{*}{\implies} \alpha_2 CDE\beta_2 \implies \alpha_2 A_1 DE\beta_2 \implies \alpha_2 A_1 A_2 E\beta_2.$$

Hence we have moved the offending productions to the "front" before any productions in the chain for CDE are actually used.

This works fine when new auxiliary variables are being introduced. How about when they are being removed? Well, suppose

$$\alpha_1 J A_2 A_3 \beta_1 \implies \alpha_1 JK A_3 \beta_1 \overset{*}{\implies} \alpha_2 JK A_3 \beta_2 \implies \alpha_2 JKLMN\beta_2.$$

Then again, we must have $\alpha_1 JK \overset{*}{\implies} \alpha_2 JK$ and $\beta_1 \overset{*}{\implies} \beta_2$. Then we could have instead used the following derivation in G':

$$\alpha_1 J A_2 A_3 \beta_1 \implies \alpha_1 JK A_3 \beta_1 \implies \alpha_1 JKLMN\beta_1 \overset{*}{\implies} \alpha_2 JKLMN\beta_2,$$

which pushes the offending production to the "back." (In the middle of the chain of productions introduced for $CDE \to JKLMN$, we get to push the offending production to the front *or* back.)

Now, by repeatedly applying this idea, we can bring together all of the productions in the chain for CDE, so they appear consecutively, in the order listed. By similar juggling, we can bring together all of the productions in the chains for other productions.

This proves the claim. Now to finish up the proof, assume without loss of generality that $CDE \rightarrow JKLMN$ is the first production used. Hence, $\alpha = \alpha_1 CDE\beta_1 \Longrightarrow^i \beta$ in G'. By the lemma, we can use all the productions in the chain for CDE immediately, and hence

$$\alpha_1 CDE\beta_1 \overset{*}{\Longrightarrow} \alpha_1 JKLMN\beta_1,$$

where α_1, β_1 contain no auxiliary variables. Hence,

$$\alpha \Longrightarrow \alpha_1 JKLMN\beta_1 \Longrightarrow^j \beta$$

in G', where $j < i$. Thus we can use induction to say that $\alpha_1 JKLMN\beta_1 \overset{*}{\Longrightarrow} \beta$ in G. But $CDE \rightarrow JKLMN$ is a production in G, so $\alpha \overset{*}{\Longrightarrow} \beta$ in G. This finishes the proof. ∎

We now turn to a machine model for the CSLs. This model, called the linear-bounded automaton or LBA, is very much like a one-tape nondeterministic Turing machine (TM), but with the following changes: the contents of the input tape is initially $\natural w \flat$, where w is the input and $\natural$ and $\flat$ are distinguished symbols, called endmarkers, that can never be changed on the tape. Note that $\natural$ and $\flat$ are tape symbols that are not contained in the input alphabet Σ. Further, the tape head can move left, right, or stay stationary, but can never move left from $\natural$ or right from $\flat$. The effect of these rules is that the space used by the LBA is limited to the length of the input. An LBA accepts if, as in the case of TMs, it enters a distinguished state called the halting state, and is usually denoted by h.

Theorem 7.1.4. *If L is context-sensitive, then it is accepted by an LBA.*

Proof. If L is context-sensitive, then L is generated by a length-increasing grammar G. We now show how to accept L with an LBA M. First, by expanding the alphabet size of M to 4-tuples, we can assume that M has four "tracks." Now we carry out the algorithm given in the proof of Theorem 6.1.2, with the following difference: we use the tracks of M instead of different tapes, and if at any time the length of the sentential form on track 2 exceeds the length of the input—which is detected by attempting to move right on $\flat$—the simulation crashes. This simulation accepts an input w if and only if there is some derivation in G in which no intermediate step is longer than $|w|$. Since G is length-increasing, w is accepted if and only if $w \in L(G)$. ∎

Theorem 7.1.5. *If L is accepted by an LBA, then L is context-sensitive.*

Proof. The idea is similar to the proof of Theorem 6.1.3. There, we created a grammar that would simulate the configurations of a TM—a nondeterministic "language generator." We apply the same general strategy here to make a length-increasing grammar, but with some additional complications.

Suppose L is accepted by an LBA M. Then we can easily convert M to an LBA M' that has the following property: it first copies its input w to a second track. It then performs the computations of M on the first track. If M ever accepts, M' writes the input w back on the tape (the two tracks disappear and become just one), moves the tape head left to scan the left endmarker ♯, and halts. This new LBA M', then, has the property that if it halts on input w, the string w is left on the tape at the end of the computation.

We now simulate the computation of M' with a length-increasing grammar. One additional problem is that at the end of a derivation we cannot simply make the state and endmarkers disappear with ϵ-productions, since these would violate the length-increasing rules. Instead, we incorporate these symbols into adjacent symbols, making new single composite symbols such as $[\sharp p X]$ and $[\sharp p X \flat]$. More precisely, we associate each permanent symbol (i.e., member of Γ) with all evanescent symbols (i.e., endmarker or state) to its left, including any symbols to the right if we are at the right end of the tape. This simply involves increasing the size of the tape alphabet.

The productions can be divided into several groups. To initialize the simulated tape, we use the productions

$$S \to [q_0 \sharp a \flat] \mid [q_0 \sharp a] S_1$$
$$S_1 \to a S_1 \mid [a \flat]$$

for all $a \in \Sigma$.
To simulate right moves of the LBA we use the productions

$$[p \sharp X \flat] \to [\sharp q X \flat]$$
$$[p \sharp X] \to [\sharp q X]$$

for states p, q, tape symbols X, and moves $\delta(p, \sharp) = (q, \sharp, R)$. We use productions

$$[p X] Z \to Y [q Z]$$
$$[p X][Z \flat] \to Y [q Z \flat]$$
$$[\sharp p X] Z \to [\sharp Y][q Z]$$
$$[\sharp p X \flat] \to [\sharp Y q \flat]$$
$$[\sharp p X][Z \flat] \to [\sharp Y][q Z \flat]$$

for moves $\delta(p, X) = (q, Y, R)$ and tape symbols Z.

To simulate stationary moves of the LBA we use the productions

$$[p\sharp X\flat] \rightarrow [q\sharp X\flat]$$
$$[p\sharp X] \rightarrow [q\sharp X]$$

for moves $\delta(p, \sharp) = (q, \sharp, S)$, productions

$$[pX] \rightarrow [qY]$$
$$[pX\flat] \rightarrow [qY\flat]$$
$$[\sharp pX] \rightarrow [\sharp qY]$$
$$[\sharp pX\flat] \rightarrow [\sharp qY\flat]$$

for all moves $\delta(p, X) = (q, Y, S)$, and productions

$$[Xp\flat] \rightarrow [Xq\flat]$$

for all moves $\delta(p, \flat) = (q, \flat, S)$.

To simulate left moves of the LBA we use the productions

$$Z[pX] \rightarrow [qZ]Y$$
$$[\sharp Z][pX] \rightarrow [\sharp qZ]Y$$
$$[\sharp Z][pX\flat] \rightarrow [\sharp qZ][Y\flat]$$
$$Z[pX\flat] \rightarrow [qZ][Y\flat]$$
$$[\sharp pX] \rightarrow [q\sharp Y]$$
$$[\sharp pX\flat] \rightarrow [q\sharp Y\flat]$$

for all productions $\delta(p, X) = (q, Y, L)$ and productions

$$[\sharp Zp\flat] \rightarrow [\sharp qZ\flat]$$
$$[Zp\flat] \rightarrow [qZ\flat]$$

for productions $\delta(p, \flat) = (q, \flat, L)$.

Finally, we add productions

$$[h\sharp X\flat] \rightarrow X$$
$$[h\sharp X]Y \rightarrow X[Y\natural]$$
$$[X\natural]Y \rightarrow X[Y\natural]$$
$$[X\natural][Y\flat] \rightarrow XY$$
$$[h\sharp X][Y\flat] \rightarrow XY$$

to simulate a left-to-right scan of the sentential form, converting all composite symbols to single symbols. Here, ♮ is a new symbol. This occurs only when the halting state h is reached. ∎

We now prove two theorems about relationship between the class of CSLs and the class of recursive languages.

Theorem 7.1.6. *Every CSL is recursive.*

Proof. Suppose L is a CSL. We give an algorithm to test membership in L that always terminates. Since L is a CSL, it is generated by some length-increasing grammar $G = (V, \Sigma, P, S)$. Hence, $x \in L$ if and only if $S \stackrel{*}{\Longrightarrow} x$. The length-increasing property implies that any intermediate sentential form in a derivation of x must be of length $\leq |x|$. We can enumerate them all, and for each pair of sentential forms, (α, β), we can determine if $\alpha \Longrightarrow \beta$. Now make a finite directed graph whose vertices are these sentential forms and whose edges are given by (α, β) when $\alpha \Longrightarrow \beta$. There is a path from S to x if and only if $S \stackrel{*}{\Longrightarrow} x$, if and only if $x \in L$. Now just use breadth-first search to determine if such a path exists. ∎

Theorem 7.1.7. *There exists a recursive language that is not a CSL.*

Proof. First we prove the following lemma: we say a TM T is *always-halting* if on any input $x \in \Sigma^*$, the TM halts with either 1 or 0 written on its tape. In this case we define $L(T) = \{x \; : \; T$ writes 1 on input $x\}$. By an *effective enumeration* of a set S we mean a TM with a write-only output tape, where the tape head moves only right and successively writes on its output tape an encoding of the elements of S such that (i) no element is written twice and (ii) every element eventually gets written. ∎

Lemma 7.1.8. *Let $M_1, M_2, \ldots$ be an effective enumeration of some set of always-halting TMs. Then there exists a recursive language L such that $L \neq L(M_i)$ for all $i \geq 1$.*

Proof. Let us enumerate the elements of $\{0, 1\}^*$ as follows: $x_0 = \epsilon$, $x_1 = 0$, $x_2 = 1$, $x_3 = 00$, and so on. Now define $L = \{x_i \; : \; M_i$ writes 0 on input $x_i\}$. Now L is recursive, because on input x_i we can determine i, then simulate M_i on x_i, and write 1 if and only if M_i writes 0. But $L \neq L(M_i)$, since $x_i \in L$ if and only if $x_i \notin L(M_i)$. ∎

We can now prove Theorem 7.1.7.

Proof. It suffices to show that we can effectively enumerate a set of always-halting TM that accept the CSLs over $\{0, 1\}$. To do so, we simply encode each CSG as a binary number, arrange them in ascending order, and create a TM accepting each using the algorithm in the proof of Theorem 7.1.6. ∎

Finally, we turn to the question of complementation of CSLs. The question of whether the CSLs were closed under complement was open for many years, until it was solved independently and nearly simultaneously by Immerman and Szelepcsényi in 1988. The technique they used, called *inductive counting*, is actually much more widely applicable. In this text, however, we restrict ourselves to its application to the context-sensitive languages.

Theorem 7.1.9. *If L is a CSL, then $\overline{L}$ is a CSL.*

Proof Idea. The basic idea is as follows: given an LBA M accepting L, we construct an LBA M' accepting $\overline{L}$. On input x, M' attempts to verify that no accepting configuration in M can be reached starting from the configuration $q_0\sharp x\flat$. To know that all configurations have been checked, M' needs to count the number of reachable configurations, a computation it carries out inductively.

Proof. Let $M = (Q, \Sigma, \Gamma, \delta, q_0, h)$ be an LBA accepting L. We can assume without loss of generality that if M accepts x of length n by reaching the halting state h, it then erases its input tape and moves the head to the left end. This means that x is accepted by M if and only if

$$q_0\sharp x\flat \overset{*}{\vdash} h\sharp B^n\flat.$$

Thus, we want to create M' that accepts x if and only if the configuration $q_0\sharp x\flat$ does not lead to $h\sharp B^n\flat$ in M.

Now if M accepts an input x, and $|x| = n$, then there is an accepting computation for x that consists of at most

$$C := |Q||\Gamma|^n(n + 2)$$

moves, since this is the number of different possible configurations of M. (A longer computation would imply that a configuration is repeated, and hence we could cut out a portion of the computation to get a shorter one.) Suppose we knew that exactly R configurations of M were reachable from $q_0\sharp x\flat$. Then we could accept $\overline{L}$ with an LBA that implements the following nondeterministic algorithm:

Input: x and R.
Set `reached` $:= 0$

For all configurations γ, $|\gamma| = n + 3$, do
(1) Guess a computation of M of s moves ($s \leq C$), beginning at $q_0 \sharp x \flat$, one move at a time.
If the computation ends at the configuration γ then
    `reached := reached+1`
    (2) If $\gamma = h \sharp B^n \flat$, then reject
(3) If `reached` $= R$ then accept
    (4) else reject

First, let us see why the algorithm works. If $x \in \overline{L}$, then some sequence of guesses in line (1) will result in each of the R reachable configurations being examined, and the variable `reached` is then incremented until `reached` $= R$. Since $q_0 \sharp x \flat$ does not lead to $h \sharp B^n \flat$, we do not reject in line (2). Thus, there is a computation that accepts in line (3).

On the other hand, if $x \notin \overline{L}$, then $q_0 \sharp x \flat \overset{*}{\vdash} h \sharp B^n \flat$. Then we either guess a computation in line (1) that terminates at $h \sharp B^n \flat$, and so we reject in line (2), or failure to guess correctly leads to some configuration being omitted from consideration. In this case the test in line (3) fails and so we reject in line (4).

It now remains to see how to determine R. Let us define R_i to be the number of configurations of M that are reachable from $q_0 \sharp x \flat$ in $\leq i$ steps. We inductively compute $R_0, R_1, \ldots$, using the following algorithm:

Input: x.
Set $R_0 := 1$ and $i := 0$
Repeat
    $i := i + 1$
    $R_i := 0$
    For all configurations β, $|\beta| = n + 3$, do { check if β is reachable }
        Set `reachable` := false
        Set `reached` := 0
        For all configurations γ, $|\gamma| = n + 3$, do { check all possible predecessors }
            (1) Guess a computation of M of $\leq i - 1$ moves beginning at $q_0 \sharp x \flat$, one move at a time.
            If the computation ends at γ then
                Set `reached` := `reached` + 1
                If $\gamma \vdash \beta$ or $\gamma = \beta$ then
                    `reachable` := true
        If `reachable` then $R_i := R_i + 1$

(2) Else if reached $\neq R_{i-1}$ then reject

Until

$$R_{i-1} = R_i$$

(3) $R := R_i$

Return(R)

Again, let us see why this algorithm works. We first argue that some sequence of guesses in line (1) will result in $R = R_i$ being returned. This is because for each configuration β reachable in $\leq j$ steps, we correctly guess either β or a predecessor configuration γ in line (1). Furthermore, the number of predecessor configurations is R_{i-1}, so the test in line (2) fails. Since $R_j \leq C = |Q||\Gamma|^n(n+2)$ and $R_j \geq R_{j-1}$ for all j, eventually we must have $R_{i-1} = R_i$ for some i.

Next, we argue that if $R = R_i$ is returned, then it is correct. The only way R can be returned in line (3) is for the test on line (2) to fail each iteration. Thus, reached $= R_{i-1}$, which guarantees that all predecessor configurations have been examined.

Finally, putting together these two algorithms gives us an algorithm to accept $\overline{L}$. It now remains to see that these algorithms can actually be implemented by an LBA M'. To do so, we use the usual trick of expanding the alphabet size so that M' can use multiple "tracks," each of which can store n symbols. Note that $\log_2 C = \log_2|Q| + n\log_2|\Gamma| + \log_2(n+2)$, so we need only $O(n)$ symbols to store a counter for the number of configurations, where the constant in the big-O depends only on $|Q|$ and Γ and not n. Similarly, we need only $O(n)$ symbols to store reached and the configurations we are examining. Finally, we need only $O(n)$ symbols to store the R_i, since we do not save all of them, but only the last two. ∎

7.2 The Chomsky hierarchy

Noam Chomsky (1928–), the influential American linguist and scholar, defined a hierarchy of language classes, which is summarized (in extended form) in Figure 7.1. It is now called the *Chomsky hierarchy*. Chomsky used the terminology "Type 3 grammar" for what we call today a regular grammar, "Type 2 grammar" for context-free grammar, and so on.

Here are some comments about the Chomsky hierarchy. First, note that nearly every class is represented by both a machine model and a grammar type. This "duality" is extremely useful in proving theorems, since one has the freedom to choose the appropriate representation. The exception is the

Abbreviation	Language class	Machine model	Grammar
REG	Regular languages	DFA, NFA, NFA-ϵ, 2DFA	Regular grammar (aka Type 3)
DCFL	Deterministic context-free languages	Deterministic PDA	LR(k) grammar, $k \geq 1$
CFL	Context-free languages	PDA	Context-free grammar (aka Type 2)
CSL	Context-sensitive languages	LBA	Context-sensitive grammar, length-increasing grammar (aka Type 1)
REC	Recursive languages	Always-halting TM	
RE	Recursively enumerable languages	TM	Unrestricted grammar (aka Type 0)

Figure 7.1: The Chomsky hierarchy

class of recursive languages, which does not have a corresponding grammar model.

Also note that each class of languages is strictly contained in the one after it.

7.3 2DPDAs and Cook's theorem

A 2DPDA is a two-way deterministic pushdown automaton. This model differs from the ordinary pushdown automaton (PDA) model as described in Section 1.5 in three ways:

- It is *deterministic*. There are no ϵ-moves, and from every configuration there is at most one move.
- It is a *two-way machine*. The input head can move left or remain stationary, as well as move right.
- It has *endmarkers*. A left endmarker ⊢ is at the left end of the input and a right endmarker ⊣ is at the right end of the input.

More formally, we define a 2DPDA to be a 9-tuple $M = (Q, \Sigma, \Gamma, ⊢, ⊣, \delta, q_0, Z_0, F)$, where

- Q is a finite nonempty set of states.
- Σ is a finite nonempty input alphabet, not containing ⊢ or ⊣.
- Γ is a finite nonempty stack alphabet.
- ⊢ and ⊣ are the left and right endmarkers.
- δ is the transition (partial) function, mapping $Q \times (\Sigma \cup \{⊢, ⊣\}) \times \Gamma \to Q \times \{-1, 0, 1\} \times \Gamma^*$. The meaning of $\delta(q, a, X) = (p, j, \alpha)$ is that in state q, scanning symbol a, and with X on top of the stack, the 2DPDA enters state p, moves left, remains stationary, or moves right according to whether

$j = -1, 0, 1$, respectively, and replaces X with the string α. If $\delta(q, a, X)$ is undefined, the machine crashes.

- $q_0 \in Q$ is the initial state.
- $Z_0 \in \Gamma$ is the initial stack symbol.
- $F \subseteq Q$ is the set of final states.

A *full configuration* is a triple (q, h, α), where q is the current state, h is an integer representing the current position of the input head (where $h = 0$ means that we are scanning the $\sharp$ sign), and α is the stack contents.

We go from one full configuration to another in an (hopefully) obvious way. For example, if $\delta(q, a, X) = (p, 1, \alpha)$, then if we are currently scanning a at position j we have $(q, j, X\beta) \vdash (p, j + 1, \alpha\beta)$. We write $\overset{*}{\vdash}$ to denote the reflexive, transitive closure of $\vdash$, and we sometimes write $\overset{*}{\vdash}_x$ to emphasize that the tape contents is x. Note that the tape contents never changes since the 2DPDA cannot write on the tape.

We define

$$L(M) = \{x \in \Sigma^* : (q_0, 0, Z_0) \overset{*}{\vdash}_x (p, i, \alpha) \text{ for some } i, 0 \le i \le |x| + 1, \alpha \in \Gamma^*,$$
$$\text{and } p \in F\}.$$

We can depict 2DPDAs graphically using a transition diagram similar to that used for deterministic finite automaton (DFAs). If $\delta(q, a, X) = (p, j, \alpha)$, we draw a transition as shown in Figure 7.2.

Example 7.3.1. The language $L = \{0^i 1^i 2^i : i \ge 1\}$ is a non-CFL that is a 2DPDA language.

To accept L, start at the left-hand side of the input. If the first symbol seen is not 0, reject. For each successive 0 seen, push a's onto the stack until a 1 is seen. When a 1 is seen, start popping off symbols and moving right on the input until Z_0 (the initial stack symbol) reappears or 2 appears in the input. If 2 appears before Z_0 encountered, reject (since there are more 0s than 1s). If 0 appears, reject (since there is a 0 after a 1). Otherwise look at the next input symbol. If it is a 1, reject (since there are more 1s than 0s). If it is a 0, reject (since there is a 0 after a 1). If you have not rejected, then the number of 0s equals the number of 1s in the first part of the string.

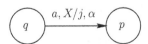

Figure 7.2: The transition $\delta(q, a, X) = (p, j, \alpha)$ depicted

Now move left until a 0 is encountered, and do the same thing with the 1s and 2s that you did with the 0s and 1s. If you have not rejected, then the number of 1s equals the number of 2s. Move right and accept.

Example 7.3.2. The language $\{ww : w \in \{0, 1\}^*\}$ is a non-CFL that is a 2DPDA language.

To see this, we use the following method: (1) first, scan the input from left to right pushing a's onto the stack until b is reached. Also keep track of the parity of the number of characters and reject if it is odd. Now move back to the beginning of the input and move right, popping two a's from the stack for each character read. When Z_0 reappears, you are at the middle of the input. (2) Now move right, pushing input symbols onto the stack until b is reached. Now push a b onto the stack. Now repeat (1); when b reappears, you are at the middle of the input. Now move left, matching input symbols against the stack contents. If all symbols match, and ♯ is reached, accept.

Example 7.3.3. The language

$$\{xcy : x, y \in \{a, b\}^* \text{ and } y \text{ is a subword of } x\}$$

is a 2DPDA language.

To see this, use the following algorithm, embodied in Figure 7.3:

1. M moves right on input until c is encountered.
2. M moves left, copying the symbols of x onto the stack until ♯ is encountered. Now $x Z_0$ (not x^R) is on the stack. Let $x = a_1 a_2 \cdots a_n$.
3. M moves right until c is encountered and then moves one symbol to the right.
4. While the symbol on top of the stack matches the next symbol of the input, pop off the symbol on top of the stack and move the input head one square to the right.
5. If the input head is scanning b, accept. If the input head is not scanning b, but Z_0 is on top of the stack, reject. Otherwise the top of stack symbol and input symbol disagree. Restore the stack by moving the input head to the left until c is reached, copying. At this point M has $a_i a_{i+1} \cdots a_n Z_0$ on the stack for some i, $1 \le i \le n$. If $i = n + 1$, M halts and rejects. Otherwise M pops a_i and moves its input head to the right to c and then one more symbol to the right. Return to step 4.

Here is a sample computation on input:

0	1	2	3	4	5	6	7	8	9	10	11	12	13	14	15
♯	a	b	b	a	b	b	a	b	a	b	c	a	b	a	b

Configuration number	State	Input position	Stack contents
0	q_0	0	Z_0
1	q_0	1	Z_0
$\vdots$	$\vdots$	$\vdots$	$\vdots$
10	q_0	10	Z_0
11	q_0	11	Z_0
12	q_1	10	Z_0
13	q_1	9	bZ_0
14	q_1	8	abZ_0
$\vdots$	$\vdots$	$\vdots$	$\vdots$
21	q_1	1	$bbabbababZ_0$
22	q_1	0	$abbabbababZ_0$
23	q_2	1	$abbabbababZ_0$
$\vdots$	$\vdots$	$\vdots$	$\vdots$
33	q_2	11	$abbabbababZ_0$
34	q_3	12	$abbabbababZ_0$
35	q_3	13	$bbabbababZ_0$
36	q_3	14	$babbababZ_0$
37	q_4	13	$babbababZ_0$
38	q_4	12	$bbabbababZ_0$
39	q_4	11	$abbabbababZ_0$
40	q_3	12	$bbabbababZ_0$
41	q_4	11	$bbabbababZ_0$
42	q_3	12	$babbababZ_0$
43	q_4	11	$babbababZ_0$
44	q_3	12	$abbababZ_0$
45	q_3	13	$bbababZ_0$
46	q_3	14	$babab Z_0$
47	q_4	13	$babab Z_0$
48	q_4	12	$bbababZ_0$
49	q_4	11	$abbababZ_0$
50	q_3	12	$bbababZ_0$
51	q_4	11	$bbababZ_0$
52	q_3	12	$bababZ_0$
53	q_4	11	$bababZ_0$
54	q_3	12	$ababZ_0$
55	q_3	13	$babZ_0$
56	q_3	14	abZ_0
57	q_3	15	bZ_0
58	q_f	15	Z_0

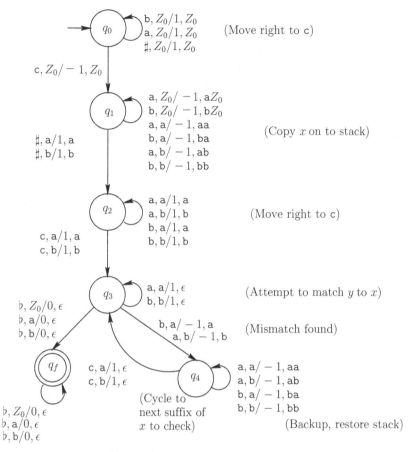

Figure 7.3: A 2DPDA for string matching

Note that the pattern-matching 2DPDA of the previous example can take $\Omega(|x||y|)$ steps on input xcy. This is $\Omega(r^2)$ if $|x| = 2r$ and $|y| = r$. The following theorem of Cook, then, is very surprising.

Theorem 7.3.4. *A 2DPDA can be simulated in linear time on a RAM.*

Our RAM model is an assembler-type machine with an infinite number of registers, $x_0, x_1, x_2, \ldots,$ where each register can hold an arbitrary integer. A RAM program contains instructions that allow a register to be loaded with a constant, to add or subtract the contents of two registers and store their sum or difference in a third, to perform indirect addressing, to do comparisons, and to read input and print output. The reader should check that these operations suffice to implement the algorithm given next.

We define a *partial configuration* to be a triple of the form (q, p, A), where q is a state of the 2DPDA, p is a position that the head is scanning, and A is the current symbol on top of the stack.

The idea of the proof is to attempt to "short-circuit" the computation of M by determining a *terminator* for each partial configuration. The terminator of a configuration i is defined to be the configuration from which, on the next move, the stack height first dips below that of i. If we reenter the configuration i, we can simply bypass all intermediate computation (which can never depend on symbols buried in the stack) and proceed directly to the terminator and perform its transition, popping the stack.

To simplify the proof, we assume without loss of generality that every move either pops, makes a horizontal move, or pushes a single additional symbol onto the stack. We use another stack S to keep track of those partial configurations whose terminator is still sought. We use an array next[ ] to store the terminators known so far.

The algorithm uses the following variables:

- q, the current state of the 2DPDA M being simulated;
- p, the current position of M's tape head;
- G, the current contents of M's stack, with the top at the left;
- i, a current partial configuration of the form $(q, p, \text{top}(G))$;
- S, a stack of lists that is used to hold partial configurations whose terminator is currently unknown;
- flags[ ], a bit array indexed by partial configurations, initially 0;
- next[ ], an array of pairs $\subseteq \mathbb{N} \times Q$ indexed by partial configurations, initially 0.

Here is the 2DPDA simulation algorithm:

```
{ initialize }
q := q_0
p := 0
G := Z_0
i := (q_0, 0, Z_0)

{ initialize simulation }
S := empty stack
push(S, empty list)
while (|δ(i)| ≠ 0) do { while it is possible to move do }
    if next[i] = 0 then
        (q', d, β) := δ(i) { get next move }
        if (|β| ≥ 1) do { horizontal move or push }
```

```
if flags[i] = 1 then
    halt and reject
    { because M was in partial configuration i at some previous time
    in the computation and the computation path has led back to
    partial configuration i at the same or higher-level of the stack;
    hence M is in an infinite loop }
else
    append i to top(S)
    flags[i] := 1
    q := q'
    p := p + d
    replace top symbol of G with β
    if |β| = 2 { push } push(S, empty list)
    i := (q, p, top(G))
if (|β| = 0) do { pop the stack }
    pop(G)
    next[i] := (q', p + d)
    for each element x in top(S)
        set next[x] := (q', p + d)
        flags[x] := 0
    pop(S)
    q := q'
    p := p + d
    i := (q, p, top(G))
else {next[i] ≠ 0; perform 'short circuit' }
    (q', p') := next[i]
    pop(G)
    q := q'
    p := p'
    for each element x in top(S)
        set next[x] := (q', p')
        flags[x] := 0
    pop(S)
    i := (q, p, top(G))
{ end do }
if i is an accepting configuration
    accept
otherwise
    reject
```

Theorem 7.3.5. *The 2DPDA simulation runs in linear time.*

First we prove two lemmas.

Lemma 7.3.6. *During the course of the simulation, every partial configuration gets pushed and popped off the stack S at most once.*

Proof. Suppose a partial configuration i is placed on the stack. When this happens, flags$[i]$ is set to 1. If the next action involving i is a push at a higher level of the stack, then we are in an infinite loop, and this is detected by checking flags$[i]$. So the next action must be a pop. At this point the next array is updated. The next time i is encountered, the next entry has been set, and so we pop, not push.   ∎

Lemma 7.3.7. *Every element of* next *is assigned at most once.*

Proof. Suppose not. Then some element, say next$[i]$, is assigned twice. But next$[i]$ gets assigned only when i is popped from S. The first time next$[i]$ is assigned, i is popped off. The next time next$[i]$ is assigned, i is popped off again. If this occurs because there was an i buried in the stack below the i that was first popped off, then there was an i encountered above another i, and we are in an infinite loop, which is detected by examining flags$[\ \ ]$. So this cannot happen.

So another i must have been pushed after the first was popped. But this cannot happen, since when i is considered for the second time, next$[i]$ was already set, so we would not push i onto the stack.   ∎

We are now ready to prove Theorem 7.3.5.

Proof. We claim that the simulation runs in time linear in the number of reachable partial configurations, which is bounded by $|Q|(|x| + 2)|\Gamma|$.

To see this, let each of the following actions cost \$1:

- appending a partial configuration to top(S);
- popping a partial configuration from top(S);
- setting next$[i]$;
- reading next$[i]$;
- pushing onto G;
- popping from G.

Now assign \$7 to each partial configuration i. The money is allocated as follows:

- We allocate $5 for reading next[$i$] when next[$i$] = 0. This can occur only once by Lemma 7.3.7, for either the stack height stays the same or goes up between the next time i is considered, in which case we are in an infinite loop, or the stack height dips below its current height. But in this latter case, i was previously appended to top(S), so when it is popped off S, next[i] is set. $2 pays for the cost of reading next[i] and appending i to top(S). The other $3 is allocated as follows: $1 pays for the cost of pushing onto G and the other $2 is "stapled" to the symbol we push onto G, for later use.
- We allocate $2 for the cost of setting next[i] and popping i from the stack S. From Lemma 7.3.7 this occurs only once for each i.

Finally, we have to account for the cost of what happens when next[i] $\neq$ 0. This is always accompanied by a pop of the stack G. So when this occurs, we can pop the stack and recover the $2 that was stored there. $1 is used to pay for reading next[i] and the other $1 is used to pay for the cost of popping the stack. ∎

7.4 Exercises

1. Under which operations in the following list is the class of CSLs closed: Union, concatenation, intersection, substitution by CSLs, inverse homomorphism, Kleene closure, positive closure?
2. Suppose we modify our PDA model as follows: instead of a finite number of nondeterministic choices, depending on the current symbol being read (or ϵ) and the current top-of-stack contents, we allow the PDA to nondeterministically replace the symbol currently on top of the stack with any member of a given CSL. More formally, we allow

$$\delta(a, X) = L(a, X),$$

where $a \in \Sigma \cup \{\epsilon\}$, and $X \in \Gamma$, where $L(a, X)$ is a CSL. We accept by empty stack.

Prove or disprove that the set of languages accepted by these more powerful PDAs is precisely the set of CSLs. (One direction is easy.)
3. Show that every context-free language is accepted by a *deterministic* LBA.
4. The *Boolean closure of the CFLs* is the class of all languages that can be obtained from CFLs by a finite number of applications of union, intersection, and complement operations. Show that if L is contained in the Boolean closure of the CFLs, then L is accepted by a deterministic LBA.
5. Show that there is a language L accepted by a deterministic LBA that is not in the Boolean closure of the CFLs.

6. Give a length-increasing grammar generating the language

$$\{0^{F_n} : n \geq 1\} = \{0, 00, 000, 00000, 00000000, \ldots\},$$

where F_n is the nth Fibonacci number, defined by $F_0 = 0$, $F_1 = 1$, and $F_n = F_{n-1} + F_{n-2}$ for $n \geq 2$.

7. Show that the set of primitive strings over $\{a, b\}$ is context-sensitive. (For the definition of primitive strings, see Section 2.3.)

8. Give an example of a CSL that is not a CFL.

9. Find a length-increasing grammar to generate the languages
   (a) $L = \{0^i 1^j 2^{\max(i,j)} : i, j \geq 1\}$;
   (b) $L = \{0^i 1^j 2^{\min(i,j)} : i, j \geq 1\}$;

10. Construct a 2DPDA to accept the language $L = \{w \in \{a, b\}^* : w$ is primitive $\}$. Conclude that L can be recognized in linear time on a RAM.

11. Show that the set of bordered words over $\{a, b\}$ is a 2DPDA language. (The definition of bordered appears in Exercise 4.16)

12. Show that the language $L = \{a^{2^n} : n \geq 1\}$ is a 2DPDA language that is not a CFL.

13. Show that the language $L = \{0^n 1^{mn} : m, n \geq 1\}$ is a 2DPDA language that is not a CFL.

14. Show that the language $L = \{0^n 1^{n^2} : n \geq 1\}$ is accepted by a 2DPDA.

15. Show that for every DFA $M = (Q, \Sigma, \delta, q_0, F)$, there exists a "small" 2DPDA M' over a unary alphabet that on input 1^n accepts iff $|\Sigma^n \cap L(M)| \geq 1$, that is, if M accepts at least one string of length n. By *small* I mean that the size of your 2DPDA (i.e., the number of transition rules) should be $O(|\Sigma||Q|)$.

7.5 Projects

1. Find out about L-systems and their applications to computer graphics. A good place to start is Prusinkiewicz and Hanan [1989] and Prusinkiewicz and Lindenmayer [1990].

7.6 Research problems

1. A *conjunctive grammar* is a generalization of context-free grammars where productions such as $A \rightarrow \alpha_1 \wedge \cdots \wedge \alpha_m, \alpha_i \in (V \cup \Sigma)^*$, are allowed. This production means A generates those words generated by all the α's. The *conjunctive languages* are those generated by conjunctive grammars. Is the family of conjunctive languages closed under complementation? This question is due to Okhotin [2006].

2. A *Boolean grammar* is a generalization of context-free grammars where productions such as $A \to \alpha_1 \wedge \cdots \wedge \alpha_m \wedge (\neg\beta_1) \wedge \cdots \wedge (\neg\beta_n)$, $\alpha_i, \beta_i \in (V \cup \Sigma)^*$, are allowed. This production means that A generates those words generated by all the α's and none of the β's. Are there any languages recognized by deterministic LBAs in $O(n^2)$ time that cannot be specified by Boolean grammars? This question is due to Okhotin [2006].

7.7 Notes on Chapter 7

7.1 Length-increasing grammars should really be called "length-nondecreasing" grammars, but the former term is the one used in the literature.

Kuroda [1964] proved the equivalence of CSLs and LBAs. The closure of the context-sensitive languages under complementation was proved independently by Immerman [1988] and Szelepcsényi [1988]. Our proof is based on notes by J. Buss.

7.2 The Chomsky hierarchy was first defined by Chomsky [1956, 1959].

7.3 2DPDAs were introduced in Gray, Harrison, and Ibarra [1967]. Aho, Hopcroft, and Ullman [1968] proved that any 2DPDA language can be recognized in $O(n^2)$ time on a RAM. This was further improved to $O(n)$ time by Cook [1972]. An exposition of Cook's proof can be found in Aho, Hopcroft, and Ullman [1974, §9.4]. Also see Jones [1977]. Our presentation is based largely on unpublished notes of Daniel Boyd.

Bibliography

Adian, S. I. (1979). *The Burnside Problem and Identities in Groups*. Springer-Verlag.

Aho, A. V., Hopcroft, J. E., and Ullman, J. D. (1968). Time and tape complexity of pushdown automaton languages. *Inf. Control* **13**, 186–206.

Aho, A. V., Hopcroft, J. E., and Ullman, J. D. (1974). *The Design and Analysis of Computer Algorithms*. Addison-Wesley.

Aho, A. V., Sethi, R., and Ullman, J. D. (1986). *Compilers: Principles, Techniques, and Tools*. Addison-Wesley.

Aho, A. V., and Ullman, J. D. (1972). *The Theory of Parsing, Translation, and Compiling*, Vol. 1. Prentice Hall.

Allouche J.-P., and Shallit, J. (1999). The ubiquitous Prouhet-Thue-Morse sequence. In C. Ding, T. Helleseth, and H. Niederreiter, editors, *Sequences and Their Applications, Proceedings of SETA '98*, pp. 1–16. Springer-Verlag.

Allouche, J.-P., and Shallit, J. (2003). *Automatic Sequences: Theory, Applications, Generalizations*. Cambridge University Press.

Angluin, D. (1987). Learning regular sets from queries and counterexamples. *Inf. Control* **75**, 87–106.

Axelrod, R. M. (1984). *The Evolution of Cooperation*. Basic Books.

Bader, C., and Moura, A. (1982). A generalization of Ogden's lemma. *J. Assoc. Comput. Mach.* **29**, 404–407.

Bar-Hillel, Y., Perles, M., and Shamir, E. (1961). On formal properties of simple phrase structure grammars. *Z. Phonetik. Sprachwiss. Kommuniationsforsch.* **14**, 143–172.

Berstel, J. (1979). *Transductions and Context-Free Languages*. Teubner.

Berstel, J. (1995). *Axel Thue's Papers on Repetitions in Words: A Translation*. Number 20 in *Publications du Laboratoire de Combinatoire et d'Informatique Mathématique*. Université du Québec à Montréal, February.

Berstel, J., and Perrin, D. (2007). The origins of combinatorics on words. *Eur. J. Comb.* **28**, 996–1022.

Birget, J.-C. (1992). Intersection and union of regular languages and state complexity. *Inf. Process. Lett.* **43**, 185–190.

Blum, N. (1996). An $O(n \log n)$ implementation of the standard method for minimizing n-state finite automata. *Inf. Process. Lett.* **57**, 65–69.

Boonyavatana, R., and Slutzki, G. (1988). The interchange or pump (di)lemmas for context-free languages. *Theo. Comput. Sci.* **56**, 321–338.

Borwein, P., and Ingalls, C. (1994). The Prouhet-Tarry-Escott problem revisited. *Enseign. Math.* **40**, 3–27.

Brady, A. H. (1983). The determination of the value of Rado's noncomputable function Σ(*k*) for four-state Turing machines. *Math. Comput.* **40**, 647–665.

Brandenburg, F.-J. (1983). Uniformly growing *k*-th power-free homomorphisms. *Theo. Comput. Sci.* **23**, 69–82.

Brauer, W. (June 1988). On minimizing finite automata. *Bull. Eur. Assoc. Theor. Comput. Sci.* No. 35, 113–116.

Brzozowski, J. (1962a). Canonical regular expressions and minimal state graphs for regular events. In *Mathematical Theory of Automata*, pp. 529–561. Polytechnic Press.

Brzozowski, J. (1962b). A survey of regular expressions and their applications. *IEEE Trans. Electr. Comput.* **11**, 324–335.

Brzozowski, J. A. (February 1989). Minimization by reversal is not new. *Bull. Eur. Assoc. Theor. Comput. Sci.* No. 37, 130.

Bucher, W. (January 1980). A density problem for context-free languages. *Bull. Eur. Assoc. Theor. Comput. Sci.* No. 10, 53.

Cantor, D. C. (1962). On the ambiguity problem of Backus systems. *J. Assoc. Comput. Mach.* **9**, 477–479.

Chaitin, G. J. (1979). Toward a mathematical definition of "life." In R. D. Levine and M. Tribus, editors, *The Maximum Entropy Formalism*, pp. 477–498. MIT Press.

Chomsky, N. (1956). Three models for the description of language. *IRE Trans. Inf. Theory* **2**, 113–124.

Chomsky, N. (1959). On certain formal properties of grammars. *Inf. Control* **2**, 137–167.

Chomsky, N., and Schützenberger, M. P. (1963). The algebraic theory of context-free languages. In P. Braffort and D. Hirschberg, editors, *Computer Programming and Formal Systems*, pp. 118–161. North-Holland, Amsterdam.

Cook, S. A. (1971). The complexity of theorem-proving procedures. In Proceedings of the Third Annual ACM Symposium on Theory of Computing, pp. 151–158. ACM Press.

Cook, S. A. (1972). Linear time simulation of deterministic two-way pushdown automata. In C. V. Freiman, editor, *Information Processing 71 (Proceedings of the IFIP Congress 71)*, Vol. 1, pp. 75–80. North-Holland.

Coppersmith, D., and Winograd, S. (1990). Matrix multiplication via arithmetic progressions. *J. Sym. Comput.* **9**, 251–280.

Crochemore, M. (1981). An optimal algorithm for computing the repetitions in a word. *Inf. Process. Lett.* **12**, 244–250.

Davis, M. (1958). *Computability and Unsolvability.* McGraw-Hill. Enlarged edition, reprinted by Dover, 1982.

Drobot, V. (1989). *Formal Languages and Automata Theory.* Computer Science Press.

Du, D.-Z., and Ko, K.-I. (2001). *Problem Solving in Automata, Languages, and Complexity.* Wiley.

Earley, J. (1970). An efficient context-free parsing algorithm. *Commun. ACM* **13**, 94–102.

Eggan, L. C. (1963). Transition graphs and the star-height of regular events. *Michigan Math. J.* **10**, 385–397.

Ehrig, H., Engels, G., Kreowski, H.-J., and Rozenberg, G., editors. (1999). *Handbook of Graph Grammars and Computing by Graph Transformation, Vol. 2: Applications, Languages, and Tools*. World Scientific.

Ehrig, H., Kreowski, H.-J., Montanari, U., and Rozenberg, G., editors. (1999). *Handbook of Graph Grammars and Computing by Graph Transformation, Vol. 2: Concurrency, Parallelism, and Distribution*. World Scientific.

Euwe, M. (1929). Mengentheoretische Betrachtungen über das Schachspiel. *Proc. Konin. Akad. Wetenschappen, Amsterdam* **32**, 633–642.

Fine, N. J., and Wilf, H. S. (1965). Uniqueness theorems for periodic functions. *Proc. Am. Math. Soc.* **16**, 109–114.

Fischer, P. C. (1963). On computability by certain classes of restricted Turing machines. In *Proceedings of the 4th IEEE Symposium on Switching Circuit Theory and Logical Design*, pp. 23–32. IEEE Press.

Floyd, R. W. (1962). On ambiguity in phrase structure languages. *Commumn. ACM* **5**, 526–534.

Gabarro, J. (February 1985). Some applications of the interchange lemma. *Bull. Eur. Assoc. Theor. Comput. Sci.* No. 25, 19–21.

Garey, M. R., and Johnson, D. S. (1979). *Computers and Intractability: A Guide to the Theory of NP-Completeness*. Freeman.

Gazdar, G., Klein, E., Pullum, G., and Sag, I. (1985). *Generalized Phrase Structure Grammar*. Harvard University Press.

Ginsburg, S. (1966). *The Mathematical Theory of Context Free Languages*. McGraw-Hill.

Ginsburg, S., and Greibach, S. A. (1966). Deterministic context-free languages. *Inf. Control* **9**, 563–582.

Ginsburg, S., and Rice, H. G. (1962). Two families of languages related to ALGOL. *J. Assoc. Comput. Mach.* **9**, 350–371.

Ginsburg, S., and Rose, G. F. (1963). Some recursively unsolvable problems in ALGOL-like languages. *J. Assoc. Comput. Mach.* **10**, 29–47.

Ginsburg, S., and Spanier, E. H. (1963). Quotients of context-free languages. *J. Assoc. Comput. Mach.* **10**, 487–492.

Ginsburg, S., and Spanier, E. H. (1966). Finite-turn pushdown automata. *J. SIAM Control* **4**, 429–453.

Glaister, I., and Shallit, J. (1996). A lower bound technique for the size of nondeterministic finite automata. *Inf. Process. Lett.* **59**, 75–77.

Goldstine, J. (1977). A simplified proof of Parikh's theorem. *Discrete Math.* **19**, 235–239.

Goldstine, J., Price, J. K., and Wotschke, D. (1982a). A pushdown automaton or a context-free grammar—which is more economical? *Theo. Comput. Sci.* **18**, 33–40.

Goldstine, J., Price, J. K., and Wotschke, D. (1982b). On reducing the number of states in a PDA. *Math. Syst. Theory* **15**, 315–321.

Gray, J. N., Harrison, M. A., and Ibarra, O. H. (1967). Two-way pushdown automata. *Inf. Control* **11**, 30–70.

Gries, D. (1973). Describing an algorithm by Hopcroft. *Acta Inf.* **2**, 97–109.

Gupta, N. (1989). On groups in which every element has finite order. *Am. Math. Mon.* **96**, 297–308.

Haines, L. H. (1969). On free monoids partially ordered by embedding. *J. Comb. Theory* **6**, 94–98.

Harju, T., and Karhumäki, J. (1997). Morphisms. In G. Rozenberg and A. Salomaa, editors, *Handbook of Formal Languages*, Vol. 1, pp. 439–510. Springer-Verlag.

Harju, T., and Nowotka, D. (2004). The equation $x^i = y^j z^k$ in a free semigroup. *Semigroup Forum* **68**, 488–490.

Harrison, M. A. (1978). *Introduction to Formal Language Theory*. Addison-Wesley.

Hashiguchi, K. (1982). Regular languages of star height one. *Inf. Control* **53**, 199–210.

Hashiguchi, K. (1988). Algorithms for determining relative star height and star height. *Inf. Comput.* **78**, 124–169.

Hopcroft, J. (1971). An $n \log n$ algorithm for minimizing states in a finite automaton. In *Theory of Machines and Computations*, pp. 189–196. Academic Press.

Hopcroft, J. E., Motwani, R., and Ullman, J. D. (2001). *Introduction to Automata Theory, Languages, and Computation*. Addison-Wesley.

Hopcroft, J. E., and Ullman, J. D. (1979). *Introduction to Automata Theory, Languages, and Computation*. Addison-Wesley.

Ibarra, O. H., and Jiang, T. (1991). Learning regular languages from counterexamples. *J. Comput. Syst. Sci.* **43**, 299–316.

Immerman, N. (1988). Nondeterministic space is closed under complementation. *SIAM J. Comput.* **17**, 935–938.

Jiang, T., and Ravikumar, B. (1993). Minimal NFA problems are hard. *SIAM J. Comput.* **22**, 1117–1141.

Jones, N. D. (1977). A note on linear-time simulation of deterministic two-way pushdown automata. *Inf. Process. Lett.* **6**, 110–112.

Kfoury, A.-J. (1988). A linear-time algorithm to decide whether a binary word contains an overlap. *RAIRO Inf. Théor. Appl.* **22**, 135–145.

Knuth, D. E. (1965). On the translation of languages from left to right. *Inf. Control* **8**, 607–639.

Kozen, D. (February 1996). On regularity-preserving functions. *Bull. Eur. Assoc. Theor. Comput. Sci.* No. 58, 131–138.

Kuroda, S. Y. (1964). Classes of languages and linear bounded automata. *Inf. Control* **7**, 207–223.

Lawson, M. V. (2004). *Finite Automata*. CRC Press.

Lewis, H. R., and Papadimitriou, C. H. (1998). *Elements of the Theory of Computation*. Prentice Hall.

Lewis II, P. M., and Stearns, R. E. (1968). Syntax-directed transduction. *J. Assoc. Comput. Mach.* **15**, 465–488.

Li, M., and Vitányi, P. (1995). A new approach to formal language theory by Kolmogorov complexity. *SIAM J. Comput.* **24**, 398–410.

Li, M., and Vitányi, P. (1997). *An Introduction to Kolmogorov Complexity and Its Applications*. Springer-Verlag.

Lin, S., and Rado, T. (1965). Computer studies of Turing machine problems. *J. Assoc. Comput. Mach.* **12**, 196–212.

Linster, B. G. (1992). Evolutionary stability in the infinitely repeated prisoners' dilemma played by two-state Moore machines. *South. Econ. J.* **58**, 880–903.

Liu, L. Y., and Weiner, P. (1973). An infinite hierarchy of intersections of context-free languages. *Math. Syst. Theory* **7**, 185–192.

Lorentz, R. J. (2001). Creating difficult instances of the Post correspondence problem. In T. Marsland and I. Frank, editors, *Computers and Games: 2nd International Conference, CG 2001*, Vol. 2063 of *Lecture Notes in Computer Science*, pp. 214–228. Springer-Verlag.

Lothaire, M. (1983). *Combinatorics on Words*, Vol. 17 of *Encyclopedia of Mathematics and Its Applications*. Addison-Wesley.

Lothaire, M. (2002). *Algebraic Combinatorics on Words*, Vol. 90 of *Encyclopedia of Mathematics and Its Applications*. Cambridge University Press.

Lyndon, R. C., and Schützenberger, M. P. (1962). The equation $a^M = b^N c^P$ in a free group. *Michigan Math. J.* **9**, 289–298.

Main, M. G. (1982). Permutations are not context-free: An application of the interchange lemma. *Inf. Process. Lett.* **15**, 68–71.

Martin, J. C. (1997). *Introduction to Languages and the Theory of Computation*. McGraw-Hill.

Marxen, H., and Buntrock, J. (1990). Attacking the busy beaver 5. *Bull. Eur. Assoc. Theor. Comput. Sci.* No. 40 (February 1990), 247–251.

Maslov, A. N. (1970). Estimates of the number of states of finite automata. *Dokl. Akad. Nauk. SSSR* **194**, 1266–1268. In Russian. English translation in *Sov. Math. Dokl.* **11**, 1373–1375.

Maurer, H. A. (1969). A direct proof of the inherent ambiguity of a simple context-free language. *J. Assoc. Comput. Mach.* **16**, 256–260.

McCulloch, W. S., and Pitts, W. (1943). A logical calculus of the ideas immanent in nervous activity. *Bull. Math. Biophy.* **5**, 115–133.

McNaughton, R., and Papert, S. (1968). The syntactic monoid of a regular event. In M. A. Arbib, editor, *Algebraic Theory of Machines, Languages, and Semigroups*, pp. 297–312. Academic Press.

Mealy, G. H. (1955). A method for synthesizing sequential circuits. *Bell Syst. Tech. J.* **34**, 1045–1079.

Moore, E. F. (1956). Gedanken experiments on sequential machines. In C. E. Shannon and J. McCarthy, editors, *Automata Studies*, pp. 129–153. Princeton University Press.

Myhill, J. (1957). Finite automata and the representation of events. Technical Report WADD TR-57-624, Wright Patterson Air Force Base, Ohio.

Nerode, A. (1958). Linear automaton transformations. *Proc. Am. Math. Soc.* **9**, 541–544.

Nozaki, A. (1979). Equivalence problem of nondeterministic finite automata. *J. Comput. Syst. Sci.* **18**, 8–17.

Ogden, W. (1968). A helpful result for proving inherent ambiguity. *Math. Syst. Theory* **2**, 191–194.

Ogden, W., Ross, R. J., and Winklmann, K. (1985). An "interchange" lemma for context-free languages. *SIAM J. Comput.* **14**, 410–415.

Okhotin, A. (2006). Nine open problems on conjunctive and Boolean grammars. Technical Report 794, Turku Centre for Computer Science, Turku, Finland, 2006.

Papadimitriou, C. H. (1994). *Computational Complexity*. Addison-Wesley.

Parikh, R. J. (1966). On context-free languages. *J. Assoc. Comput. Mach.* **13**, 570–581.

Perrin, D., and Pin, J.-E. (2003). *Infinite Words: Automata, Semigroups, Logic, and Games*. Academic Press.

Pilling, D. L. (1973). Commutative regular equations and Parikh's theorem. *J. Lond. Math. Soc.* **6**, 663–666.

Post, E. (1946). A variant of a recursively unsolvable problem. *Bull. Am. Math. Soc.* **52**, 264–268.

Prusinkiewicz, P., and Hanan, J. (1989). *Lindenmayer Systems, Fractals, and Plants*, Vol. 79 of *Lecture Notes in Biomathematics*. Springer-Verlag.

Prusinkiewicz, P., and Lindenmayer, A. (1990). *The Algorithmic Beauty of Plants*. Springer-Verlag.

Rabin, M. O., and Scott, D. (1959). Finite automata and their decision problems. *IBM J. Res. Dev.* **3**, 114–125.

Rado, T. (1962). On non-computable functions. *Bell Syst. Tech. J.* **41**, 877–884.

Robson, J. M. (1989). Separating strings with small automata. *Inf. Process. Lett.* **30**, 209–214.

Rosenkrantz, D. J., and Stearns, R. E. (1970). Properties of deterministic top-down grammars. *Inf. Control* **17**, 226–256.

Ross, R., and Winklmann, K. (1982). Repetitive strings are not context-free. *RAIRO Inf. Théor. Appl.* **16**, 191–199.

Rozenberg, G. (1997) editor. *Handbook of Graph Grammars and Computing by Graph Transformation, Vol. 1: Foundations*. World Scientific.

Rubinstein, A. (1986). Finite automata play the repeated prisoner's dilemma. *J. Econ. Theory* **39**, 83–96.

Schützenberger, M. P. (1963). On context-free languages and pushdown automata. *Inf. Control* **6**, 246–264.

Seiferas, J. I., and McNaughton, R. (1976). Regularity-preserving relations. *Theor. Comput. Sci.* **2**, 147–154.

Shepherdson, J. C. (1959). The reduction of two-way automata to one-way automata. *IBM J. Res. Dev.* **3**, 198–200.

Shieber, S. M. (1985). Evidence against the context-freeness of natural language. *Linguist. Phil.* **8**, 333–343.

Shyr, H. J., and Thierrin, G. (1977). Disjunctive languages and codes. In M. Karpiński, editor, *Fundamentals of Computation Theory: Proceedings of the 1977 International FCT-Conference*, Vol. 56 of *Lecture Notes in Computer Science*, pp. 171–176. Springer.

Stearns, R. E., and Hartmanis, J. (1963). Regularity preserving modifications of regular expressions. *Inf. Control* **6**, 55–69.

Strachey, C. (1965). An impossible program. *Comput. J.* **7**, 313.

Szelepcsényi, R. (1988). The method of forced enumeration for nondeterministic automata. *Acta Inf.* **26**, 279–284.

Thomas, W. (1991). Automata on infinite objects. In J. van Leeuwen, editor, *Handbook of Theoretical Computer Science, Vol. B (Formal Models and Semantics)*, pp. 133–191. MIT Press.

Thornton, R. J. (2003). *The Lexicon of Intentionally Ambiguous Recommendations*. Sourcebooks.

Thue, A. (1906). Über unendliche Zeichenreihen. *Norske vid. Selsk. Skr. Mat. Nat. Kl.* **7**, 1–22. Reprinted in T. Nagell, editor, *Selected Mathematical Papers of Axel Thue*, pp. 139–158. Universitetsforlaget, Oslo, 1977.

Thue, A. (1912). Über die gegenseitige Lage gleicher Teile gewisser Zeichenreihen. *Norske vid. Selsk. Skr. Mat. Nat. Kl.* **1**, 1–67. Reprinted in T. Nagell, editor, *Selected Mathematical Papers of Axel Thue*, pp. 413–478, Universitetsforlaget, Oslo, 1977.

Turing, A. M. (1936). On computable numbers, with an application to the Entschei-dungsproblem. *Proc. Lond. Math. Soc.* **42**, 230–265.

Urbanek, F. (1990). A simple completeness proof for Earley's algorithm. *Bull. Eur. Assoc. Theor. Comput. Sci.* No. 42, 194.

Valiant, L. (1975). General context-free recognition in less than cubic time. *J. Comput. Syst. Sci.* **10**, 308–315.

Wolfram, S. (1984). Computation theory of cellular automata. *Commun. Math. Phys.* **96**, 15–57. Reprinted in S. Wolfram, editor, *Cellular Automata and Complexity: Collected Papers*, pp. 159–202. Addison-Wesley, 1994.

Wolfram, S. (2002). *A New Kind of Science*. Wolfram Media.

Wood, D. (1987). *Theory of Computation*. Wiley.

Woods, D. R. (1978). Elementary problem proposal E 2692. *Am. Math. Mon.* **85**, 48. Solution by D. Robbins, **86** (1979), 394–395.

Wright, E. M. (1959). Prouhet's 1851 solution of the Tarry-Escott problem of 1910. *Am. Math. Mon.* **66**, 199–201.

Younger, D. H. (1967). Recognition and parsing of context-free languages in time n^3. *Inf. Control* **10**, 189–208.

Yu, S. (1997). Regular languages. In G. Rozenberg and A. Salomaa, editors, *Handbook of Formal Languages*, Vol. 1, pp. 41–110. Springer-Verlag.

Yu, S., Zhuang, Q., and Salomaa, K. (1994). The state complexities of some basic operations on regular languages. *Theor. Comput. Sci.* **125**, 315–328.

Zhang, G.-Q. (1999). Automata, Boolean matrices, and ultimate periodicity. *Inf. Comput.* **152**, 138–154.

Zhao, L. (2003). Tackling Post's correspondence problem. In J. Schaeffer, M. Müller, and Y. Björnsson, editors, *Computers and Games, 3rd International Conference, CG 2002*, Vol. 2883 of *Lecture Notes in Computer Science*, pp. 326–344. Springer-Verlag.

Index

Printed in the United States
By Bookmasters